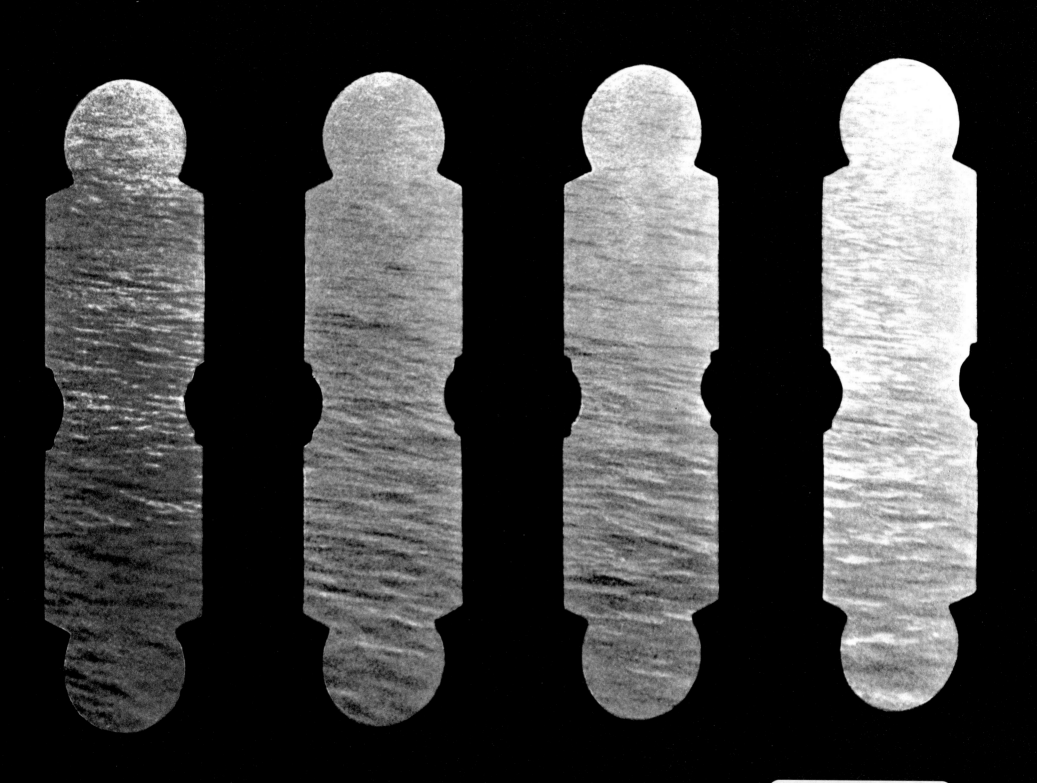

GREAT RIVERS OF EUROPE

GREAT RIVE

RS OF EUROPE

INTRODUCTION BY ALAN BULLOCK

WEIDENFELD AND NICOLSON

20 NEW BOND STREET LONDON W1

©1966 by George Weidenfeld and Nicolson Ltd, London

Designed by Leslie McCombie Associates for George Weidenfeld and Nicolson Ltd

Filmset by Graphic Film Limited, Dublin, Ireland

Printed in Switzerland by Conzett & Huber, Zurich

CONTENTS

INTRODUCTION

ALAN BULLOCK

ONE of the natural features of Europe can compare in size with those of other continents. Its highest mountains, the Alps, are little more than half the height of the Himalayas; its lakes not even half the size of a score in Africa and North America. The greatest of European rivers, the Danube, and the Volga, are outdistanced by the Nile, the Mississippi and the Amazon. In length, breadth or volume; in the size of the area they drain, the height of their waterfalls, or the depth of their gorges, none of the rivers described in this book holds a place among the natural wonders of the world. Their claim to distinction is a different one.

Thanks to its smaller scale, and even more to its temperate climate, no landscape in the world is so much the work of man as that of Europe. There are few parts of the continent where you can travel for long without coming upon the signs of settlement and cultivation, continuous for centuries past. The hills and plains, the woods and fields through which its rivers flow are a human as much as a natural setting, and it is from this setting, rich in legend and history; from the towns and cities, the tumult and peace, splendour and squalor of the human lives lived out on their banks, that these rivers derive their fame.

The importance of her rivers in Europe's history springs from the surprising variety of purposes which they have been made to serve. They were gateways for invaders, like the Vikings and the Normans; lines of advance for armies; defensive positions capable of being held against an enemy, as the Dutch proved again and again. The number of battles named after a river or a riverside village is no coincidence: there can hardly be a bridgehead on either side of the Rhine which has not been fought for a hundred times in the course of history, and the same must be true of the Danube and the Elbe. Rivers played an essential part in the strategy of the great European commanders—Wallenstein, Turenne,

Marlborough, Napoleon—and the same names recur in the twentieth century: the Marne and the Somme in 1914–16; the Tagus in the Spanish Civil War; the Loire in 1940; the Volga during the battle for Stalingrad; the Rhine, the Danube and the Elbe in the final campaigns of 1944–5.

But war is only part of the picture: much more important, cumulatively, has been the part Europe's rivers have played in her economy. For centuries merchants travelled and carried their merchandise by river boat; even today millions of tons of goods are shipped by barge up and down the principal rivers of Europe, and her greatest ports—London, Rotterdam, Hamburg, Antwerp—stand at the mouths of rivers.

Water-borne traffic, however, only partly accounts for the importance of rivers in the network of European communications. The engineer searching for the easiest line of advance for a road or railway has frequently found it along a river valley, especially in hilly or mountainous country. Many of the most spectacular stretches of road and rail bring both together on the narrow margin of a river bank, with all three crossing and re-crossing in a complicated pattern of curves, tunnels and bridges. There are no more exciting journeys in Europe than those which carry the traveller from Milan north to the St Gothard up the valley of the Ticino, or over the Arlberg Pass to Innsbruck by the side of the Inn.

And of all the natural obstacles which the engineer has to overcome, none is more frequent than running water: Europe's bridges, from Roman times to our own, form an unequalled series of monuments to the skill of her engineers, and many of them are as remarkable for the grace of their proportions as for their strength.

The development of agriculture and industry has been as closely linked with the river system of the continent as communications. Europe's rivers have watered her flocks and herds and irrigated her crops. The legendary fertility of Lombardy, to take only one example, is derived from the plentiful supply of water provided by

the Po and its tributaries. Each district along the river valleys has its own speciality, a trout done in a particularly delicious way, a cheese or fruit with the local *vin du pays* to wash it down. Some of the finest of all vintages are grown on the terraces laid out along the steep banks of the Rhine, the Moselle and the Danube, while the Garonne has been a wine-grower's river since the Middle Ages.

For centuries water power was employed to turn the wheels of the corn mills. The first cloth mills were built alongside rivers for the same reason: water power and transport by river and canal were the forerunners in the early industrial revolution of steampower and the railways. Access to ample supplies of water was often as necessary for industrial processes as for agriculture, and in our own time a growing proportion of Europe's electricity supply is derived from the hydro-electric works situated on her river banks.

The part which they have played in war and her economy would endow Europe's rivers with political importance without further need of explanation. But this has been magnified by two further factors, the suitability of river sites for settlement and the use of rivers to mark frontiers and boundaries.

All but a handful of Europe's most famous cities stand on rivers. To take only the ten rivers described in this volume, their cities include seven capitals, London, Paris, Rome, Vienna, Budapest, Belgrade, Lisbon, not to mention ports like Hamburg and Rotterdam; the Rhineland cities, Cologne, Düsseldorf, Strasbourg, Basel, and others as renowned as Dresden, Magdeburg, Ulm, Orleans, Toledo and Nizhni Novgorod.

In a famous phrase, John Burns called the Thames flowing through London 'liquid history'. London and the Thames, Paris and the Seine, Rome and the Tiber, Vienna and the Danube, these are the stages on which some of the most dramatic scenes of European history have been enacted with an incomparable cast of players

that has included, at one time or another—think of Rome alone—half the great names of history. To imagine any of these without its river—London without the Thames, Paris without the Seine—is to rob it of its historical as well as its physical character. Neither London nor Paris would ever have been founded if it had not been for the river which could be most conveniently forded at this particular spot, and without the Thames and the Seine, the history not merely of the capitals themselves but of England and France would have been different.

To the eye that can read, then, each successive chapter of Europe's history has left its record in the buildings along her riverbanks, from the Popes' Castel Sant' Angelo, which the Emperor Hadrian built as a mausoleum, to the jagged ruins of Dresden's Frauenkirche destroyed by British bombs on the night of 13 February 1944. Lisbon, rising white above the Tagus, was rebuilt after the Great Earthquake of 1755; Stalingrad (its names, once Tsaritsyn, now Volgograd, an historical record in themselves) after the greatest battle of Hitler's war. The cathedrals of the Rhineland are matched by the chateaux of the Loire, the *quais* of the Seine fronting Notre Dame and The Louvre by the wharves and warehouses of the Thames between the Traitors' Gate of the Tower of London and Wren's palace at Greenwich. It was Wordsworth, the poet of the English countryside, who wrote, looking at the view over the river from Westminster Bridge towards St Paul's:

Earth has not anything to show more fair;
Dull would he be of soul who could pass by
A sight so touching in its majesty;
This City now doth like a garment wear
The beauty of the morning; silent, bare,
Ships, towers, domes, theatres, and temples lie
Open unto the fields and to the sky;
All bright and glittering in the smokeless air . . .

Much of the history of Europe has been dominated by

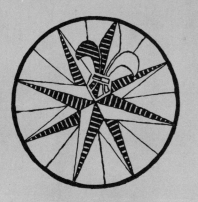

THE
RIVERS
OF
EUROPE

Kilometres 0   100   200   300   400
Miles 0   50   100   150   200   250

OSLO

NORWAY

STOCKH

NORTH SEA

SWEDEN

EDINBURGH

NEWCASTLE

DENMARK
COPENHAGEN

LIVERPOOL
MANCHESTER

HAMBURG

BIRMINGHAM
GREAT BRITAIN

WEST
GERMANY

BERLIN

River Thames
OXFORD
LONDON

AMSTERDAM

HOLLAND

River Elbe

River Oder

BRUSSELS

COLOGNE
BONN

EAST
GERMANY

LE HAVRE
ROUEN

BELGIUM

FRANKFURT

PRAGUE

PARIS

River Seine

River Rhine

CZECHOSLOVAI

NANTES

ORLEANS

River Danube

FRANCE

River Loire

BASLE

BERNE

VIENNA

SWITZERLAND

AUSTRIA

BORDEAUX

LYONS

River Rhône

River Garonne

MILAN

River Po

VENICE

TRIESTE

TURIN

PORTUGAL

MARSEILLES

BE

LISBON

River Tagus

MADRID

River Tiber

ADRIATIC
SEA

SPAIN

ROME

ITALY

MEDITERRANEAN SEA

BALTIC SEA

LENINGRAD

River Volga

KAZAN

GORKI

MOSCOW

KUYBISHEV

River Vistula

ARSAW

UNION OF SOVIET SOCIALIST REPUBLICS

LAND

River Don

River Volga

VOLGOGRAD

KIEV

River Dnieper

ASTRAKHAN

CASPIAN
SEA

UDAPEST

UNGARY

SEA OF
AZOV

RUMANIA

DE

BUCHAREST

River Danube

BLACK SEA

OSLAVIA

BULGARIA

SOFIA

TURKEY

territorial disputes: the claims of a ruler, a city state or a nation to occupy a particular piece of land and deny it to others. And there are few of Europe's rivers which have not, at one time or another, served to mark the frontiers under dispute. A classic example is the Rhine, which the French proclaimed the 'natural frontier' of France, and the Germans as stubbornly persisted in regarding as the 'German Rhine'. The secular conflict between the Teutonic and Slav peoples, out of which grew the power of Brandenburg–Prussia, was a fight for the successive river lines of Elbe, Oder, Vistula, Niemen; and one of the bitterest disputes of our own time has been the Polish claim, backed by the Russians, to push the frontier between Poland and Germany back to the Oder-Neisse line. Further south, the 'natural frontier' of the Danube has been a perennial source of conflict between the different peoples living along its banks, from Bratislava and the Banat to Bessarabia and the Dobrudja.

Europe's rivers are so much bound up with her politics and wars, the struggle for power, territory and wealth, that it is easy to overlook the other side of their history, the part they have played in the private life of generation after generation of Europeans.

A whole volume, and a singularly attractive one, might be devoted to the pleasures of the river, pleasures described a thousand times in every European literature, from the Roman to the Russian, and repeated in our own individual experience. Some are active pleasures: bathing, skating, and boating. It would be hard to think of three more universal or wholly delightful human activities. 'Nice? It's the *only* thing,' said the Water Rat in *The Wind in the Willows*. 'Believe me, my young friend, there is *nothing* – absolutely nothing – half so much worth doing as simply messing about in boats.'

Others are more contemplative pleasures: a walk along the riverbank, a winter walk with the sun sinking red across the frozen fields, a spring walk with the light glistening like quicksilver on the still naked trees, a summer walk with great white clouds reflected in the water and the sense of time stilled in the heat of a July day. The most philosophical of outdoor occupations, fishing, belongs to the river; and no food or drink ever tasted better than on a summer picnic with the boat drawn into the shade of the bank. The river and its delights are a part of the magic world of childhood and family life from which the light never fades.

To these I would add the pleasures of travelling by river steamer, the slow rounding of a bend to discover what lies beyond the bluff, the excitement of tying up at an unfamiliar town waiting to be explored. The charm of river travel lies in its unhurried pace, with time to observe the fields and woods, the houses along the water's edge, and the changing mood of the sky to which the river's mood responds. To explore Europe by riverboat is to see it, from a different angle, and at a different tempo, much closer to that of earlier centuries before the power of observation was blurred and lost in the speed of the train, the motor car and the aeroplane.

It is the painters who can most vividly recall what the riverside world of that older Europe was like: the sweep of the Tagus gorge at Toledo seen through El Greco's eyes; Canaletto's views of the eighteenth-century Thames, or Vermeer's Water Gate at Delft, hanging in a room in William of Orange's Prinsenhof from which you can still look out and see the same scene he painted across the Old Rhine. For me, it is the Seine which is pre-eminently the painter's river, the Seine with that intricate movement of light across its fields and rooftops which fascinated the Impressionists and has challenged the skill of every painter who ever lived in Paris.

There are a hundred other rivers which might have been included besides the ten chosen for this volume: the Arno with Florence and Pisa; the Vistula, the Dnieper and the Dniester; the Rhone and the Garonne; the Meuse, the Scheldt and the Moselle. But the greatest are here, and they are more than enough to illustrate the theme which runs through all the essays in this volume, the wealth of associations, mythological, historical, literary, personal, which has gathered round each of the rivers of Europe. It is the combination of these associations with their physical characteristics which gives them their character and fame.

W. H. Auden once pointed out that there is no device in poetry that has more the effect of an incantation than a list of proper names, as Homer demonstrated with his famous catalogue of ships in the Second Book of the *Iliad*. River names have the same magical effect. We have only to hear spoken or come across on the printed page the words 'Rhine' or 'Danube', 'Volga' or 'Tiber', for a whole series of images to flicker through our minds, transporting us to other lands and other times. The pages that follow are a *catalogue raisonné* of such names, with the images illustrated, the allusions caught and pinned down, the associations documented. No good catalogue fails to provide delight as well as instruction, and he will be a full reader who, when he has come to the end of this one, does not echo Izaak Walton's remark in *The Compleat Angler*: 'I love any discourse of rivers.'

THE DANUBE

BASIL DAVIDSON

'The Blue Danube' of Johann Strauss' famous waltz
is the Danube of the nineteenth century and the gaiety
and brilliance of the Vienna of that age. But the
Danube is blue for only part of its length, and has
echoed to the tramp of armed warriors as well as the
subtle tread of courtiers

GERMANY CZECHOSLOVAKIA

Black Forest

Regensburg

Passau

Dürnstein

VIENNA

Linz

Melk
Pöchlarn

Bratislava

BUDAPEST

Ulm

Lech

Isar

Inn

snaueschingen

AUSTRIA HUNGA

River Drava

River Sava

Heraldic Shields of
Vienna during first
Turkish siege 1529

THE DANUBE

Y

Melk Monastery

Kriemhild leaving the Danube

Vienna at time of Turkish Siege 1680

The Cathedral at Ulm

The Cathedral at Regensburg

USSR

RUMANIA

Y

THE BLACK SEA

River Tisza

Ismail

Galati

Braila

Novi Sad

BUCHAREST

Fruskagora Mtns

The Iron Gates

BELGRADE

Giurgiu

Ruse

Sturgeon fishing

SOFIA

GOSLAVIA BULGARIA

Kilometres
0   50   100

Miles
0   25   50   75   100

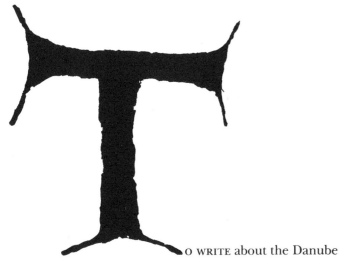

To WRITE about the Danube is to embark upon the life story of a large part of Europe. Unlike every other long river between the Urals and the Bay of Biscay, this majestic stream has never been the possession of any single state or even of any single empire, whether Frank or Slav, Magyar, Teuton or Turk. Through all such geo-political obsessions the Danube has moved with serene impartiality. More than three hundred often furious tributaries pour their hurrying national waters into the Danube, but the Danube placidly swallows them all, and is hustled from its comfortable pace only by the occasional accident of tectonic disturbance still more ancient than itself. However variously named, the Danube survives all national declensions and con-

jugations. Persistently, reassuringly, it follows a European course. Its *genius loci* is an internationally minded sprite, its guardian nymphs are many-tongued: Donau, Duna, Dunava, Dunarea—they are all the same river whose name the Romans, borrowing from vanished Celts before them, called Danubius.

All this means that to travel with the Danube is a European experience, and perhaps an essential one. There may be no better way of growing into the knowledge of why Europe, even this middle Europe of so many snarling conflicts in the past, has been more than the sum of its parts; and of why these parts, however little they may have seemed to belong to each other (much less love each other), have remained members of one body and segments of one civilisation. Even since

the Second World War, when Europe has divided itself more emphatically than at any time for centuries, this immense river has continued to make its point with true Danubian insistence. It has continued to flow from west to east, carrying the waters of Western Germany into the Black Sea and uniting, with a nicely casual irony, the lands of the west with the lands of the east.

But all this, one may object, is a romantic view of the matter. Statistically considered, this is simply the biggest river of Europe. From its origins in south-western Germany, where the Breg and the Brigach rush out of the Black Forest and join their waters at Donaueschingen, the Danube flows to the Black Sea over a course of about 1750 miles, declining as it does so from a height of 2187 feet above sea level and gathering force from

A famous crossing of the Danube by Trajan's Roman Legions during his conquest of Dacia in A.D. 101–102 is recorded on Trajan's Column in Rome. To punish the rebellious Dacians and to ensure their future obedience, Trajan forced them to hew a road out of the bare rocks lining the southern bank of the river, and build a bridge of stone at the point where the Danube crosses what is now the Hungarian–Bulgarian border

RIGHT The abbey and church of Durnstein in the Wachau valley, seen from the castle where King Richard Coeur-de-Lion, captured and imprisoned by Duke Leopold VI of Prussia on his way home from the Third Crusade (1189–92), was discovered by his minstrel Blondel and ransomed for 150,000 silver marks. Nearby, in 1805, Napoleon's troops defeated a Russian army led by General Kutusov, who, helped by the Russian winter, was later to force Napoleon to retreat from Moscow after the battle of Borodino

RIGHT *The reputed source of the river is this spring rising in the castle yard of Donaueschingen on the southern slopes of the Black Forest. The second largest river in Europe, the Danube flows 1,750 miles eastward from here to the Black Sea*

BELOW *On a sheer cliff 130 feet above the river in the Wachau valley stands the castle of Schonbuhl, built between 1819–21. This sequestered defile is reputed to be the loveliest river valley in all Europe*

RIGHT *A drawing by Albrecht Altdorfer (c. 1480–1538), the most important artist of the Danube school, shows how the river boils and surges through the rock-bound Strudel to the wide valley of the Blue Danube on the approaches to Vienna*

OPPOSITE *After cutting deep gorges through the Swabian Alps, the river reaches Sigmaringen, where the castle of the Hohenzollerns rises sheer from the water, dominating every approach. Built on the site of an earlier, much besieged fortress by the Russian King Willian IV, the father of the first German Emperor, the castle was the family seat of the Hohenzollern dynasty*

tributaries which drain 300,000 square miles. Its volume gains imposingly but steadily. At Passau, where the Danube enters Austria from Bavaria, its average flow is at the rate of about 730 cubic metres every second, while at Vienna the flow is about 1600, at Budapest about 2300, at the Iron Gates about 5840, and at Tulcea, nearing the sea, about 7230 cubic metres. Low draught tugs and barges navigate the Danube over a distance of more than 1500 miles. In colour its waters range from a rare hint of blue to a more general brown or sepia or even sorrel at certain times of the year, or else to pale reflections of a dull and thunderous sky. I have once seen the Danube frozen entirely over as far down as the Hungarian plain: then it became a half mile width of ice, peaked and piled by the hidden current into summits that glittered to begin with but afterwards, hoaring over, were blurred with dusty shadow. Hungarian and Yugoslav gunners shelled the Danube on that occasion, partly to get it moving again and partly out of sheer artillery panache; theirs, so far as I remember, were the first shots of the Second World War in that part of the world. They had remarkably less effect than others fired at other targets later on; for the river, as I recall, moved in its own good time.

Yet the sober facts tell little. This river flows with the drive, fury and final slowing down of life itself. Unfolding growth and onward movement, a bursting through of barriers and compartments: all this seems to get itself embodied in stupendous undertones of fate that are proper to the Danube. In its youth, far west in high Bavaria, it leaps and hustles like any other mountain stream. Through the blue-green flanks and forest gorges of the Schwabian Alps it hurries into adolescence, glittering, impatient, and breaks from the hills at Ulm, where manhood begins. Turning north to Regensburg, our urgent river sweeps through lowland Bavaria and ambition takes a hold: about here, the Danube divides itself from its neighbours. Down from the mountains of Tirol come Iller and Lech, Isar and Inn, salmon-leaping, taking no thought for the morrow and appropriately having none: their future is to nourish the Danube, afterwards no mere mountain stream like others of its kind. Then come Traun and Enns, Ybbs, Erlauf, Traison and others of their soon-spent sort, and this is already the Austrian Danube, the Blue Danube of Viennese tradition, more than a hundred miles of pastoral bliss, one of the loveliest lengths of riparian scenery anywhere in the world. With Vienna we are already on the skirts of middle age, carrying more weight, moving not so fast, glittering no longer in the fond insouciance of youth. This is where the Danube, mature and confident, really enters on its grand career, its European vocation. It flows on through Vienna, goes beneath a haggard castle on a cliff, leaves the pleasant city of Bratislava on its left-hand side and turns southward into Hungary, heading for the Black Sea. There follow, as one might say, years of steady progress, not untouched by one or two adventures (flowing out of the plains, for example, the Danube is suddenly embraced by tall black rocks, is narrowed from a mile in width to a fearful spate of less than two hundred yards across and then at last ejected into south-eastern Europe with no dignity at all); and through all these years the Danube proceeds upon its way, conducting its European mission, connecting Yugoslavia with Rumania, Rumania with Bulgaria, until venerable age comes slowly on the verge of giant marshes. Through these the Danube shuffles by a dozen idle streams and wanders forgetfully away into the sea, its destiny complete.

There are other ways of considering this river. Its monuments are many and remarkable. The peoples who live along its banks are highly various. One may also recall one's own memories. Mine are mostly of the middle Danube, of the broad slow beauty of the river's middle age, the Danube of the plains of Hungary and Yugoslavia. Here one may still travel for days on the deck of a flat-bottomed steamer through green and yellow meadows fringed with bullrush reeds and wind-blown trees, patiently, for the paddles are in no hurry and nor are the peasants who stagger aboard every hour or so from trembling wooden quays. This is where one begins to sip coffee in the Turkish style, poured from slender beakers into small china cups; and grows aware of the smell and noise of middle Europe, of paprika and plum-brandy and peasant gear, of the hammering nag of the Magyar tongue, its accent always on the first syllable of every word, and the onward hint of new lands and peoples waiting to be found. One sits and takes one's time, and looks out ahead every now and then for the towers of Buda and the parliament of Pest. There, after a final surging of paddles, the steamer puts you ashore until it is ready to depart, soon after dawn, for the lands of the south and east. A long day later the little hills of the Fruška Gora will raise a line along the south, and then, passing under the battlements of Petrovaradin, you are soon tying up at Belgrade, with Europe once again quite different from the day before.

There is a great deal to be said for this mode of travel

HOOGHSTET

on the Danube. It puts things in their right perspective. Whether along its banks or on its waters, the Danube has always been a passage way for movements of people. Nameless Indo-Europeans came this way, moving westward: so did the Romans, moving eastward. And westward after them, looking for loot and land, came all manner of Asian folk, Huns and Avars, Slavs and Turks, while eastward again, though more often for loot than land, went Franks and Bavarians, Crusaders, latterday Germans. There is scarcely a single long reach of the river without its famous battlefield. Here it was, on Mohács field in 1526, that the knights of the last Hungarian king, Lajos II, went down in glorious defeat before the armies of Suleiman the Magnificent. Every bridgehead on the Bavarian and Austrian Danube was taken and retaken during the religious wars of the seventeenth century or the Napoleonic invasion of the nineteenth.

Diversity of scene matches variety of history. In Bavaria it is all hills and valleys. In that country you can walk all day through high trees and then at evening

ABOVE LEFT *The Duke of Marlborough, son of the first Sir Winston Churchill and ancestor of the last. His defeat of a superior French force at Blenheim—his most famous victory—was a triumph of leadership and tactics*

ABOVE RIGHT *Prince Eugene of Savoy, commander of the right wing in the battle, was an implacable enemy of King Louis XIV. Although of French ancestry, he entered the service of France's arch-enemy, the Emperor of Austria, in 1683*

LEFT *The Blenheim Tapestry depicts Marshal Tallard, the Commander of the combined French and Bavarian armies, surrendering to the Allied forces of England and Austria under the Duke of Marlborough after his defeat at the battle of Blenheim, near the Danube, in 1704. The captured French Royal Standard in the hands of a British Grenadier (left foreground) symbolizes a victory which earned Marlborough the admiration of his Queen, the thanks of a grateful nation, and Blenheim Palace, where this tapestry now hangs*

make down to the riverbank through pine-smoke and the scent of resin, while southern hills climb away above you to the sky. You can stand there, half way down, and see the mountains piled and pinnacled beyond an evergreen blur of valley sapling, and feel that the world itself is like a lifetime, one range of peaks for ever furled and spread beyond the ones immediately in front. You can eat trout and schnitzel, drink agreeably, sleep in the odour of pine planks and clean old pillows. You can follow on down to Vienna, a city of unmatched urbanity, and continue again to Bratislava, where you will get the hint and tone of Slavonic Europe for the first time, not yet at full strength but still the taste and sip of the thing, sliding curiously on the tongue after the sensuously different pleasures of Germany and Austria.

Leaving aside the cities for a while, you can go on down through the wide Hungarian plain to the foothills of Yugoslavia. Here the Danube passes through the Vojvodina, the Captaincy, so named because through many years it was a sharp-contested frontier land. Old Serbia planted military settlers here, and so did old Hungary and old Rumania, and others as well. They lived as their successors still live, in large villages of varying prosperity, each nursing their sense of being 'separate and better', and hopeful of the chance to prove it. Theirs is a land of limitless plains, or so it will appear to you: with your feet in the mud of a Vojvodina village, you can accept that the world is really flat, and that the plains run on until they tumble off the edge. You can cross the Danube and climb a few hundred feet into the hills of Srem which the Romans called Sirmium, and find that the impression stays with you. Looking northward here across the river, there is nothing but a panorama of pastel greens and browns with a village picked out now and then by the white fingered tower of a church or a dark clump of poplars.

And how prosperous they are, these villages. Even in the midst of the Second World War, loping down from the hungry hills of Bosnia, partisan detachments found them stuffed with food, their lofts lined with long sides of bacon, their ovens warm with crisp loaves of wheaten bread, their commons scattered with fat white geese like the distant sails of a grand regatta. For me, at any rate, this is the dramatic heartland of middle Europe, a place where peace and war have

OPPOSITE LEFT *A modern view of Regensburg's stone bridge, which was built in the twelfth century and was, for the times, an engineering miracle.*

OPPOSITE RIGHT *Passau, built on a rocky tongue of land shaped smooth by the confluence of the rivers Inn and Liz with the Danube, has one of the most beautiful settings in Europe. In the twelfth century, the land-owning Bishop Ulrich built a fortress here, aptly called Oberhaus, from which he could impose his will on his rebellious tenantry*

For more than eight hundred years a stout Romanesque stone bridge has linked Regensburg, now called Ratisbon, to the ancient Bavarian town of Stadt-im-hof. This flourishing centre of commerce at the most northerly bend of the Danube, with its palatial homes and fine churches — among them the so-called 'Scottish Church' built by Irish monks in the thirteenth century — has survived the last war as it did the religious wars of the sixteenth century

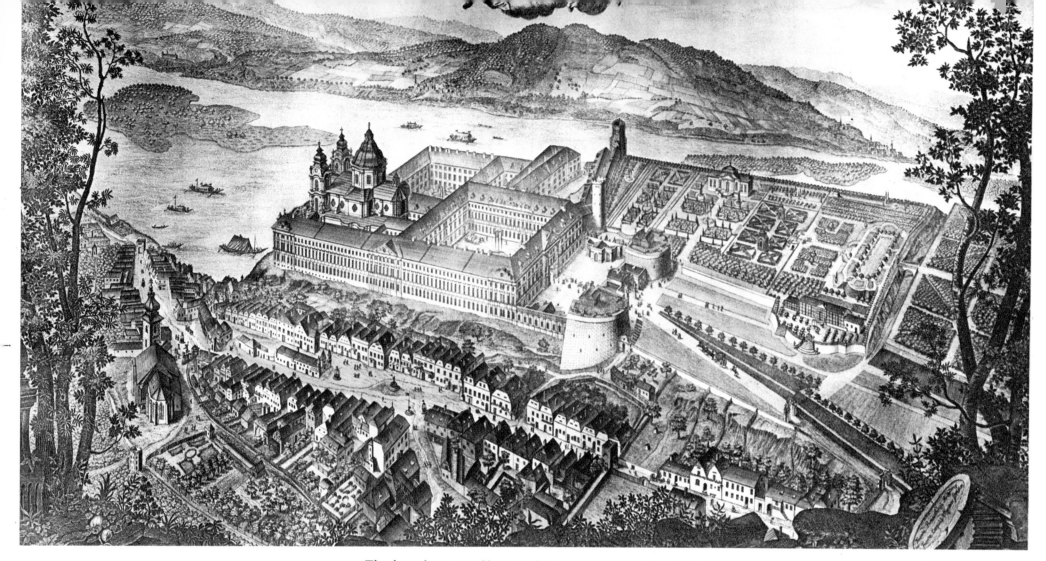

The eleventh-century Abbey of Melk after its restoration in 1708. More a palace than a monastery, it was formerly the home of the margraves of Babenberg, some of whom are buried in its church, which is decorated in red marble and gold. Its 30,000 volume library contains a priceless collection of incunabula, and its art gallery is justly famous. The ancient fortress of Melk is mentioned in the famous German epic, Nibelungenlied. Although an Abbey, it was besieged several times and was fortified by Napoleon after the battle of Aspern in 1809

OPPOSITE *The Benedictine Abbey at Weltenburg is outwardly simple but magnificent inside. Its beautiful church, built in 1818, is the masterpiece of two famous brothers, Cosmas and Egid Asam, one a painter and architect, the other a sculptor. Here the Danube is overtopped by rocks rising sheer from the water. Unable to tow their boats from the banks, boatmen inch them upstream by means of iron rings fixed in the rock face*

always played a narrow counterpoint. I think of a time in 1944 when I lived a hidden kind of life in a little town called Palanka, a sprawling assemblage of huts and houses that you will see on the left hand side as the river steamer turns east for Novi Sad and Belgrade. My hosts were a Serbian woman and her daughter, the daughter's lover was a Slovak serving in the Hungarian army, while the troops splashing by in their trucks outside were local Germans or other folk who served the Nazi side. Yet they were all people of the Danube. They were all people of the Vojvodina.

Even as far down as this, though, you are only half way along the Danube. There follows a punctuation mark and a long slow passage to the sea. The punc-

tuation mark occurs between Yugoslavia and Rumania at the Kazan Defile and the Iron Gates. This is where the comfortable Danube suddenly gets its middle-aged spread into a terribly tight corset, not once but twice, and rushes into the Balkans at a wildly dangerous pace. But it soon recovers. A long slow passage to the sea draws an otherwise featureless frontier between Bulgaria and Rumania. Travelling this stretch, you arrive in the course of quite a long time at the opposing river ports of Giurgiu and Ruse, and are faced with the site of a classical Balkan situation: with the long-standing impossibility of agreement between two neighbouring peoples who might well have had, one is bound to think, everything to gain from agreement.

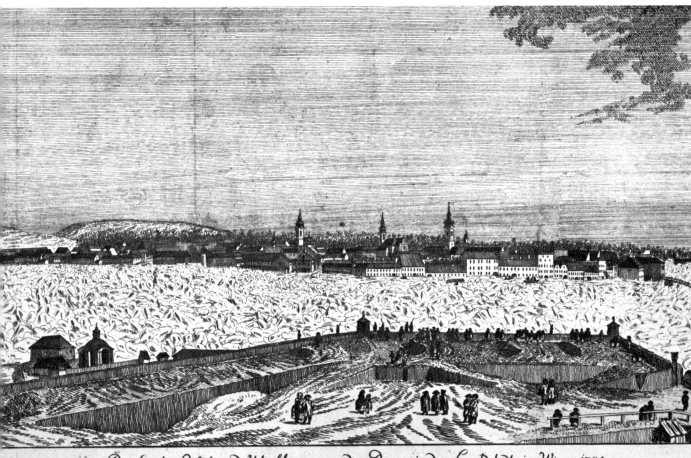

Der starcke Eisstoß und Ueberschwemmung der Donau in der Leopoldstadt in Wien. 1784.

When winter comes and stretches of the river freeze, as (above) on the outskirts of Vienna (shown in a late eighteenth-century engraving) or (right) in the windswept marshes of Hungary, strong undercurrents tear and toss the ice into jagged piles, making the river impassable for miles

Thus the railway from Sofia, which is the capital of Bulgaria, runs north to Ruse, and the railway from Bucharest, which is the capital of Rumania, runs south to Giurgiu, while in between there lies a mile of placid water over which nobody until the other day had ever managed to build a bridge. Now that they have finally done so there may be real substance in the claim that Balkan Europe has at last moved into a new life. Even so, I would guess that you may still enjoy the energetic sensation of being absolutely Rumanian in Giurgiu and unmovably Bulgarian in Ruse.

And then to complete the variety of scene you can move on down through Braila to the great delta itself, and linger in that strange marsh country for a while, a paradise for wading and water birds if not for human beings, before going out into the Black Sea through the Sulina Channel. Quite large sea-going vessels have used this channel for many years: its clearing and re-gular dredging are among the few achievements of human co-operation along the whole river, being first embarked on by the International Danube Commission of 1856. In those days the mouths of the mighty Danube were navigable to nothing but rowing boats and punts. 'The entrance to the Sulina branch,' wrote the Commission's chief engineer in 1873, 'was a wild open seaboard strewn with wrecks, the hulls and masts of which, sticking out of the submerged sandbanks, gave to mariners the only guide to where the deepest channel was to be found'; and even the deepest channel was only a few feet deep at the best of times. Now all that is long since changed. The wrecked hulls and masts have given way to quays and cranes. Personally, I should like to see them again. They mark the termination of the Danube with a dignity and emphasis which must have been altogether absent in the past.

These few impressions may suggest a little of this

OPPOSITE *Approaching the valley of the Blue Danube, the stream crashes and roars over rapids and between jutting rocks into a whirlpool in places only fifteen feet wide–the fearsome Strudel. According to legend, only virtuous young maidens can cross it in safety. Others risk being dragged down by the Nix, an amorous monster living in the depths*

Der Strudel-Strom in der Donau.

Vienna still keeps much of the pastoral charm of this early nineteenth-century engraving by Bittwiller – a prospect of Vienna and its environs seen from the village of Nussdorf

river's wonderful diversity of scene. One could lovingly add to them. Nowhere else in Europe, I should think, is there anything to compare with the pristine hush and the hint of far-reaching years, piling back from our own time as the hills pile back on either side, the blue hills of Transylvania and the black hills of Bulgaria, that enliven and overlie the country of the lower Danube. One finds repeatedly a sense of space and slow time that has a value of its own. Wait for duck in dawn reeds along the Tisza, not far from where that lazy river joins the Danube near Novi Sad, or stroll for hares among the water meadows of the Sava, twenty miles or so upstream from its confluence with the Danube at Belgrade, or merely sit and watch for anything you like in any of these quiet lands, and you will be likely to relax and grow into a state of quite remarkable contentment. You may need hours to get home again, but there is no

hurry: even if your boots are soaked, you know that you will come to no harm. There is something about the country that tells you so. Travel in a Backa *kola* through the heat-haze of a harvest summer, two sleepy horses kicking up the dust in front of you so that it burns in your nose like snuff and curls out behind you in a tiny thunder cloud; or take a meal of Banat ham and cakes washed down with the wines of Balaton, the sweet wines of Badacsonyi or the dry wines of Tihány; or move on a little further and sleep the slow night in any of half a hundred slumbering single-storeyed towns, their house walls prinked in old azure or vermilion between the linden-trees, agreeable aspects you will notice before yielding to their good goose quilts and mattresses; and in all this, as well as in much else too, you may connect yourself with a Europe that has never yet managed to get itself into the guide books. This

BELOW 'Knights of the last Hungarian King going down in glorious defeat before the armies of Suleiman' — a woodcut from the Czech Chronicle depicting the battle of Mohács, which was fought on the banks of the Danube in 1526. Lewis II, King of Bohemia and Hungary, perished in the battle, and all of central and southern Hungary passed under the rule of Suleiman I, sultan of Turkey from 1520–66

is, above all, the country of the nineteenth-century Magyar painters, the Courbets and Corots of middle Europe, Munkácsi and his like; the land and people of Bartok's music and Dvorak's dances, of Serbian flutes and songs, of Bulgarian myth and Rumanian legend. It is probably the least known of Europe's great and memorable regions.

The upper Danube, the German Danube, is a different matter. This was the country of Europe's wealth and progress in the Middle Ages. From Donaueschingen down to Vienna, close on 500 miles, the towns and cities of the Bavarian and the Austrian Danube are all monuments to spending and splendour. This is the Danube of the powers and potentates of old Germany, of the great merchant cities of the Holy Roman Empire and the Counter Reformation. These places are inexhaustibly splendid. They must be taken carefully, and one at a time, or abundance will soon induce surfeit.

Their architecture is a procession of all the great styles of middle Europe from the forts of the Romans to the clear high angles of Romanesque and on through various Gothic adventures to the baroque of the Counter Reformation and its *envoi* in rococo, not forgetting the municipal efforts of the nineteenth century and the glass and concrete of our own time. Their churches and minsters are positively encrusted with the wood and stone sculpture of the masters of the Middle Ages and of later times. Their palaces and *städtische Museen* are packed with the engravings and paintings of Dürer and his peers. Their history is nothing if not peculiar and abundant; and its very key note is extravagance.

This so typical note of the upper Danube is heard almost from the beginning. Even while the youthful river is still thrusting down the gorges of the Schwabian Alps there is Sigmaringen with its Hohenzollern castle

LEFT *Suleiman's ambitions did not end with Hungary. He entered Austria in 1529, and besieged Vienna for twenty-four days, as seen in this engraving which shows the tents of the vast Turkish army surrounding the embattled city. The siege was unsuccessful, however, and in 1533 peace was finally made*

BELOW *War between the Turks and the Austrians broke out again in 1682, and in the following year Turkish armies under the leadership of Kara Mustafa besieged Vienna for the second time – again unsuccessfully. This engraving shows the storming of Tabor, Leopoldstadt (a district of Vienna) and the bridge across the Danube wrecked by the Turks*

ABOVE *The riverside at Pest is much the same today as it was in 1856, sixteen years before the cities of Buda and Pest were joined to form the capital of independent Hungary*

RIGHT *The Basilica of the Archbishop dominates Esztergom, the ancient capital of Hungary where the Kings of Hungary were crowned. The dome of the Basilica, modelled on St Peter's in Rome, looks incongruous on the banks of the Danube*

ABOVE *Captured by Sultan Suleiman the Magnificent in 1541 and garrisoned by 12,000 janissaries (a special guard corps composed of Christian citizens of the Turkish Empire), Buda remained in Turkish hands for nearly 150 years, the frontier post where Christianity faced Islam*

on a crag. At Ulm, where the hills release the Danube into lowland Bavaria, there stands the famous minster whose spire looks out for miles across these fertile valleys, another note of human extravagance in a country often given to extremes of ambition and behaviour. It was from the Adlerbastei at Ulm that the tailor Albrecht Ludwig Berblingen, right in character, launched himself on a homemade glider no later than 1811 and fell into the Danube, an Icarus of truly Bavarian ingenuity. But the superb city of Regensburg is where the German Danube, here at the river's most northerly point, attains the peak and summit of its old magnificence.

The Celtic founders of Regensburg called their settlement Radasbona, or something to that effect: near enough, in any case, for later generations to latinise the name into Ratisbon, leaving it for Bavarian patriot-

The floodlit Hungarian Parliament Building reflected in the Danube. The huge limestone edifice has a centre dome 315 feet high, with wings for the House of Representatives and the House of Magnates. Ninety statues adorn its façade

ism to insist on Regensburg in still later times. In AD 159 the Romans guarded its military value with a cohort. Evicted by the Germans, they returned with a legion and stayed for a long time. Fragments of their buildings have survived. In 1245 the Holy Roman Emperor fixed his capital here, for Ratisbon was then the wealthiest of all the south German trading cities, being overtaken only in the fifteenth century by Augsburg, Nuremberg and Vienna. Its cathedral was founded in the middle of the thirteenth century and completed in the sixteenth; by this time Ratisbon had physically become what in a large sense it has since remained, an architectural and artistic museum of the Middle Ages, in some respects almost perfect but for its modern ensnarlment in the traffic problem. Several of the most enflamed of all the sessions of the old imperial Reichstag were held in Ratisbon-Regensburg, notably that

of 1541, when Eck and Melancthon argued their doctrinal differences while the battles of the Reformation trampled and ravaged in the wings. Here, too, during the Diet of 1532, the Emperor and his impoverished courtiers sat in wait for news of the Turks, who, with 40,000 warriors cooking mutton round their fires at Budapest, seemed bound to seize the whole of middle Europe, a moment in history which might have altered everything but which ended, as such moments fortunately may, in the bathos of indecision and retreat. Through all these to-ings and fro-ings Regensburg suffered with the rest. The Protestants took it in 1630, and the Catholics took it back again, while in 1809 the troops of Napoleon duly burned the southern quarters of the city. Compared with all that ravaging the bombs of World War II had oddly small effect. Only one old building, a Romanesque church, suffered much damage.

Nowadays these cities are very much part of the modern world. Early in the 1960s Bavaria was said to have a higher rate of industrial growth than any other part of Germany, which meant, in fact, than any other part of Europe. Yet they still have their feet in the past. You cannot really think of them apart from their history. And in this respect, as I have said, extravagance has been the key note. It was in these cities that the anti-witch hysteria of the sixteenth century reached some of its most curious forms, outdoing even the mental paralysis of James VI's Scotland. In 1595 – and examples are abundantly recorded – the governor of Ingolstadt on the upper Danube presided over the trial of a girl of twelve and a boy of nine, children of 'a soldier

OVERLEAF *Buda, on the right bank of the Danube, seen from Pest, on the left bank. The two cities were united in 1872*

35

The famous 'Iron Gates' along the 'Kissura' the last great defile on the way to the sea. Eight miles of cataracts and rapids, of which the most important is the Iron Gates, narrow the deep and mighty stream to two-thirds of its former width, and a shelf of rock succeeded by a jagged reef force it through a channel only 360 feet wide

in the Ingolstadt lifeguards and a witch who was executed'. These children were recalcitrant. They would not confess. Yet 'by birching them it was elicited that they could ride in the air and had learned it from their mother . . .' Unhappily, even with the aid of birching and sundry other appropriate torments, the children could not get their stories to agree. And as their statements refused to tally, 'distressing confusion and perplexity arose in the college of judges'. At Regensburg in the same year the lawyers and clergy likewise had to deal with a girl witch who insisted that 'the devil entered her in the shape of a fly, and that she had often been in and out of hell with the devil'. Two jurists opined that this was the devil's fault rather than the girl's, and were content to recommend that 'she should be not punished with death by fire, but only be stretched a few times by way of warning, then be put in the pillory, have her cheeks burned through and sent into

perpetual exile'. The goggling stone gargoyles of Regensburg and its sister cities had plenty to amuse them. One is not surprised to learn that it was at Ingolstadt, according to local tradition, where Faust studied the magical arts.

Here too, along the German Danube, the knights and nobles of the Holy Roman Empire competed most royally in all those flights of high living for which the Germans as a people were later to acquire, quite often against all justice, so bibulous a reputation. It may be that Bavaria has the highest intake of beer of any country in the world: nothing that modern Bavarians may do, however, will be likely to rival the vinous triumphs of their princely ancestors. These drank by the barrel as a matter of decency and daily routine, gambled and whored, quarrelled, belched and fought as no other community of men and women (for the princely women were grand topers too) has probably ever

done. 'Folly and drink with good honest blows are spice to the banquet,' declared one of them, stating what was clearly the social norm, 'and still better if there's blood spilt as well, for then you can drink another glass to end the skirmish. And what would life be like without drink? It wasn't for nothing that God gave us princes our rich vineyards.' Sometimes the servants had to put up with more than even they could take: a certain duchess, it was complained on one occasion, 'is beyond measure idiotic and merry when intoxicated'. And no wonder. It is not known whether anyone along the Danube could outdrink the famous North German imbiber, Veit von Bassenheim, who was able to empty at one draught, and three times running, a silver beaker which held eight bottles of wine; but it is perfectly certain that many tried. The princesses, while not at table, could also win fabulous reputations for magnificence of dress, being womanfully aped in this

In the quieter waters of the Danube delta, a vast and desolate stretch of lakes, marshes and reeds, fishermen earn a scanty living in home-made boats of unusual design. Although the Rumanian government has created iron, steel and chemical industries in Galati and Braila, the principal delta ports, the area is largely underdeveloped

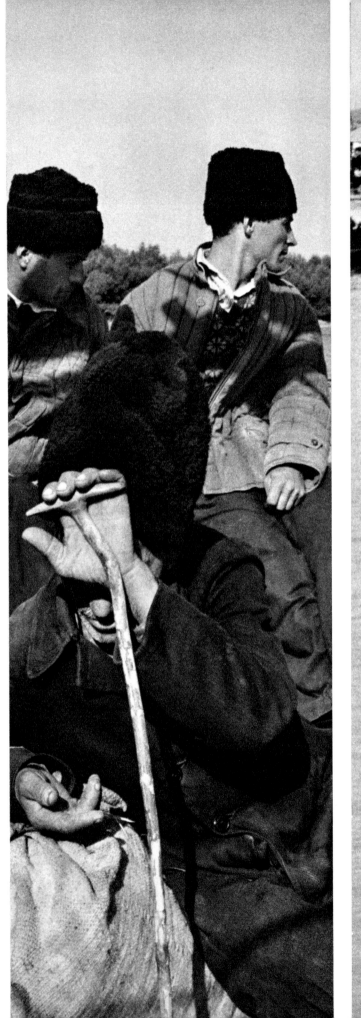

by the rich burghers' wives of these wonderful Danube towns. They crowned their heads with pearls, dribbled rubies down their breasts, slung chains of gold around their waists, and girdled their hips with strings of sapphire and turquoise.

Clergy and tax payers disliked this kind of thing: understandably, for they had to pay for it. But it made no difference. Indeed, no sooner was the Reformation tamed and the old Empire splintered into its princely parts, than the spending of the rich seems to have reached still greater heights of gay abandonment. Not even the grim religious wars had curbed it; on the contrary, the bestial destruction of the Catholic–Protestant campaigns appears to have given to high living a new and sweeter edge. Chroniclers of the period believed they were living in a time of unexampled depravity out of which they were never likely to climb. In 1610 a physician of Ingolstadt inveighed against this 'collapse of standards' in a book which became notorious. Public bathing was now the rage with those who could afford it. But 'of what goes on in these bathing places,' he warned, 'I should have to write a special huge book, and then I should not be finished with the subject . . . If the town authorities knew of this terrible

vice and iniquity, as well as do God and the bathers, they would never permit such scandalous abodes of vice to remain in their towns.' No doubt we can recognise the cry: time past was not so different, after all, from time present. The moral frontiers were breaking down.

The artists understood, if not the moralists. The old grotesqueries of medieval inhibition flowed into the new and popular merriment and invention of Breughel and Bosch, whose works had their due reflection with painters in the Danube cities. A new and secular naturalism shocked by its often lyrical reaction from monastic norms and habits. It became possible to paint nudity. And at the same time, life being what it was, horror and violence inspired

OPPOSITE LEFT *On a steamer plying between Galatz, Rumania, and the Black Sea port of Sulina. The first steamer passed the Iron Gates in 1846*

LEFT *On the banks of the Danube Canal at Vilcov, Rumania, in the Danube delta*

BELOW *A floating water mill on the Danube in Rumania*

astonishing works. 'It is no longer the pure and sacred which delights,' wrote a critic of the late sixteenth century, 'but the gruesome art of counterfeiting ghosts and devils; for it has come to this, that artists are more anxious to inspire terror by their works than to give consolation.' Once again the complaint is recognisable: an old world was passing away. 'Young men and maidens run wild about the streets and roads all night, beating drums and disturbing a whole village with their yelling. And when they have turned everything upside down, shoved carts and carriages into the stream and smashed them up, climbed into houses down the chimney, and broken doors and windows, they are mighty pleased with their performance, think it quite masterly, and expect to be praised for it.' Yet the old world of the German Danube about which those sixteenth century words were written has at any rate left us the physical appearance and in-

tegument, often marvellously intact, of its strange and furious being.

After the Reformation there came the Counter Reformation; architecturally, this meant baroque. Things quietened down. Life grew steadier, even boringly so. The new establishment, nothing if not respectable and *buergherlich* for all its princely titles, ruled with a new style, prosy and unadventurous. Yet even these rulers could not quell the genius of the German Danube. Baroque rose above itself, achieved a special kind of glory within the obsessive demand for regularity and order. Almost every riverside town or village acquired its handsome white rectangular church complete with bulbed tower, green-coppered and capped with a tiny spire. Some are marvels of their sort, none more so than the Benedictine church and monastery at Melk on the Austrian Danube, the old Medeliki of the Nibelungenlied. Built between 1702 and 1736 to the design of Jakob

OPPOSITE *Tow flax, which grows plentifully in the inlets and creeks of the river's delta region, is harvested from punts*

The floodland channels of the Danube delta are a paradise for wading and water birds. The majestic White Pelicans were once numbered in hundreds of thousands, but today only two or three thousand pairs remain

Prandtauer, a master of his day, this great patterned pile stands superbly on a granite peak above the river. Vienna is packed with such splendours. Even the basilica of the archbishopric of Hungary, Esztergom, becomes glorious by its position, raised in majesty above the broad brown flood, although in architecture it is no more than a rather commonplace copy of St. Peter's in Rome, built between 1821 and 1856 in the ninth century of Esztergom's archiepiscopal existence.

The cities of the lower Danube, by contrast, have little or no historical distinction in their architecture, while Giurgiu and Ruse, Braila and the rest have none at all. Both Budapest and Belgrade suffered very great damage in the Second World War, though losing little of much artistic value, and both have since been the scene of far-reaching reconstruction. Today they are modern cities on nineteenth-century foundations, which is not to say that they and their smaller neighbours do not have a charm of their own. There is nothing more enjoyable in Europe, to offer a personal opinion, than a winter swim in one of Buda's snow-surrounded pools of hot spring water, when the bracing sulphurous steam lifts a foot-deep belt of warmth above the water, or, if your season should be summer, than a bottle of cool Csopaki drunk in some pleasant garden on the little island that divides Buda from Pest. There is nothing more stirring to the historical imagination, not even along the whole dramatic course of the Danube, than to stand on the cliffs of the Kalemegdan Garden in old Belgrade, and consider how the fate-laden waters of the Sava meet the mile wide Danube, mingling the rivers of the west with the rivers of the south, and joining together the history of the Germans and the Magyars, the Croats and Serbs and Slovenes, before flowing on to the far south-east.

The peoples of the Danube have not found it easy to live with their frontier-defying river. Efforts at international agreement about how to behave along the Danube began in 1856 and have continued with varying

RIGHT *Water buffalo cooling off in the muddy stream, while on land, wolves, foxes, wild boars and hares range from the mountains to the riverbank in search of food, shelter and breeding grounds*

OPPOSITE *In the Danube delta the production of caviare is a major industry. The prize catch is the Great Sturgeon, which can be as much as thirty feet long, weigh a ton and a half and yield 220 lb of caviare. Sturgeon enter the mouth of the river to spawn, and penetrate as far as the Iron Gates*

success. Much has been talked of securing the 'freedom of the Danube' as an international waterway, and many learned conferences have met to this effect, producing between them a large if more or less completely unreadable library of reports. All this has marched in step, though erratically, with the growth of river traffic, itself a product both of steam and oil propulsion as well as of better standards of living in the lower Danubian lands. Progress has been slow. Some notion of the relative poverty of these peoples during the first half of the twentieth century may be had from comparing figures of river traffic on the Danube and the Rhine: of the order of five to seven million tons a year on the Danube during the 1930s, traffic on the Rhine was ten times greater.

Many changes have occurred since the Second World War, not least in the economic field, and all the lower Danubian countries are now embarked on industrialisa-

tion. The problem of agreeing on Danube conventions has eased through two circumstances: the end of internecine wars (though not by any means yet of rivalries) and the sharing of common economic aims and means. On paper these have produced a real effort at integration, though practice still lags far behind. Generally, though, the abyss of welfare and comfort that used to separate the upper Danube lands from their neighbours to the east and south has greatly narrowed. Sleepy river towns like Novi Sad are no longer what they were. Novi Sad, indeed, has grown into something of a small metropolis, far bigger and more prosperous than before, while rumour even speaks of Palanka, little riverside Palanka where I hid in 1944 and watched the German army ploughing through the mud outside, as having got itself a fish restaurant that is quite *hors classe*. I find this a good thought after all the wars and worries, and I happily believe it.

A world away from the Blue Danube of song, people live and work on the shores of the river where slow, deep and serene, it flows into the Black Sea

THE ELBE

JOSEPH WECHSBERG

An allegorical representation of the god of the Elbe, a river of dark memories whose waters have divided enemies more often than its bridges have united friends

BALTIC SEA

DENMARK

NORTH SEA

THE ELBE

W E S T
G E R M A N Y

Altona
Hamburg

Wittenberge

River Havel

Spandau
BERLIN

Brandenburg

Memorial Church

Magdeburg
Cathedral

POLAND

GERMANY

CZECHOSLOVAKIA

AUSTRIA

Dessau

Wittenberg
Martin Luther: The Reformation

Torgau
Americans & Russians join hands across the Elbe, 1945

Leipzig

River Saale

1813 Napoleon defeated by Russian Armies

Meissen Cathedral

Dresden before the bombing of 1945

Decin

River Ohre (Eger)

Usti
Cathedral

River Berounka

River Vltava

Mělník

PRAGUE

River Isar

River Sazava

The Reisengebirge
The Source

Hradec
Králové

Kolin

Kilometres 0 10 20 30 40
Miles 0 10 20 30 40 5

In a rockstrewn meadow high up in the Czechoslovakian mountains, a well marks the source of the river which flows nearly 700 miles to the North Sea

O
F ALL the great rivers of Europe none has been more tragically affected by past and recent history than the Elbe. *Fata viam invenient*, wrote Virgil. The Fates have indeed found their way along the Elbe.

A great river has its profile and personality, its far-away echo and contemporary life, its destiny and fascination. To each man it has its own meaning. The poet dreams of the river's myths and the composer evokes the music of its waters. The mapmaker draws its course, the historian its past, the merchant its trade possibilities, the philosopher wonders about the eternal flow of its waters and the military man considers it a strategic obstacle or a bridgehead to victory.

But there are few myths around the Elbe and very little poetry, none of it good. The Rhine, dearly beloved by romanticists, has been called a melted emerald, and the Rhône a dissolved sapphire. The Danube, which is rarely blue and not always beautiful, will remain so for ever in the minds of men, owing to Johann Strauss' bittersweet waltzes. Great painters have immortalised

the Seine and the Arno; historians love the Marne and Biblical scholars the Jordan; and Russia's novelists have recreated the dramatic stories of the Don and the Volga.

The mighty Elbe has often influenced the course of Europe's civilisation, yet the mythmakers, the poets, the composers, the painters, the novelists ignore it. But warriors, statesmen, kings, and dictators have always known it well. To them the Elbe was a flowing fortress that had to be conquered, a barrier that had to be broken down. Mystic-minded Germans have called the Rhine their *Schicksalsstrom*, river of destiny. Yet it is really the Elbe that deserves that name. The Rhine is now a happy river where people sing of love and wine, and speak of *rapprochement* and business. The Elbe is a river of tears.

The Elbe, Germany's second-largest river, has never been a unifying force between nations, always a boundary. In 9 B.C. the Elbe marked the farthest northern

advance of the Romans who called it Albis. In the fifth century German tribes occupied the land west of the Elbe, pushed there by Slavonic tribes, who had occupied the ridges east of the river. Four hundred years later there came the first of many German eastward movements, all of them unsuccessful. For the past fifteen centuries a continuous ebb and flow of great human tides has swept across the Elbe's slow, grey waters.

To the historian most rivers are roads along which nations seem to be drawn toward their ultimate destiny. The Elbe is an exception: peoples never moved alongside the river that separated two civilisations, Germans and Slavs. Strategically, it was rarely a serious obstacle and has been crossed many times since the dawn of history. All the battles and crusades fought around the Elbe – crusades for new territory and more power, for faith and conversion, business and trade – moved *across* the Elbe, always from west to east. All were repulsed in the opposite direction.

Only once the Elbe enjoyed a brief moment of glory.

A rich and fertile river valley stretches from Velký Černošek, a typical Czech village of vineyards and orchards, to the foothills of the Mittelgebirge, a highland region of Germany

At 4.40 on the afternoon of 26 April 1945, elements of the 69th Division of the United States First Army met spearheads of the 58th Guards Division of the Ukrainian First Army on the Elbe bridge near Torgau. The Red Army and the American forces which had been 2300 miles apart when their painful, killing march toward victory began, had at long last established contact. The most hellish war in mankind's history was almost over. 'The Meeting at the Elbe' was hailed by many people as the symbol of a bright, new future.

Alas, the moment of togetherness was brief. Today the source of the Elbe is high up in the windswept mountains of Communist Czechoslovakia, almost in the geographical centre of Europe. Its estuary is near Hamburg, a symbol of Capitalist trade and power. At the lighthouse 'Alte Liebe' (Old Love) the Elbe flows into the North Sea.

Old Love... For many people it is just that, a melancholy river of nostalgia, a memory of better days and lost homes. Today the Elbe forms the strangest boundary

in Europe, between West and East Germany. The electrified barbed-wire frontier runs only twelve miles east of Hamburg, and south of Lübeck to the Elbe above Lauenburg, thence along the river for 38 miles. An old German folk song tells about two *Königskinder*, the children of warring kings.

> *Sie konnten zusammen nicht kommen,*
> *Das Wasser war viel zu tief.*

'They couldn't get together – the water was much too deep.' A great many people on both banks of the Elbe feel that the water is getting deeper all the time.

The Germans call the Elbe a 'German' river because for 496 miles out of its total of 724, the river flows through the two Germanys. But the Elbe is a child of the mountains of Bohemia where it was christened 'Labe'. It listened to fairy tales in its native Krkonoš (Riesengebirge) where its source is on the Elbe Meadows, at an altitude of 4000 feet, below the wind-swept

Hohes Rad. A small well and a plaque indicate the spot. Standing there as a little boy many years ago, I wondered whether I would be able to stop the flow of the mighty stream by throwing pebbles and sand into the small source... Nearby was Agnetendorf, where the eminent German playwright, Gerhart Hauptmann, had his home.

One of Hauptmann's dramas, *Die Weber* (The Weavers) concerns the plight of the poor, hard-working people of the mountains. Poor people dream of good fairies that bring them sudden wealth, and the Riesengebirge has its mountain-god, called Rübezahl, a Sudeten-German, lower-echelon version of Wotan. Rübezahl is the tutelary saint of bearded foresters and lost orphans. Alas, he didn't bring the people sudden wealth. They had to learn to trust the skill of their hands, and they did very well in the course of the centuries. This is the country of famous glass blowers, ceramics artists, of porcelain makers and builders of musical instruments.

In these lonely, lovely mountains the Elbe – I use the

51

Near Mělník, Czechoslovakia, where the Elbe is joined by its most famous tributary, the Moldau, and can be navigated by barges, the river cuts deep gorges round sandstone rocks many hundreds of feet high

BOTTOM RIGHT *Barges being towed past the landing stage at the tiny German village of Rathen, located at the base of the Bastei, an enormous sheer cliff 640 feet high*

BOTTOM LEFT *The Bohemian plain from the summit of the Schrammstein, one of the rugged masses of weatherworn rock that stand like fortresses guarding the Elbe where it leaves the mountains*

German name to avoid confusion–is still an exuberant foaming stream, jumping happily down the rocks, joining up with a playmate, the Weisswasser, at the resort of Spindlerúv Mlýn (Spindlermühle), flowing past the town of Vrchlabí (once known as Hohenelbe). As it approaches the plains, it becomes more sedate, flowing past the mysterious baroque castle of Kukus, once the residence of Count Franz Anton Sporck, a Bohemian mystic and pietist, who summoned to his court the Tyrolian sculptor Matthias Braun, a pupil of Bernini. Braun made Kukus into an Eastern outpost of Roman baroque. He cut immense sandstone figures in the woods, building a cathedral under the trees.

Mystics have always been attracted by the majestic, monotonous waters of the river. Wallenstein, the strange, controversial generalissimus of the Thirty Years' War, was born in the village of Hermanitz near the Elbe, and later, before he was murdered, lived in mystic seclusion near the river. Hundreds of books have been written about this enigmatic man. Another

great mystic, Charles IV, king of Bohemia, emperor of the 'Holy Roman Empire of the German Nation' was also fascinated by the river. He built himself Karlštejn Castle in Bohemia with a chapel whose ceiling shows the solar system. The walls were adorned with gold leaf and a thousand polished semi-precious stones. Later he had another castle built in Tangermünde, overlooking the Elbe, halfway between Magdeburg and Hamburg. Theoderich of Prague and Thomas of Modena covered the walls with his beloved semi-precious stones, and twelve Bohemian nobles were installed as guardians of the Emperor's 'grail'.

Mysticism was not the only reason that made Charles IV build his castle on the lower part of the Elbe. He was a man of great vision. This was the golden epoch of the Hanse and Charles IV dreamed of making the Elbe the great trade route of his empire, 'the golden river' that would connect Prague with Hamburg, and would become a network of trade routes reaching out as far east as Breslau and Königsberg. He encouraged com-

mercial alliances with the Hanse towns, had plans drawn up for the regulation of the Elbe, an audacious scheme with dams and river ports that was centuries ahead of its time. But after his death in 1378, with the Hussite wars approaching, the great scheme was forgotten.

Leaving the mountains, the Elbe now enters the rich Bohemian plains, Bohemia's most fertile lowland and historically an important prize that was contested for centuries between Slavs and Germans. But the biggest contest was between Austria and Prussia in the eighteenth century when a formidable coalition of continental powers under Austria tried to destroy Frederick the Great. Much of the action of the Seven Years' War was fought along the banks of the Elbe.

On 29 August 1756, the Prussian troops invaded Saxony and occupied Dresden. Frederick the Great moved up from his headquarters at Pirna near Dresden. The Austrians, taken by surprise, were defeated near the Elbe town of Lobositz. The Prussians laid siege

53

to Prague, and the end of the war seemed near. But Frederick the Great was decisively defeated at Kolin, an old town overlooking the river. The battle lasted only five and a half hours but the Prussians lost eighteen per cent of their troops, and as a result Frederick had to abandon all of Bohemia. In Kolin's thirteenth-century Church of St Bartholomew which was later rebuilt by the great Gothic architect Peter Parler, Frederick the Great spent one of the saddest hours of his life. Later the Prussians and Austrians met again at the Elbe, at the fortress of Torgau, in a battle which paralysed both sides. When the war was over, the Elbe was still flowing slowly, majestically, but its banks were literally drenched with blood.

And a hundred years later Prussians and Austrians met once more near their river of destiny, at Königgrätz, in 1866. This time the Prussians were victorious, and the consequences of the engagement, the consolidation of a united Germany under the leadership of Bismarck's Prussia, have never been forgotten. The Elbe in Bohemia is still only a young river, but it already has melancholy memories of a sad, unhappy childhood.

At Mělník there is the junction of the Elbe with its most famous tributary, the Vltava (Moldau). The river becomes navigable for barges. The Vltava collects the waters of the Forest of Šumava and brings them to the Elbe. It is the national river of Bohemia, the reflection of the country's history, the very image of the Czech soul, and it was immortalised by the country's greatest composer. Bedrich Smetana wrote the tone poem *Vltava*, a movement in his masterpiece *Má Vlast*, (My Country). The great, sad history of Smetana's country is evoked by his work. There are the faraway sounds of Vyšehrad, where the heroic past begins, and the muted trumpets of Tábor where the past fades into the myth. The country's hopes and defeats, its unhappy history and bucolic charm are all in Smetana's music. The romantic sweep of the waters of the Vltava comes to life in the concert halls of the world.

The wines of Mělník are the best in Bohemia. They have been produced there since the beginning of the thirteenth century; the vines grow well in the hilly country between Prague to the south and the spas of Karlovy Vary (Carlsbad) and Mariánské Lázně (Marienbad) to the north. The river flows past Říp, a 'holy' mountain that mysteriously rises out of the plains; and there is Roudnice, where Cola di Rienzi (1313–54), the Roman tribune, was imprisoned before Charles IV delivered him to Pope Clement VI at Avignon in 1352.

Twenty miles below Mělník the Elbe receives its second important Bohemian river, the Ohře (Eger). The countryside is called 'Golden Rod', an idyllic landscape with orchards and fields, a paradise on earth.

Abruptly the idyll is broken. There is the old Austrian fortress of Leitmeritz (Litoměřice) where Gavrilo Princip was imprisoned – the man who fired the shots in Sarajevo that led to the First World War. Across the river is the Czech fortress of Terezín (Theresienstadt), which was a notorious Nazi concentration camp during the Second World War. No matter where the Elbe flows it always seems to meet tragedy sooner or later. Alfred Kubin who translated the dark, strange world of Kafka into his dark, strange drawings, was born not far from here.

For a while there is sheer beauty, however. The Elbe valley between Leitmeritz and Dresden has been compared to the landscape of the Rhine between Bingen and Koblenz. Every great river has some romance in its past, and the romance of the Elbe is found here. The colours of the countryside are deep and the light is soft. At Velký Černošek, where the Elbe crosses the Porta Bohemica into the Mittelgebirge, the northernmost vines of Bohemia are planted. German and Bohemian painters who dreamed of Italy but were too poor to go there, would come to the valley of the Elbe to paint in its diffused light. No visible memories of the cruel past disturb the wanderer. Near Ústí (Aussig) the ruin of Schreckenstein ('stone of terror') up on a high hill overlooks the Elbe, but the river below is dotted with excursion boats and there is the sound of music.

People from the north were always drawn toward this part of Europe, so rich in tales and traditions, bloodshed and beauty. The fields of Bohemia, the old castles, the great baroque towers of Prague. Heinrich von Kleist, the great German playwright, after a journey to the Elbe wrote: 'We arrived in Bohemia near Lobositz at the southern rim of the Erzgebirge, where the Elbe enters the mountains. It made me think of a young maiden that appears suddenly among a group of men. The river makes its entrance; shy and lovely and slim

A view of Königstein, Saxony, in the eighteenth century, with its fortress perched like an eagle's nest 700 feet above the little town on the river

it appears among the powerful rocks, the men. It seems staggered by the tall figures. They crowd around the river, want to block its way, desirous to see the lovely face of the virgin. But she doesn't stay on. Her cheeks reddened, she smiles sweetly, and gracefully winds through the rocks on her way... It was one of these soft, sweet, half-dusk days that bring to the mind a sense of nostalgia and the hidden wishes of the heart.'

One understands why the Germans say '*die* Elbe'. It's a feminine river, soft and shy, sad and suffering. Not a masculine, heroic, dominating stream like '*der* Rhein'.

The rounded hills recede, the plains disappear in a haze, and the Elbe crosses the Mittelgebirge, cutting through the fantastically sculptured region of hard, cretaceous sandstone that for some unfathomable reason has been called 'Saxony's Switzerland'. The analogy is all wrong. This is the sinister never-never land of Kafka's *Castle,* not the meadows-and-Alphorn symphony of Schiller's *Wilhelm Tell.* A bizarre nightmare formation. Unlike the castles of the Rhine which were built by men, the castles of the Elbe were built by God.

And in the very middle of this formidable landscape, where the river is narrow, accompanied by a road and a railroad, a few wooden towers stand, with machine guns on top and sentries. Why this fortified border between two members of the Soviet Satellite family? To keep the Czechs from escaping to East Germany or the East Germans from running away into Bohemia? This boundary is not a Kafka nightmare, but a real one.

Now the Labe becomes officially the Elbe, a German river, with a split personality, like the country itself. Near Schandau, once a summer resort for well-to-do bourgeois, now a vacation spa for the workers and peasants of the German Democratic Republic, is the fortress of Königstein where the Germans kept high-ranking prisoners during the last war. Generals always had special privileges – why shouldn't they have their own prison fortress?

Farther downstream is the castle of Pillnitz, once a summer residence of the kings of Saxony. In Pöppelmann's 'Wasserpalais' Emperor Leopold II and Frederick William II of Prussia met in August 1791, to discuss plans against the consequences of the French Revolution... And now, as it reaches Dresden, the Elbe approaches its moment of glory.

TOP *The Castle of Pillnitz or 'Water Palace', built on the Elbe for Augustus the Strong (1670–1733), King of Poland and Elector of Saxony*

ABOVE *The side-wheel steamer Königin Maria on the Elbe near Dresden in 1836, twenty years after the first steamboat had appeared on the river*

LEFT *A painting by the nineteenth-century artist Anton Schiffer of one of the first paddle-wheel steamers on the Elbe, in the rocky, winding valley below Königstein. On the left, the peaks of the Bastei rise high above the river*

OVERLEAF *Dresden in the eighteenth century, by Bernardo Bellotto (1720–80), whose accurate detail was invaluable in the reconstruction of the city which was all but razed by Allied bombs in World War II. On the right of the Augustus Bridge, named for Augustus the Strong, is the Catholic Hofkirche, the Court Church, with its 280 foot tower still under construction and fifty-nine sandstone statues of saints. Behind the bridge is the Frauenkirche, built in 1726 by Lutheran citizens as a protest against the conversion of Augustus the Strong to Catholicism*

tourists and Red Army soldiers relax after the rigours of sightseeing.

The end of the German Florence came the night of 13 February 1945 – *Faschingsdienstag*, the last day of the carnival – when the Royal Air Force dropped 300 tons of phosphorous bombs on the historic Altstadt. The attack lasted fourteen minutes. It was followed three hours later by a second Royal Air Force attack, and the next day by a third, when 300 Flying Fortresses of the United States Eighth Air Force bombed the city.

Gerhart Hauptmann, then 83 years old, watched the raids from Weidner's Sanatorium on Loschwitzhöhe overlooking the city, and later wrote; 'He who no longer knows how to cry learns to cry again at the end of Dresden . . .'

Dresden, as people had known it, was dead. Gone was the Frauenkirche from whose dome Goethe had looked in 1768 at the city that was destroyed after the Seven Years' War. In 1813 Napoleon had stored munitions there with no ill consequences for the building. In 1945 Hermann Göring was using it as a warehouse for millions of feet of Luftwaffe reconnaissance film. This time its luck ran out. The films exploded and the church burned out. Also destroyed was the Hofkirche, and the castle. Only a few broken walls remain. On the golden mosaic of a jagged wall an old inscription had survived:

'Wie alte Zeit

Dein Volk Dir wahrt

Die alte deutsche Treue.'

(As in old times your nation keeps its old German faith.) Many people here wish the inscription had disappeared instead of the castle . . .

And gone was the greatest treasure of all, the magnificent Zwinger, one of the world's great art galleries which ranked with the Louvre, the Prado, the Uffize, and the Vatican Museum, and contained some of the world's most celebrated paintings, Raphael's 'Sistine Madonna', masterpieces by Titian, Giorgione, Veronese, Correggio, Vermeer, Tintoretto, Murillo, many Rembrandts, among them the wonderful 'Selfportrait with

Flowing in from the nearby mountains, the Elbe formed a graceful curve as it entered the beautiful city, making a graceful bow to a great queen. It seemed to bring the lush colours of the wooden hills and the enchanted countryside right into the town, and with it a sense of peace and tranquillity. Like the Arno at Florence and the Seine at Paris, the Elbe was always a functional part of the city's architectural plan. The lovely baroque palaces, churches, theatres, terraces that adorned its banks, the splendid bridges that crossed it – all might have been designed expressly to create spectacular mirror effects in the water, especially at night. The river was an integral part of the city. Dresden without the Elbe was as unimaginable as Budapest without the Danube. It was hard to say whose beauty was greater – the city's or the river's.

The magnificent baroque structures alongside the silvery band of the river gave Dresden a sense of harmony and an appearance of nobility. The great German humanist, Johann Gottfried Herder, called Dresden 'the German Florence'. The Dresdeners themselves spoke of 'Elbflorenz'. And the German historian Edward Winkelmann said it was 'the German Athens'.

Dresden was a feminine city of great charm, and the Elbe was the mirror of its beauty. Its landmark was the beautiful Frauenkirche with its vaulted dome, which the Lutheran citizens built after 1726 as a protest against the Elector, Augustus the Strong, who had taken the Catholic faith so he could be crowned King of Polonia. The Frauenkirche had a beautiful organ, a masterpiece of Gottfried Silbermann, the Stradivari of organ builders.

Across from it stood the castle, and next to it the late-baroque Catholic Hofkirche with a slim, elegant spire and its girdle of sandstone saints which, seen from across the Elbe, looked like filigree. Gaetano Chiaveri, the Italian builder, brought stucco and terrazzo workers from his native Italy. They lived in the 'Italian village' in small houses on the bank of the Elbe. Today the name has survived in a state-owned restaurant where

Saskia'. Across the square stood the Dresden Staatsoper, one of Gottfried Semper's great theatres, forming a harmonious whole with the great buildings around it.

Some Dresdeners, with their strange passion for Wagnerian supertragedy, now find grim satisfaction in claiming that Dresden suffered more from bombs than any other city in Germany. Anybody who saw Berlin at the end of the war would find it hard to imagine a more heavily damaged city, but when it was all over and statistics could be computed with mathematical nicety, it was found there were 16 cubic metres of rubble for every inhabitant of Berlin, while each Dresdener could boast 43 cubic metres.

In fact, Dresden was almost as badly smashed as was Warsaw when the Germans had finished with it. And both the historic old towns of Dresden and Warsaw were restored with the help of Canaletto, the Venetian eighteenth-century painter who fell in love with Dresden at first sight as he later fell in love with Warsaw. His scrupulously exact paintings were used by the Polish architects supervising the reconstruction of Warsaw's Staré Miasto (Old City), and by the German architects who rebuilt some of Dresden's more historic buildings. Some people in Dresden and Warsaw now see a deeper poetic justice in the heritage of Canaletto.

The restoration of the Zwinger was completed, after enormous difficulties and fourteen years of work. Piece by piece the portals and pavilions, the statuettes and rococo ornaments were recreated, the remains of the copper roof were salvaged, and each ornamental leaf was lovingly repaired and restored to its place. The Hofkirche was restored but the jagged remains of the Frauenkirche will be left as a horrid memorial to the supreme folly of war. Dresden has again half a million people. The East German government calls it 'a city of industry, science and the arts, a centre in the heavily populated Elbe region, the third-largest industrial region in the German Democratic Republic'. Few of its former inhabitants would recognise the new city.

Fifteen miles farther north-west the Elbe flows past the late-Gothic Albrechtsburg overlooking Meissen, the birthplace of European hard-paste porcelain. Its inventor was Johann Friedrich Boettger, an apothecary apprentice from Berlin who was said to be a promising alchemist. The impecunious king of Prussia tried to seize Boettger. The 'alchemist' fled to Saxony where he was promptly seized by the police of the not-so-impecunious Elector who needed more gold for his mistresses and canvasses. Boettger was installed first at the Jungferbastei, an Elbe fortress, and later at the Albrechtsburg

ABOVE *Albrechtsburg Castle at Meissen, fifteen miles north of Dresden on the Elbe, in 1800. Here, ninety-two years earlier, the imprisoned alchemist J. F. Böttger had discovered the secret of porcelain-making, a Chinese art, which was to make Meissen world famous*

RIGHT Spanish Lovers *from the Italian Comedy series, a classic example of Meissen ware by the great designer and innovator, Johann Joachim Kaendler*

On 23 September 1697, the Elbe overflowed its banks and inundated the surrounding countryside, as shown in this contemporary engraving of the disaster. Serious flooding still occurs from the spring snow-melt in March

where he and his workers were virtual prisoners. In 1709 he submitted a memorandum claiming discovery of 'the good white porcelain with the finest glaze and all painting belonging to it'. The following year the State Porcelain Manufacture was established 'whose products will rival those of Asia'. Its golden era began in 1731 when Johann Joachim Kaendler made his great masterpieces there. After over 250 years Meissen's 'blue onion' patterns are still its most popular designs.

Meissen escaped destruction during the war though the SS blew up the stone bridge over the Elbe a few hours before they ran away. A new bridge was built. From Meissen's Frauenkirche every noon the lovely sound of its porcelain glockenspiel fills the air.

The Elbe continues its journey past Torgau which Napoleon made into a fortress, and Wittenberg, where Martin Luther nailed his 95 theses to the entrance of the Schlosskirche, and where he and his pupil Melancthon lie buried. Half-way between Dresden and Hamburg is Magdeburg, the old fortress of the German

ABOVE Martin Luther *by Lucas Cranach the Elder (1472–1553), the leading painter of the German Reformation period. The Great Reformer lived near the Elbe from the age of fourteen, when he was sent to Magdeburg to study*

RIGHT *Jesus Being Baptised in the Elbe in the Presence of Luther and the Prince's Family, an allegory by Lucas Cranach the Younger (1515–85) to console the imprisoned Elector of Saxony for his defeat and capture at the Battle of Muhlberg in 1547 by the Catholic emperor, Charles V*

BELOW *The fortress town of Wittenberg, cradle of the Reformation, where Luther received the decisive illumination of justification by faith, nailed his ninety-five theses to the castle door and burned the Papal Bull of excommunication*

MAGDEBURG.

colonisers, once the easternmost bastion of the Occidental World, with a beautiful old cathedral, a synthesis of French and German Gothic. From here water traffic reaches out in all directions: to Prague in the south, to Berlin in the east, through the Mittelland Canal to Hanover in the west, through the Dortmund-Ems Canal to the Ruhr and the Rhine, and to Hamburg in the north.

From Magdeburg to Hamburg the Elbe is a river of the plains, bordered by many marshes. There were bad floods here in spring when the flow of the river is at its maximum, or in summer after heavy rainstorms, but now the marshes are drained and have become strips of fertile farmland.

The character of the land is different on both banks. The land between Elbe and Rhine is flat and monotonous. To the east there are depressions bordered by dry, high, wooded ridges. (Prussia means 'land of spruce'.) This is the land of eternal strife, of attempts to cross the river to convert the people in the East and colonise the land. Since Charlemagne countless rulers have had these ambitions. There was Henry I the Fowler (the basso king in Wagner's *Lohengrin*) who defeated the Havelli. Gero, margrave of the East Saxon Mark; Otto the Great, who founded the bishopric of Brandenburg; Lothair of Saxony who renewed the

OPPOSITE LEFT *An engraving by Matheus Merian (1593–1650) showing the storming, sacking and burning of Magdeburg, a stronghold of the German Protestant Princes during the Thirty Years' War, by von Tilly, the General of the Catholic League, in 1631*

OPPOSITE RIGHT *A portrait by Van Dyck of Albrecht von Wallenstein (1583–1634), the soldier-statesman who, during the Thirty Years' War, fought a brilliant series of campaigns for Ferdinand, Emperor of Austria, and defeated Count Mansfeld's English mercenaries at Dessau, near the Elbe. The ruthless and brutal Wallenstein later became distrusted and was assassinated*

OPPOSITE BELOW *The Cathedral of St Maurice and St Katherine at Magdeburg, one of the earliest examples of German Gothic architecture, was built on the site of a church erected by Otto the Great, the tenth-century founder of Austria*

RIGHT *The Battle of Muhlberg in 1547, when the Catholic army of Charles V surprised the Protestants commanded by the Elector of Saxony, forced a crossing of the Elbe and seized control of the ford at Schirmenitz*

BELOW *4.40 p.m., 26 April 1945. At a partially wrecked bridge near Torgau, American and Russian soldiers join hands across the river which now, twenty years later, forms part of the barrier between East and West*

attack in 1106; and many others. In the thirteenth century towns were founded, among them Berlin. The marshy lands were drained. The knights of the Teutonic Order occupied the new farmlands. Later the Junker grew up here, county aristrocrats with immense properties who developed a tight hold over the peasants, and have since become an evil symbol of feudalism.

Dynasties came and went – Wittelsbach, Luxembourg, Hohenzollern – but the tide of history remained as unchanged as the flow of the Elbe; always it was the Germans who wanted to push back the Slavs, and the Germans' attacks were always repulsed. They nearly succeeded under Hitler when the Germans went farther east than any other army before, but the end came inexorably and terrifyingly. Today Slavonic power is back again at the Elbe, as it was fifteen centuries ago.

Of Germany's two great waterways only the north–south trade artery of the Rhine remained intact. The east-west system of the Elbe which was connected through the Saale, the Havel and a network of lakes and canals with the Baltic and the Oder, was badly afflicted by the division of Germany. Of the two great sections of the Elbe's water traffic – from Hamburg to Berlin, and from Czechoslovakia to Hamburg – much

LEFT *These multi-storey merchants' houses on the Nicolai Canal in old Hamburg were built in the seventeenth century, with warehouses on the upper floors and pulleys for lifting cargo from boats below*

OPPOSITE *A painting by Valentine Ruth (1827–1905), the marine artist and lithographer, of the Wooden House in Hamburg. Its size and splendours testified to the wealth and power the sea and the Elbe together brought this great trading city*

was cut off. In an easterly direction all traffic now ends in Berlin. And the trade between Hamburg and Prague has dwindled. It is hard to realise that before 1938 half the goods that reached Hamburg were water-borne, that the density of traffic along the lower Elbe was almost as great as that on the Rhine.

The recovery of the port of Hamburg is one of the miracles of post-war Germany. Eighty-five miles from the mouth of the Elbe, Hamburg breathes the smell of the sea. The waters of the Elbe are everywhere in Hamburg – in its tributary, the Alster, in its lovely lakes, the Binnen–Alster and Aussen–Alster, that have earned Hamburg the name of the German Venice. The title seems particularly fitting at night, when you walk along Jungfernstieg, and see the lighted buildings reflected in the water. The Elbe is part of the city. People talk about the changing tide as they talk elsewhere about the weather. To the Hamburgers, the Elbe is almost a human being, a member of the family. They know how much they owe to it. 'Without the Elbe,' an economic expert said recently, 'Hamburg might be today a small, obscure village.' But Hamburg has the Elbe and as a result ten million people live within a 90-mile radius around the proud Gothic Hamburg City Hall. A similar concentration of people exists on the continent of Europe only around Paris, Frankfurt and Düsseldorf.

They are a very special breed, the people of Hamburg. Since 1189, when Frederick Barbarossa, Holy Roman Emperor, grateful for Hamburg's help during one of the Crusades, granted the burghers the right 'to pass to and fro with their ships and goods, from the sea to the said city, free of any duty and charge", the people of the Free Port of Hamburg have been proud of their independence. Their city is ruled by its own council. In 1266 when some Hamburg merchants were living in

OPPOSITE *A passenger launch on the Elbe at Hamburg, painted by the Post-Impressionist, Albert Marquet (1875–1947), with the simplicity that was his special gift*

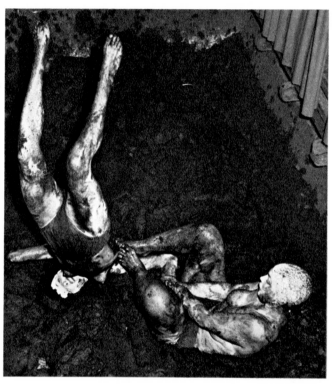

Labour and leisure in the Hamburg dockyard quarter

(Top row) From one of Hamburg's newest bridges spectators look out over the vast industrial and shipping centre

(Bottom row) Hamburg dock workers spend off-hours in conversation over good German beer in the harbour bars, while in a city famous for its infamous night life, one of the chief tourist attractions is women wrestlers (or, for those in search of more bizarre entertainment, women wrestling barebreasted in mud)

69

London, King Henry III of England recognized them as members of the Hansa–a trade league–'quod ipsi habeant hansam suam' (that they have their own league).

Like Venice in its great days, Hamburg is in effect a city–state. For centuries its shipbuilders and merchant princes considered themselves the equals of nobility in other parts of Germany. Hamburg's old families – the Petersens, Godeffroys, Chapeaurouges, Sievekings–repeatedly refused to accept titles from German rulers. Kaiser William II, on an official visit to the city, was greeted by the mayor of Hamburg as 'Lieber Bundesgenosse' ('Dear Ally') which delighted the citizens and irritated the Kaiser. He may have forgotten that the Hanseatic League once was an armed alliance and successfully waged war against Denmark.

Some of the powerful old shipping magnates still live in their beautiful houses in splendid isolation along the Alster but the tide is running against them. Hamburg has become the largest industrial city in Germany and the most modern port in Europe. It seems incredible–it is only a little over twenty years since *die Katastrophe* when the port and city, after nine days of saturation bombing in midsummer of 1943, were turned into a shambles. Hamburg has even overcome the supreme handicap of having lost much of its former Elbe trade.

The new Hamburg is one of the cultural centres of Germany. The old legend of the 'cold' North Germans who were interested only in money no longer exists there. Since the end of the war publishers have come here from Leipzig and Berlin, musicians and painters from Dresden. Hamburg may justifiably be called West Germany's Athens, with its great Kunsthalle, State Opera, Philharmonic, its excellent theatres, well-run radio station, film studios and newspapers.

Hamburg's heartbeat can be felt as one follows the Elbe toward its estuary, past enormous shipyards, brand-new port installations, beautiful houses, large factories. There is traffic, excitement, the sound of foghorns, the racket of riveters. The sounds and the work never stop; this is an immensely alive river.

In its lowest part the Elbe is divided by some islands into several branches which unite again five miles before reaching their goal. Gradually the greyish water of the river takes on the greenish-blue shades of the open sea. The river has now become an enormous, ten-mile-wide stream, as wide as a large lake. Having overcome at long last the trials of history and the tribulations of the past, the great Elbe now flows with supreme confidence and unrestrained power into the sea.

150 years after the first paddle-wheel steamship churned up the Elbe, little more than 100 years after a cart ferry came into operation across the estuary and only twenty-two years after almost total destruction in war, Hamburg is Germany's second largest city and chief port — a magnificent climax to the journey that begins seven hundred miles away in a well in the Czechoslovakian mountains

THE LOIRE

FREDA WHITE

The closing lines of a sonnet by the French Renaissance poet
Joachim du Bellay, written while he was working in Rome in
1553–58. These lines, reproduced from a 1573 edition of his
works, express the poet's longing for the natural beauty of the
Loire valley and for his home at Liré not far from Nantes

Plus me plaiſt le ſeiour qu ont baſty mes ayeux,
  Que des palais Romains le front audacieux:
Plus que le marbre dur me plaiſt l'ardoiſe fine,
Plus mon Loyre Gaulois, que le Tybre Latin,
  Plus mon petit Lyré, que le mont Palatin,
  Et plus que l'air marin la doulceur Angeuine.

THE LOIRE

MANCHE

CALVADOS

ORNE

EURE ET
LOIRE

LO

Châteaudun

Orléans

Beau

Kilometres 0 10 20 30 40 50

Miles 0 10 20 30 40 50

SARTHE

Che

Blois

Rochambeau

MAYENNE

Le Mans

River Loir

River Sarthe

River Mayenne

Amboise

CÔTES
DU
NORD

Craon

Sablé

Le Lude

Tours

Chenonceaux

River Oudon

Villandry

VILAINE

Langeais

ILLE ET

La Loire

Montgeoffroy

Azay le Rideau

Usse

Angers

Saumur

Chinon

MORBIHAN

Brissac

MAINE
ET
LOIRE

Montreuil Bellay

River Thouet

River

VIENNE

Nantes

LOIRE
ATLANTIQUE

River Sèvre

St Nazaire

VENDÉE

DEUX
SÈVRES

THE ATLANTIC

CHA

THERE ARE four great French rivers, the Rhône, the Garonne, the Loire and the Seine. For many Frenchmen and for most foreigners the Loire – which has been the scene of so many dramatic moments in French history, and whose châteaux are among the most beautiful examples of Renaissance architecture – has come to symbolise France herself.

The Loire is the longest river that flows through all its course within the borders of France. It is 1000 kilometres – 600 miles – long. It rises at the top of the Vivarais, the inner range of the northern Cévennes. For a long distance it runs almost due north and then it takes a north-westerly direction in a great curve at whose apex stands the city of Orléans. At this point it encounters low hills, just tall enough to deflect it towards the south-west and to hold it in this course until it reaches the Atlantic at Nantes.

The little stream, which at the outset is so narrow that a strong jumper can leap it from bank to bank, receives tributaries from either side. Many of these, especially the Allier, come in before it turns on the Orléans bend. After that a whole series of rivers, the Cher, the Indre, the Vienne run north-westerly down from the Massif Central into the Loire, each in its own valley. On the north side the Loir roughly parallels the Loire, separated from it by the cornlands of the Beauce. Confusingly it bears the same name, except for the omission of the feminine 'e'. It joins the Sarthe and the Mayenne above Angers, and, renamed the Maine, flows into the Loire near Nantes. There the Loire finds the root of the long estuary where the waters of the river mingle with the tides of the Atlantic.

In high summer you can lean on the parapet of the bridge of Tours and regard the shrunken Loire dividing round shoals and sandbanks. You might think you could paddle across it – and indeed the bridge marks an ancient ford – but you had better not try for the river is deeper than it appears. In Autumn after the November rains and again in March when the snows melt in the Massif Central and the water comes down to the plains in

ABOVE *Not far from its source the Loire (right) is joined by its first tributary*

LEFT *The farmhouse which stands at the source of the Loire at the foot of the peak of the Gerbier de Jonc in the Vivrais mountains*

spate, the Loire brims its banks. In many years it floods the country round about and inundation lies for miles over the fields. The Cher especially is subject to violent risings. From the castle-ridge of Chinon on the Vienne you can look at a waste of water, lapping on the door-sills of the houses in the street below, stretching away to the horizon. The grey flood reflects the low heavy sky; the ruined castle has the melancholy of a dream. But long before the summer travellers come that way, the floods have subsided, leaving the year's deposit of the alluvial silt that makes the riches of the Loire farming. The sky has lifted to the high pale blue of spring. Small clouds sail across it from the west. The river is calm and silvery blue, between the embankments from which roads run between poplar avenues just in leaf. Flowers in meadow and orchard shine with vernal white and yellow. Then the country can truly claim its title of 'the Garden of France'.

Spring, too, is the time to follow the Loire from its mountain sources. They lie at the heart of the Massif

Central. The whole of that region is called the 'water-tower of France', because rivers run from it to every point of the compass. Millions of years ago the mountain mass used to be a series of ranges of hard rock, granite, sandstone, and slate, rimmed round by lower plateau of limestone and chalk. Those softer rocks were left bare when the seas of even earlier ages sank away, leaving behind them the petrified bones of fishes, sometimes to a depth of thousands of feet. The Massif, as we know it now, was shaped by the Great Foldings of fifty million years ago, when the whole of Europe was wrenched and split by an age of volcanic convulsions. In many places great peaks rose up, burst, and poured lava down their slopes. In others the rock-crust was blown up in blisters that did not break, but formed the 'domes' common in the Massif. Whole ranges were turned topsy-turvy. The limestone rim cracked like china into canyons and gulfs. The Pyrenees and Alps, new ranges thrown up by the Foldings, wrinkled up the southern and eastern sides of the Massif Central, which are steep, often precipitous,

The eleventh-century chapel of St Michel d'Aiguille perched on a needle of volcanic rock 250 feet above the ancient town of Le Puy. Originally the site of a temple to Mercury, this dome of rock thrusting up dramatically from the surrounding land is characteristic of the countryside near the source of the Loire

while the northern and western slopes are far gentler.

This history of elemental violence explains the strange course of the Massif rivers. The Rhône runs north to south beneath the steep eastern side of the mountains. But in the inner hills the Vivarais, the highest of the Cévennes ranges, rise like a wall. On their western side the rivers run north, and among them, a few miles from its source, the Loire.

The springs of the Loire rise at about 4,500 feet on the Gerbier de Jonc, a tall, slender cone of a mountain that is well called the 'Reed-Stack'. The Gerbier sheds the three burns that are collectively named the Loire Sources to the south. Below the peak they are turned by the slope up to the col of the Pal, and are trapped for hydro-electricity at the reservoir of Lapalisse. Their overflow is carried through a tunnel under the col to the power-station of Montpezat, on the eastern side of the range. From the reservoir the Loire turns north. Lapalisse is a great feat of engineering, and amid the desolation of the mountains, the peaks and scree, and the desert of blowing grass, it has not meant the destruction of too much natural beauty.

Downstream from Chambles near St Etienne the river winds between wooded outcrops of rock to a rich valley of vineyards, orchards and plantations

After leaving Montepezat the upper Loire flows through a succession of narrow gorges. Above its right side tower the great shoulders of the Vivarais; on its left the Veley, a chain of volcanic domes. The roads do not follow the river deep within its cliffs. But at Arlempdes, an ancient *bourg*, you can see them from the bridge, and if the weather is dry and the water low, you can walk a path in the riverbed to the village of Goudet.

The hills of the Loire sources are used for summer grazing – they are snowbound for months of the year – and also have an abundance of wild-flowers. Their westward-facing slopes have never known the plough, and are a paradise for botanists. There is a fair in July at the village of Ste Eulalie of medicinal plants gathered in the mountains.

As the gorges descend, there are breaks in the cliffs. One such admits the road from Le Puy, as well as the railway line down the valley. It is a small inconspicuous line; you may travel the road for days and never see a train. Le Puy is the best place for the exploration of the upper Loire. It is an astonishing city. It stands on a dyke in the bed of an ancient lake emptied by earthquake, its terrifying landscape studded with needles and surrounded by cliffs. A dyke is an upright block of hard rock laid bare by the wearing away of the softer stone surrounding it. On one such the cathedral is built, its façade projecting from the rock and sustained on pillars. On another the magical little chapel of St Michel d'Aiguille crowns a needle rock 250 feet high.

'Magical' is the word that explains Le Puy. It owes its origin to a miracle. According to legend a slab from a Stone-Age dolmen lay on the dyke and a woman, sick with fever, lay down to sleep on it and woke cured. The bishop of the Veley witnessed to the miracle and one of his successors moved his cathedral to this spot. From a practical point of view the place was a natural fortress, and could be defended against the heathen invading Franks. The church still stands over the haunted Fever-Stone; but its power in the Middle Ages emanated from a most holy and miraculous Black Virgin. Pilgrims came to worship at her shrine for centuries. They still come, in the modern revival of pilgrimages, though the original Virgin was destroyed in the Revolution, and another now sits on her throne. St Michel, too, suc-ceeded an older faith; his chapel stands on what was once a temple of Mercury – like him a messenger of the Gods, like him winged, a slayer of dragons. Le Puy is electric with the transmission of faiths.

The people of this desperately poor country have lived for long on the pilgrims. The Bishop of Le Puy was their feudal lord. He was appointed by the King of France and later shared the revenues with him in the system of '*Pariage*', but the Veley formed the borderland of the domains of the Dukes of Guienne. When the Angevin line owned it as the heritage of Eleanor of Guienne, it became involved in the wars between the French and English kings. It passed to the Capets when Philippe Auguste defeated John Lackland in 1204. But the French kings, like the Dukes of Guienne, left this remote region to the rule of its bishops.

Not that the bishops were without their rivals. The local barons built castles and tyrannised over their tenants, as they did everywhere in France. The chief of them were the Polignacs. Their immense *château-fort* built on a dyke near Le Puy, was the fortress of the 'Kings of the Mountains'. It was magical too, for in the

Roman period it was a temple of Apollo, where a statue of the god uttered oracles. The Polignacs were an enduring race; the Renaissance château of Lavoûte-Polignac, down in the Loire valley, still belongs to one of them.

The road through the gorges below Le Puy is very beautiful. It runs by the river where there is room for it, but it has to take off and traverse the slopes above the gorges where they are too overhung to hold it. From these higher points there is a view up the narrow rising valley to where the Gerbier de Jonc stands sentinel beside the mass of the Vivarais. Villages, castles ruined or converted to town halls and schools, churches, are strung down the valley. The Priory of Chamalières, is an outstanding Auvergnat Romanesque church. At Aurec the gorges are made of hard waterproof rock, granite and slate, and this has enabled the engineers to dam them for electricity. It has been done by barring the river at either end, and turning it for sixteen miles into a narrow lake; the cliffs do the rest; it is one of the few such schemes not to hurt the beauty of the scenery.

The Upper Loire is not a natural route of travel; and there lies the clue to its long seclusion. It was only broken in the nineteenth century by a spillover from St Etienne at Firmigny. But the Col of the Pal is too high and too long snowbound for much use. The hills were haunted by packs of wolves till two centuries ago. The Romans made a road up the eastern side of the Cévennes, but it followed the Chassejac to the divide and thence the Allier to Moulins, which was a junction on their network of military roads centred at Bourges. The Loire kept its long seclusion. But at the end of the gorges, at Grangent, it entered another world.

The Middle Loire is a waterway serving the commerce of central France. The hills of the Lyonnais still hold it on the eastern side, but they are nothing like so impenetrable as the Vivarais. On the west the Forez slope down to a plateau of many streams and marshes. It lies

LEFT *The massive towers of the moated château of Sully. It was here in 1429 that Joan of Arc prevailed upon the Dauphin to be crowned king of France. Later the château was the home of the Duc de Sully, Henry IV's chief Minister, whose far-reaching reforms did much to restore the shattered economy of France after the wars between Catholics and Protestants which divided France during the second half of the sixteenth century*

OPPOSITE *The picturesque town of Gien, about thirty miles east of Orléans, which was twice devastated during the Second World War. The line of gabled houses seen across the river and the twelve-arched stone bridge have since been rebuilt. The château behind, originally built in 1500, was also damaged and has been extensively restored*

OPPOSITE *The Loire at Orléans during the summer months when the level of the river is low. On the left is the beautiful seventeenth-century cathedral of the Holy Cross*

RIGHT *A contemporary engraving showing the construction of the bridge at Orléans in 1755. Today it has been replaced by a more modern bridge*

1000 feet above sea-level and is difficult to cultivate. But a *route nationale* comes in from St Etienne to run above the right bank of the river, and at Feurs it is crossed by the straight Roman road from Lyons to Thiers.

Roads cause trade, and are caused by it. There seems no other reason why this poor country should support the considerable manufacturing town of Roanne, save that the road from Lyons to Moulins crosses the Loire at that point. But at Roanne the Loire waters, if not the Loire itself, become part of the trading complex of central France.

The river road north of Roanne is not of the first importance. Of course there must always have been one; the whole country was threaded with paths and bridle-ways older even than the Roman roads. But the three centuries of Roman rule left the paved streets traced by their engineers, armed with surveying tools and an ample supply of slave labour. After their departure, there was little road-building for many centuries. But people got about the country in a surprising way. The pedlars and pilgrims, the shepherds and the men at arms, used the immemorial tracks.

There was always the river itself, and in the old days rivers served commerce better than roads. The Loire by this stage has plenty of water for small craft. Yet it still remained a difficult waterway. Shoals, currents and floods made navigation hard; and for the long reaches running little west of north the direction of the river rendered it almost impossible. The current would carry boats downstream. But on the return journey, where sail might have helped, the wind was against them. North winds are the rarest in western Europe.

The solution found by the French in modern times is canalisation. The Loire canal begins at Roanne and follows the left side of the river all the way to Chatillon. At Decize it joins the system of Burgundy, and at Briare it crosses the Loire and connects with the northern complex of canals. From Orléans another canal, begun under the encouragement of Henry IV's minister, Sully, joins the Seine network. This canal still makes Orléans a busy inland port. Thus the Loire above Orléans is left to itself. It remains a country river, with old spas like Pouges and Bourbon-Lancy on its banks,

and camps where the youth of France flock with their canoes. The commerce of the Loire downstream from Orléans was another story. There the current carried boats to the sea, and the west wind blew them back. Every ford became a bridge, and every bridgehead a market. Trading towns grew up, Orléans, Blois, Tours, Saumur, Angers, Nantes. In the later Middle Ages there were some industries, such as the entrancing *mille-fleurs* tapestries, and the silk and cloth-of-gold weaving of Tours. But the flourishing commerce of the Loire Basin suffered a series of blows. The Bourbon kings no longer kept their court on the Loire, after Henry IV won Paris. A century later, the Revocation of the Edict of Nantes undermined the prosperity of Tours and Saumur, for the weavers were Protestant, and emigrated to escape persecution. The Revolution emptied the châteaux; the wealthy customers of the markets were gone. After the Revolution the riverbed was already sanding up, when the coming of the railway ended its traffic; for the trade of Nantes was carried by rail. Nantes is still a great port, but the Loire today is an idle river.

The lower course of the Loire, below Gien, lies open to invasion: on the north to the plain of northern Europe, on the south to armies coming up over the rolling country of the Bourbonnais and Berri. The Loire basin was a natural target for the racial migrations that followed each other for a thousand years of the Christian era. To the barbarian tribes pressed by famine and curiosity out of the East, the equable climate, the cultivated valleys, must have seemed the fulfilment of their dreams, after the barren wastes and black forests from which they came. The first invasion recorded in written history, came from the south. The Romans gave France roads, law and order, towns, agriculture including the vine, peasant slavery, the Latin tongue, and Roman Catholic christianity. After the barbarians battered in the imperial frontiers and the legions marched away, their imprint remained – except for law and order, which decayed under the rule of nomadic tribes, which in this region were the Franks. They were not the first. In the third century Attila the Hun himself reached the walls of Orléans at the head of his abhorred horsemen, but

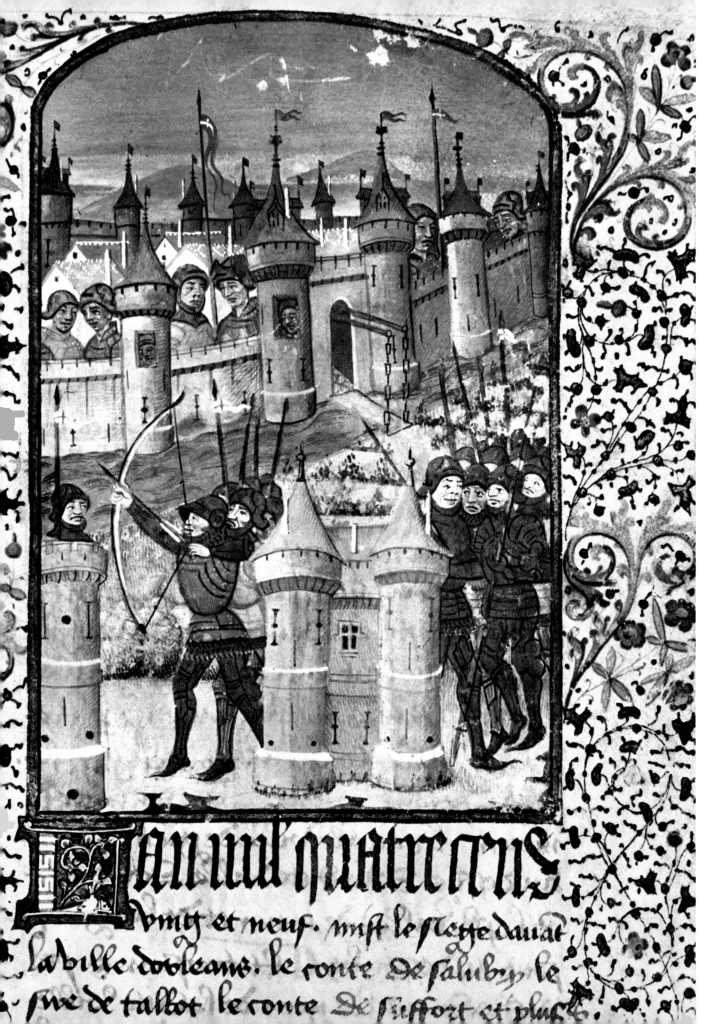

was repelled by Bishop St Gatien, who rallied the people. The Franks of the fifth century came to stay. They destroyed the civilisation of Rome, and imposed upon their Gallic subjects a domination by a class of warriors, trained for nothing but fighting and served by all others. The conversion of the conqueror Clovis to Roman christianity, however, was a turning point in French, and indeed in world history. For he used it as a pretext for making war against the far more civilised Arian Visigoths, who ruled France to the Loire. His victory at Vouglié in 506 began their gradual retreat and disappearance. With it the Roman Church was preserved as the orthodoxy of the West; and the subjection of the south of France to the north was under way.

Meantime, as the dark and savage years went by, the Church kept some candles burning in the abbeys. Tours was honoured as the shrine of St Martin, the soldier–missionary, and pilgrims came to it from far lands. The Bishop Gregory, and Alcuin, under Charlemagne, made the abbey a centre of learning. St Benoît-sur-Loire, where the body of St Benedict lay, became something like a university. But the dangers of invasion were not ended; and one, the flooding of Saracens from the south in the great wave of Moslem conquest, was stopped by the founder of the line of Charlemagne, Charles Martel, in a victory at Poitiers in 732. The last threat came from the sea. In the tenth century the Normans took Nantes and sailed up the Loire burning and looting as they went; they destroyed the basilica of St Martin, and the abbey of St Benoît. In the end they were dislodged from Angers, which they had made their pirates' den, and were bought off by being given Normandy to settle.

The greatest of the Franks, Charlemagne, had ruled his far too extensive empire by setting its provinces under trusted counts. As his line decayed and the empire fell apart, the counts handed their governments from father to son, and the feudal system was established. They paid formal homage to the kings, but in fact each of the lords was sovereign in his little state. And when Hughues Capet usurped the throne, he was only a rather small baron among the holders of the great fiefs.

This was true of the Loire seigneurs. Their early medieval history is the delight of French children, for it is rich in tales of blood and magic. Who could forget the name of Foulques Nerra, Black Foulques of Black Anjou, or of his enemy Tibault le Tricheur, Tibault the Cheat of Blois? Foulques was the legendary Bad Baron. He built twenty castles and fought without ceasing; he committed vile crimes, and smitten by remorse did penance for them by going on pilgrimage to Jerusalem, being scourged all the way. The whole of Anjou is dotted with the stumps of Foulques' castles. Another of his line married a she-devil. She refused to enter a church, so he had her forced into the Cathedral, her wrists manacled and attached by chains to two knights. At the Elevation of the Host she uttered a piercing yell, snapped the chains as if they were straws, and flew out of the window – legendary, but psychologically true. It is a fact that the Angevins, all of whom to the last man with a drop of their blood in his veins were subject to ungovernable rages, used to boast, like Richard Coeur-de-Lion, that it was all the fault of their grand-dame the fiend.

This violent breed suddenly sprang into world history when red-headed Henri of Anjou married the Duchess Eleanor of Guienne. She had been queen of France, but Louis VII divorced her in 1152. Within two months she married Henri, and took with her her lands, about half of France. Henri himself inherited the crown of England two years later through his Norman mother. The pair governed an empire from the Tweed to the Pyrenees, and from the Atlantic to the Veley. The power of the Capet kings, which did not encompass much beyond the Île de France and the Orléannais, was a feeble thing in comparison.

The rivalries between Capets and Plantaganets cost France three centuries of war. In the earlier stages they were typical dynastic quarrels; the question of nationality played no part, for the Angevins were just as French as the kings of France. The first round went to the Plantaganets; Louis VII was no match for Henry II and Richard Coeur-de-Lion, with their great castle at Chinon. But when Philippe Auguste faced the lamentable John Lackland, the positions were reversed. Philippe won a great victory and confiscated the French lands of John. Louis IX (St Louis) restored the domains of Eleanor to Henry III, but not Anjou or Maine. These he gave to his brother Charles, as Charles of Anjou.

Some French historian ought to write a book called 'French Kings and their Brothers'. The kings, as their lands expanded, had to delegate their government to others; and they had small reason to trust their peers, the great counts. So they formed a habit of choosing their own brothers; and little good it did them. A succession of younger sons were made Dukes of Orléans; they varied from being a nuisance like Louis XIV's brother 'Monsieur'; to being traitors, like Gaston d'Orléans. France owed a debt to one of them, Charles l'Orléans, who, it is true, did lose the battle of Agincourt, but who, as a prisoner in the Tower of London, wrote some of the loveliest poetry in the French language.

OPPOSITE *The Siege of Orléans depicted in an illumination from a fifteenth-century chronicle. For eight months in 1428–29 the city held off the English besiegers, until it was relieved by a French army inspired by Joan of Arc*

RIGHT *The earliest known portrait of Joan of Arc taken from a miniature of 1451. Three decisive events in the life of this most famous of French heroines took place in the Loire valley: her first meeting with the Dauphin at Chinon in 1429, the relief of Orléans, and her visit to the château of Sully to persuade the Dauphin to be crowned at Rheims*

Jehanne La pucelle

A portrait by Clouet of François I (1494–1547) the cavalier king of France who built the magnificent château of Chambord and made important additions to the châteaux at Amboise and Blois. François made his court a great centre of Renaissance culture and following his unsuccessful campaign in Italy against the Emperor Charles V he summoned to France some of the greatest Italian artists, including Leonardo da Vinci, Cellini, and del Rosso

The last phase of the Hundred Years' War had more resemblance to a nationalistic struggle, if only because Henry V of England's victory was due to the English longbowmen. It was involved for the French king with an old-fashioned dynastic quarrel, for the Dukes of Burgundy were allied with the English on account of a vendetta against the Valois. After Agincourt the position of the French seemed hopeless. They were confined to the south side of the Loire, with the enemy pressing in upon them. Their king was the uncrowned, self-distrustful Dauphin Charles. The English were besieging Orléans, though with insufficient strength to cut it off, except on the side of the French army at Blois. But then, from far Lorraine, came the shepherd-girl, Jehanne d'Arc.

This is not the place to tell that tale. But a single small event may be described to explain its meaning. Joan came up the Loire with a small force and supplies for the beleaguered city; only to find that the French leaders had brought her to the wrong side of the stream, the south, while Orléans lay on the north. Also the wind was

The Château of Chambord built by François I and the scene of many court pageants. Its ornate skyline of domes and pinnacles makes it the most elaborate of the châteaux of the Loire

blowing downstream. The French general, Dunois, rowed across from Orléans to tell her that she could not get past the English against the wind. Joan was a shepherd-girl; shepherds know all about winds. 'Wait!' she said. The wind faltered, dropped, and began to blow upstream.

Dunois did not, in fact, attempt to relieve Orléans that day, the day of the most famous wind that ever blew on the Loire, the 28 May 1429. But the soldiers and the people of Orléans took the change of wind for a miracle, or at least for a sign. When she got inside the city they welcomed her as the messenger of God. There followed her brief campaign, victory at Patay, followed by defeat and capture, trial by the Inquisition and death at the stake at Rouen. The English threw her ashes into the Seine, but they could not drown the spirit she inspired. In 1453, after a final defeat on the Dordogne, they left France.

Now some have said that Joan's mission was the first instance of national patriotism, as distinct from loyalty to a king or a leader. Joan, in heaven with the Spartans of Thermopylae and the Scots of Bannockburn, would laugh at that. But it was an appeal to the pure sort of patriotism that seeks nothing for itself. In France it won the war, because it was then the only thing that could have won. The tragedy is that so many have confused that devotion with the false patriotism which the French call *gloire*, the glory of aggressive war. The evil tradition came down to the rulers of France from the ferocious Franks; it was that policy that was repeatedly, in the future, to wreck the France that the spirit of Joan had set free.

But nobody can accuse France of the pursuit of glory during the last invasion of the Loire, that of 1940. The German army followed the retreat of the French across the Loire, and they sent the Luftwaffe before them. There was some resistance; they were bound to bomb military objectives. At Tours the French themselves blew up the bridge over the Loire, and the Germans destroyed the whole heart of the eighteenth-century city. The cadets of Saumur put up a gallant, hopeless fight, but the town was wrecked. But the systematic massacre of refugees on the roads was sheer Nazi terrorism. And it was not the end. In 1944, when the Americans under Patton were pursuing the retreating Germans across France to the east, the American Air Force bombed many places on the Loire.

The tale of damage was frightful; the gaps show still. Gien, for instance was twice reduced to rubble. Nantes, which as a submarine port had been a target for British bombing was badly damaged even before the Germans on their departure tried to sabotage it and destroyed half the harbour. But it is hard to forgive the destruction of art treasures in places which were not military strong-points at all. What excuse can be urged for bombing St Benoît-sur-Loire, or for dropping bombs on the castle of Amboise, inhabited by a few old pensioners, and breaking the lovely carvings of its chapel of St Hubert?

Still, despite these wars, the Loire basin remains extraordinarily rich in artistic monuments. The churches are the oldest in the country. They include some of the finest Romanesque abbeys in France: St Benoît-sur-Loire, Fontrevault, where Henry II of England, his

85

LEFT *The spiral staircase in the open tower of the château of Blois, said to have been designed by Leonardo da Vinci for his patron François I*

ABOVE *Henri, Duc de Guise, the great Catholic leader during the Wars of Religion. His power became so immense that the king, Henri III, felt it threatened the crown and ordered the assassination of the duke at the château of Blois in December 1588*

ABOVE RIGHT *A view from across the river of Blois and the high-pitched Mansard roofs of the late seventeenth-century wing of the Château, designed by Jules Mansart, great-nephew of the famous French architect who gave his name to this style*

wife Eleanor of Guienne, and their son Richard Coeur-de-Lion lie under their carven effigies, the cathedral of Angers. Perhaps the most famous church of the Gothic period is the cathedral of Tours, which contains glorious stained glass. So does the cathedral of Angers. Anjou in its great period developed a form of Gothic architecture of its own, with flat apse, tall narrow arches, and slender lancet windows as good for glass as the Romanesque. The French call this style 'Angevin' and the English 'Early English', but it is the same from Ripon to the border of Perigord, since the church-builders must have been in touch throughout that great empire. There is much of this later Gothic that was still built during the Renaissance period; the chapel of St Hubert at Amboise is a perfect example of it. The chapel of the Château d'Ussé, about six miles west of Tours is a charming, purely Renaissance church, carved like a jewel-casket.

The modern traveller, however, seeks the Loire for its castles, the famous châteaux. The great river itself and all its incoming tributaries are set with castles. They are, of course, similar to those built in the fifteenth and sixteenth centuries all over France; but their number and beauty is due to a series of historic coincidences. The main one was that Charles VII and the later Valois never liked to live in their ancestral capital of Paris. That city housed too many turbulent spirits; it could be roused to riots and killing by the sermon of a Capucin friar; perhaps it knew French kings too well to love them much. In any case the kings preferred the Loire, deep in their own domains. They liked its pleasant climate, the country so well suited for hunting, with its open or forested uplands dividing the river valleys. Almost all the nobility of France was addicted to the hunt. Among the many taboos of that strange way of living called chivalry, was one which decreed that gentlemen should not dirty their hands with manual toil. The only stain allowed on the hands of the French nobility was the stain of blood. When they were not killing men, they were forever hunting animals. They gladly followed the court to Amboise or Blois. Loches,

OPPOSITE *The château of Chenonceau built partly on an island and partly on a bridge over the Cher, a tributary of the Loire. The delicate reflections of the château and the bridge in the river make Chenonceau one of the most beautiful of all French châteaux. It was begun in 1515 and continued first by Diane de Poitiers, mistress of Henri II, and later by his wife Catherine de' Medici, both of whose monograms can be seen on the walls*

OPPOSITE *The fifteenth-century château of Amboise built on a terrace above the Loire between Blois and Tours. On the left is the huge round Tour des Minimes containing an immense spiral staircase*

LEFT *A sketch of Amboise by Leonardo da Vinci. He came to France in 1517 under the patronage of François I and worked at Amboise for nearly three years until his death in 1519*

BELOW LEFT *Charles VIII (1470–98), an ill-favoured and politically maladroit king, was born and brought up at Amboise and retired there in 1494 with booty acquired during his brief campaign in Italy*

BELOW RIGHT *In 1560 twelve hundred Huguenots were brutally massacred at Amboise by the Catholic party following a Protestant conspiracy. The execution of the victims, many of whom were hung from the walls of the château, was watched by François II and his court who were in residence at Amboise at the time*

LEFT *Only a single pier remains of the bridge across the Loire at Écure, between Tours and Blois — one example of the devastation by bombing suffered in this area during the Second World War*

OPPOSITE *A contemporary record of the massacre of Huguenots at Tours in July 1562, when 200 men, women and children were killed and their bodies hurled into the Loire*

where Charles VII lived with gentle, lovely, Agnes Sorel, was still a fortified castle. But Louis XI, though he retired to it in his fear-crazed old age, emerged to build a decent *manoir* at Plessis-les-Tours. Charles VIII was a man of the Renaissance. Even before he started his foreign adventures he began to rebuild Amboise and he returned from Italy with painters and builders. François I was the builder par excellence. He raised at Chambord the most elaborate of all the châteaux, whose circle of towers burgeons into a fantastic crown of domes and pinnacles. The castles of the Loire were following a deliberate fashion set by royalty.

Considering the influx of Italian artists – François I established Leonardo da Vinci himself at Amboise – it might seem curious that the Loire châteaux do not resemble Italian palazzos of the same period. But the native character of the new castles was determined by a tradition of the Middle Ages. In the past nobody was allowed to fortify his house, expecially with a tower, except by leave of his feudal superior. The ownership of a towered dwelling came to be taken as a patent of baronal status. The Renaissance lords would never have dreamed of building a new *manoir* without towers. The result was an extremely beautiful style of architecture, for the combination of the round towers with the straight exteriors of the new living wings creates a delightful effect.

Of course the simplest thing to do was just to add some modern rooms at the side of the old *donjon*. This is what happened to the castle at Sully, upstream from Orléans, the town from which Henri IV's great minister took his ducal title. From the river it seems just a

line of *donjons* with pointed roofs. But the *corps de logis* lies behind them. Another idea was to preserve the exterior as a fortress capable of defence, but to soften the interior court with windowed rooms. Langeais, about twenty miles below Tours, is the best-known example, but Châteaudun on the Loir, the castle of Dunois, the companion of Joan of Arc, is a more interesting example. The great general would never have lived in a castle incapable of defence, and the exterior has uncompromising buttressed walls; but the inner court has two storeys of large rooms with tall elegant Renaissance windows, and a staircase with bal-

conies at each storey. The Chapel at Châteaudun also has a line of realistically carved statues of saints, which are amongst the finest examples of fifteenth-century sculpture.

However, the castles soon discarded any pretence of military purpose. The towers remained; but their battlements and platforms for archery were converted into ornamental external galleries. The towers still held stairs, but the old defensible spiral was turned into decoration – the most famous is in the royal castle of Blois, a carven stair held in an octagonal cage as fine as filigree. The most beautiful of the staircases is at Azay-le-Rideau.

A great beauty of the Loire castles is their colour. The early ones combined brown brick and stone. But the later castles are made of local white limestone, a most lovely material. It is as white as marble, but without the hard gloss of that stone; its texture has the appearance of the petals of a waterlily.

The great age of château-building was also the age of the Renaissance women, who were often as well educated and as absorbed in the new arts as the men. The two most beautiful of all the châteaux are Chenonceau, about twenty miles east of Tours, built partly on an island in the Cher and partly on a bridge, and Azay-le-Rideau in the valley of the Indre. They were both built under the supervision of women whose husbands, being royal ministers of finance, could not only afford the luxury, but were too busy to interfere in the details

of the building. In both cases, disgrace overtook the fortunes of the financiers. François I seized Chenonceau, but neglected it; both his daughter-in-law Catherine de' Medici, and his son's beautiful mistress Diane de Poitiers coveted it. As long as Henri II lived, Diane was the real queen of France and she owned Chenonceau; but when he died Catherine turned her out and added her own initial of C to the enlaced mongram of D and H on the walls.

The age was one of brilliant hope, of art and learning. But it still carried the burden of its medieval heritage. François I might in many ways be the finished product of a new age; but his son Henri II was killed in a tournament like any baron of earlier times. Men built the lovely castles for pleasure, not for war. Yet when the new learning brought new religion, the brutality of the past reached out and caught the people in its grip. The intelligence of the Renaissance was not applied by the kings to problems of the Reformation. At Tours, many years before the massacre of St Bartholomew, the Catholics massacred the Protestants. There was no means of gaining toleration except by influencing the king himself. It was in an attempt to destroy the power of the fanatical Guises over François II that a band of Protestants became involved in the Conspiracy of Amboise in 1560. They were betrayed and ambushed. Twelve hundred of them were executed at Amboise, and hung from the balconies of the château. Catherine brought François II and his wife, the lovely Mary Queen of

Scots, to watch the agonies of the dying as though to a show. The court never returned to Amboise after that.

After the thirty years of religious wars, the country was laid waste and too full of bitterness to revive the gaiety of the Renaissance. An era came to an end when Henri III summoned Duke Henri of Guise to negotiate with him at the Château de Blois, and had him murdered by his bodyguard on the threshold of his cabinet. Later Henri III himself was killed by an assassin's knife, and Henry IV, the first of the Bourbons and one of the few kings that the people of France remember with love, was too busy winning Paris, and trying to heal the wounds of war, to spare time for hunting on the Loire.

Gradually over the years the châteaux fell into decay. When Louis XIV left Chambord to the tenancy of various pensioners of the crown and moved the court to Versailles he hastened the process. In the nineteenth century, however, the passion for romantic history brought a great revival of interest in the châteaux of the Loire and the period of restoration began. At Villandry, for example, two generations of owners have recreated the magnificent formal Renaissance gardens. Nowadays many of the châteaux have been restored and some are open to the public – Chenonceau, Chambord, Azay-le-Rideau, and Cheverney, for examples. Others have survived the vicissitudes of war and revolution and have been passed down from generation to generation of the same family. One of these is the Château d'Ussé – the most beautiful of all the châteaux in the Loire valley. It is like something made by enchantment. It was indeed the setting chosen by Perrault for the Sleeping Beauty in his *Contes des Fées*.

Times change. Geography changes too, but much more slowly. The *Pays de la Loire* are still the river valleys, the uplands are still infertile, and to tell the truth scarcely beautiful. It is the river valleys that yield vegetables and fruit, and the slopes above them that grow the grapes for the light, delicately-scented wine. The real people of the Loire live in the low white houses of the villages, or in the caves cut into the cliffs under the vineyards. Above their work stretches the sky of the

OPPOSITE *The Loire at Saumur crossed by a great twelve-arched bridge. Once a flourishing Protestant stronghold, its prosperity declined after the Revocation of the Edict of Nantes (which had given a measure of toleration to Protestants) in 1685, when more than two-thirds of the population fled. On the left is the twelfth-century church of St Pierre with its wooden spire*

The junction of the Loire with the Vienne at Candes. In the foreground is the roof of St Martin's church, built on the site of the cell where the saint died in 397

THE LOIRE

Loire, and the air, which is as delicate as their wine, holds the landscape in a clear bubble of light.

Joachim du Bellay, the Renaissance poet, came from Liré, far down the Loire near Nantes. While serving with the French ambassador in Rome he wrote his *Regrets*. One of these sonnets – well known by all French children – is a moving expression of du Bellay's longing for his home by the Loire. There have been many attempts to render this sonnet into English poetry, but none of them have succeeded in capturing its spirit. A prose translation reads:

'Happy is the man who, like Ulysses, comes safely to the end of his journey, or like the winner of the golden fleece returns home full of experience and wisdom to live the rest of his days among his kin. Alas, when shall I see again the smoke rising from the chimneys of my village, and when shall I stand once more in my little garden, which for me is far more than a whole province? The home built by my forbears pleases me far more than the grandeur of Roman palaces, and delicate slate more than hard marble. The Gallic Loire means far more to me than the Latin Tiber, the little town of Liré than the Palatine, and dearer to me than the sea breezes of Rome are the sweet airs of Anjou.

Heureux qui, comme Ulysse, a fait un beau voyage,
Ou comme cestuy la qui conquit la toison,
Et puis est retourné, plein d'usage et raison,
Vivre entre ses parents le reste de son age.
Quand reverrai'je, Helas! de mon petit village
Fumer la cheminée? et en quelle saison
Reverrai'je le clos de ma pauvre maison,
Qui m'est une province et beaucoup davantage?
Plus me plait le séjour qu'ont bati mes aieux,
Que des palais romains le front audacieux.
Plus que le marbre dur me plait l'ardoise fine.
Plus mon Loire gaulois que la Tibre latin.
Plus mon petit Liré, que le mont Palatin,
Et plus que l'air marin la douceur angevine.

Nantes, an important port and industrial centre, and the last great city on the Loire before it flows into the Atlantic thirty miles later. ABOVE *an eighteenth-century view of the quayside and* BELOW *the harbour today*

THE PO

H. V. MORTON

An allegorical representation of the Po, depicting the river as strong, virile and life-giving. An engraving made in 1538 by the Duke of Mantua's architect, G. B. Scultori

Mantua in the 16th century

Ravenna mosaic

THE PO

PIEDMONT

SWITZERLAND

Lake Maggiore

Lake Como

MILAN • Milan Cathedral

River Adda

River Ticino

River Sesia

River Stura

River Dora

Hannibal crossed the Alps 218 BC

TURIN •

River Pellice

The Source

Mount Viso

The Superga (1731)

River Tanaro

Casale Monferrato

Cement Works

Coperto Bridge • Pavia

Marengo 1800
Napoleon defeated the Austrians

Piacenza

14th Century Gothic Portal
of San Antonino

River Trebbia

Kilometres 0 10 20 30 40

Miles 0 10 20 25

TRENTINO
ALTO ADIGE

Dolomite Mountains

Lake Garda

The Villa Capra

Vicenza

The Roman Amphitheatre
Verona

LOMBARDY

Leo the Great confronted
Attila the Hun 452 AD

Padua

Padua Basilica of St Anthony

VENICE

GULF OF
VENICE

The Tonazzo (1250)
Cremona
Stradivari Violins

Mantua

VENETO

Petrol Refinery

River Parma

Parma

Parma Cathedral

Bologna
12th Century
Leaning Towers

Bologna

Po di Volano

Ferrara

Porto Tolle

EMILIA

ROMAGNA

Ravenna

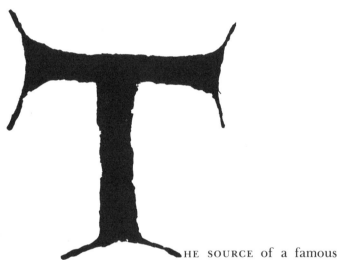

THE SOURCE of a famous river cannot fail to stir the imagination. It is almost as though, with a foreknowledge of the future, one had seen Shakespeare or Michelangelo in his cradle. That a spring, bubbling through the fern, or a mountain stream slipping from ledge to ledge, should grow into a mighty river bearing lights and towers upon its banks and ships upon its waters, arouses wonder in the mind, and may even seem to be symbolic of life itself. Pliny was aware of this, and, writing of the source of the Po, or the Padus as it was called in his day, said that the river originated 'in a manner that merits an inspection by the curious'.

Since he wrote those words curiosity has led many a mountaineer to an inaccessible spot above Cressolo in the Cottian Alps, midway between Nice and Turin, where a stream descends from two sombre, chilly tarns. From the time of the ancient Greek historian, Polybius, this has been recognised as the main stream of the Po, Padus, Eridanus or Bodincus, to give the river the four names it has borne in the course of its long history. It was Polybius, who, writing a century before the birth of Christ and quoting an older writer, hazarded a guess about the derivation of the name, Padus. The word, he said, was Celtic in origin and referred to the pine trees that grew near the source upon the slopes of Monte Viso.

The mountain torrent, descending rapidly, begins its three hundred mile long sprawl to the Adriatic Sea across the great plain of Northern Italy. It is, of course, the greatest river in Italy and the life-giver of the northern plain; without it, Lombardy would have been a desert instead of the green land it is, a land dotted with famous cities each one of which has a history that goes back for 2,000 years. Less romantically, one might call it the main drain of Lombardy, Emilia and the Veneto: the channel that carries off the water which flows south from the Swiss and Austrian Alps and north from the Apennines.

Its tributaries are too numerous to mention. The south, or right, bank receives countless streams from the Apennines, some of which become dry in summer, but on the north bank the rivers come tumbling down ice-green with the melted snows of the high Alps even

The Po bubbles to the surface at Monte Viso in the Cottian Alps and falls, a mountain torrent, to the Saluzzi plain 600 feet below. Hannibal and his elephants almost certainly crossed the Alps near the river's source, and followed the infant Po to the plain

OPPOSITE *In the lovely valley of Mescolina the villages of Cebbia and Andergia cluster on the banks, out of reach of any but the worst winter floods. The Po valley, fed by hundreds of tributaries flowing from the lakes in the north and from the Cottian and Ligurian Alps, dominates northern Italy*

in the heat of August, when the Lombardy peasant is cutting his seventh crop of hay. Among those tributaries is Milton's 'smooth-sliding Mincius', south of Mantua, which, in its turn, is nourished by Lake Garda, the Lacus Benicus where Catullus lived at 'olive-silvery Sirmio', and where today the local people point with pride to a massive ruin which one has not the heart to tell them is almost certainly not that of the poet's villa. Virgil, too, was a child of the Mantuan countryside. The first farms he saw, and the first bee-skips, were upon land irrigated by the Po and the Mincio,

and once in a moment of pride, as he remembered that fair scene, he called the Po *fluviorum rex*.

The Po is a river that avoids nearly all the famous towns along its course, or should one say that the towns have drawn away, afraid of such a turbulent companion? Turin alone stands astride both banks of the Po, and one remembers how the river, as it slides beneath the bridges, lends beauty to the stately rectangularity of that city. But the Po is still a young river there: only some thirty miles away the Cottian Alps, where it rises, lift their frosted pinnacles against the southern sky. But after Turin no other city stands upon both banks of the river. The Po runs south of Pavia, it touches Piacenza and Cremona, it flows to the south of Mantua and to the north of Ferrara, before it winds its way eastward to that wild delta of sandbanks and *lidi* which it has been building up for centuries.

The great plain of the Po has witnessed a continuous pageant of mighty events. When the mists of history part we see the Etruscans there, a still mysterious people to whom legend has credited a genius for engineering. They are believed to have been the first

to drain, embank and harness the Po. After them came the Gauls. Those warriors, who sacked Rome in 390 B.C. and set the Capitoline geese cackling, marched south from the Po valley and in retaliation the Romans conquered them and colonised Cisalpine Gaul, a region which included the modern Lombardy. The traveller of to-day who knows that Gauls, Romans, and Lombards after them, were dairy farmers and pig breeders, will appreciate the continuity of history as he enjoys the buttered rice of Milan, the hams of Parma and the pigs' trotters of Modena, not to mention the rich delicacies of the headquarters of Italian gastronomy, a city which is said to have enriched the English language with 'Polony', a word believed to be a corruption of 'Bologna'.

One of the most celebrated events in ancient history took place on the plain of the Po when Hannibal, the Carthaginian general, crossed the Alps in 218 B.C. and advanced upon Rome with an army that included a corps of war elephants. As neither Polybius nor Livy, the two writers who describe this extraordinary feat, mention the Alpine pass used by Hannibal, the

problem has inspired a formidable literature, which has had a peculiar attraction for the English historical detective. The latest theory is that of Sir Gavin de Beer, who believes convincingly that Hannibal led his army through the Col de la Traversette, sometimes called the Col de Viso, and followed the infant Po down to the plain and to the city which is now Turin. If so, one of the most notable tableaux of history occurred at the source of the river when Hannibal, assembling his army in the unmelted snows of Monte Viso, pointed down to the distant sunlit valley and indicated the southward direction of Rome.

The final drama in what is called 'the fall' of the Roman Empire was staged upon the great plain of northern Italy. To the west stands Milan, to the east, Ravenna. In the fourth century, when the Teutonic pressures on the imperial frontiers became severe, the western emperors removed their capital from Rome to Milan, and when, in the next century, the tribes came pouring across the Alps, the last Caesars fled from Milan to the moated security of Ravenna. There, enfolded by the waters of the Po, which in those days flowed south of

OPPOSITE LEFT *The old port of Classis depicted in a sixth-century mosaic in St Appollinaris Nuova, one of the many early Christian basilicas in Ravenna. Classis was enlarged by Augustus to hold 250 ships, an arsenal and building yards. Ravenna became the capital of the Empire in the 5th century* A.D. *and the greatest centre of Byzantine civilization in the west*

OPPOSITE RIGHT *A statue of the Younger Pliny on the façade of Como Cathedral. Both he and his uncle owned villas on the shores of Lake Como*
BELOW *The Grotte di Catullo, the ruins of a Roman villa of the Constantine period at Sirmione on Lake Garda, where Catullus, the Roman poet and epigrammatist, had a country house*

A mosaic portrait of Virgil Between His Muses. *The greatest of the Latin poets was one of many famous Italians born near the Po. The son of a farmer from Andes near Mantua, he spent many years in Lombardy, where he wrote most of the* Eclogues, *pastoral poems describing the Mantuan countryside*

The meeting between Leo the Great and Attila the Hun on the banks of the Mincio in 452 A.D., as depicted by Raphael nearly 1,100 years later. Attila and his army were encamped near Mantua preparing to march on Rome, and Leo's intervention saved the city and much of Italy from the ravages of the barbarian Huns

CENTRE *Saints Liberata and Faustina Crossing The Po, a fourteenth-century fresco in the museum at Como. Overcome by the sight of a woman weeping for her dead husband, the two sisters vowed never to marry, fled from their parents and home at the foot of the Cottian Alps and joined the Benedictine Order at Como*

RIGHT *The Triumph of Vice, a fresco by Cosmè Tura and Francesco del Cossa in the famous Room of the Months in the Palazzo Schifonia near Ferrara. This was the seat of the Este family, one of the most important families in northern Italy and distinguished patrons of the arts during the Renaissance period*

its present course, the last shadowy emperor abdicated in A.D. 475 and handed the diadem to the barbarian, Odoacer. And the Dark Ages began.

Except perhaps to the scientist and the naturalist, a great river is significant only in relation to the human deeds accomplished along its banks. Thus to most people the tiny Rubicon, which is scarcely visible in summer, is more interesting than the mighty Amazon; and, as one reviews the pageant of the Po valley, the mind twists and turns in time just as the river itself bends back upon its course. Fascinating as the retreats and disasters which led to Ravenna are in retrospect, they were preceded by centuries of ordered, disciplined life. How pleasant Cisalpine Gaul must have been during the Pax Romana. Roman engineers dyked and embanked the river and planned a system of irrigation which never really broke down completely during the barbarian invasions. Ancient cities were rebuilt, new cities were founded. One of the great consular roads,

the Via Emilia, was constructed from Ariminum (Rimini) on the east, to Placentia (Piacenza) on the west, where it met the Po; and this road still runs today across the level landscape, as firm and straight as ever.

Rich Romans, attracted to the green valley and the wooded hills where Alpine rivers tumbled to the plain, built their villas there. The sails of their yachts slanted across the blueness of Lacus Verbanus, which we call Lake Maggiore, or Lacus Larius, which we know as Como, and the cultured, leisured life which developed there, the libraries, the baths, the centrally-heated houses, was not to be known again, after the breakdown of Roman government in the fifth century, until the rise of the princely courts of the Renaissance. Both the Plinys, uncle and nephew, had villas on Larius; Catullus, as we have seen, retired to Sirmione; and Virgil, born at Mantua, went to school at Cremona.

The Po became a main artery of trade. Varro said that the Cisalpine farmers monopolised the pig in-

dustry and cured all the bacon for Rome. What happened to the butter must be conjectural. To the Romans, it was a barbarian grease useful as ointment, and Pliny, repressing a shudder, noted also that it was 'held as the most delicate of food among barbarous nations, and one which distinguished the wealthy from the multitude at large'.

A regular service of packet boats known as *cursoriae* traversed the Po and also the Ticino, linking Milan and Pavia with Ravenna and the Adriatic, and thus the entire length of the now deserted river was used by the Romans. A fascinating letter has survived from the end of the Roman period in which a traveller described how he took a *cursoria* on the Ticino and sailed happily down the Po all the way to Ravenna. The writer was a distinguished and wealthy dilettante named Apollinaris Sidonius, who had estates in what is now southern France. His letters give a surprising picture of country-house life during the barbarian invasions.

Though his district had been conquered by the Visigoths, he and his friends still had hot water in their luxurious baths and cooks in the kitchen. They gave dinner parties and visited each other and, save for an increase in highway robbery, might still have been living in the Augustan, or at least the Theodosian Age. Strange-looking barbarians passed through the district without apparently smashing a window: Burgundians, who dressed their hair with rancid butter and ate revolting stews; Herulians, noted as runners, who tattooed their cheeks a blue-green; Goths in fur tunics; blue-eyed Saxons, who sacrificed victims to sea gods; savage little Huns with flat noses and wispy beards, who leaned on the withers of shaggy ponies – all these passed across the landscape. Yet the dinner parties continued in Auvergne; and Sidonius sat with poised stylus in his heated library, composing tortuous Latin prose.

He described his voyage down the Po in a letter, probably written in the year A.D. 467, to a fellow dilettante named Herenius, who lived at Lugudunum, now Lyons. In the course of it Sidonius described how he travelled by post-horse across France, how he painlessly crossed the Alps and descended into the valley of the Po. 'On the Ticino,' he wrote, 'I boarded the packet known as the cursoria which soon bore me to the Po; be sure I laughed over those convivial songs of ours about Phaethon's sisters and their unnatural tears of amber gum.'

What the convivial songs were, we do not, alas, know, but in the reference to Phaethon and his sisters, he was referring to the legend of Phaethon who, unable to control the Chariot of the Sun, crashed into the river Eridanus, which was said to have been the Po. The 'tears of amber gum' were those shed by his three sisters, the Heliades, who were transformed into poplar trees, since when these trees, says the legend, have always wept sorrow in the form of gum. From this reference, one might surely believe that the poplar trees

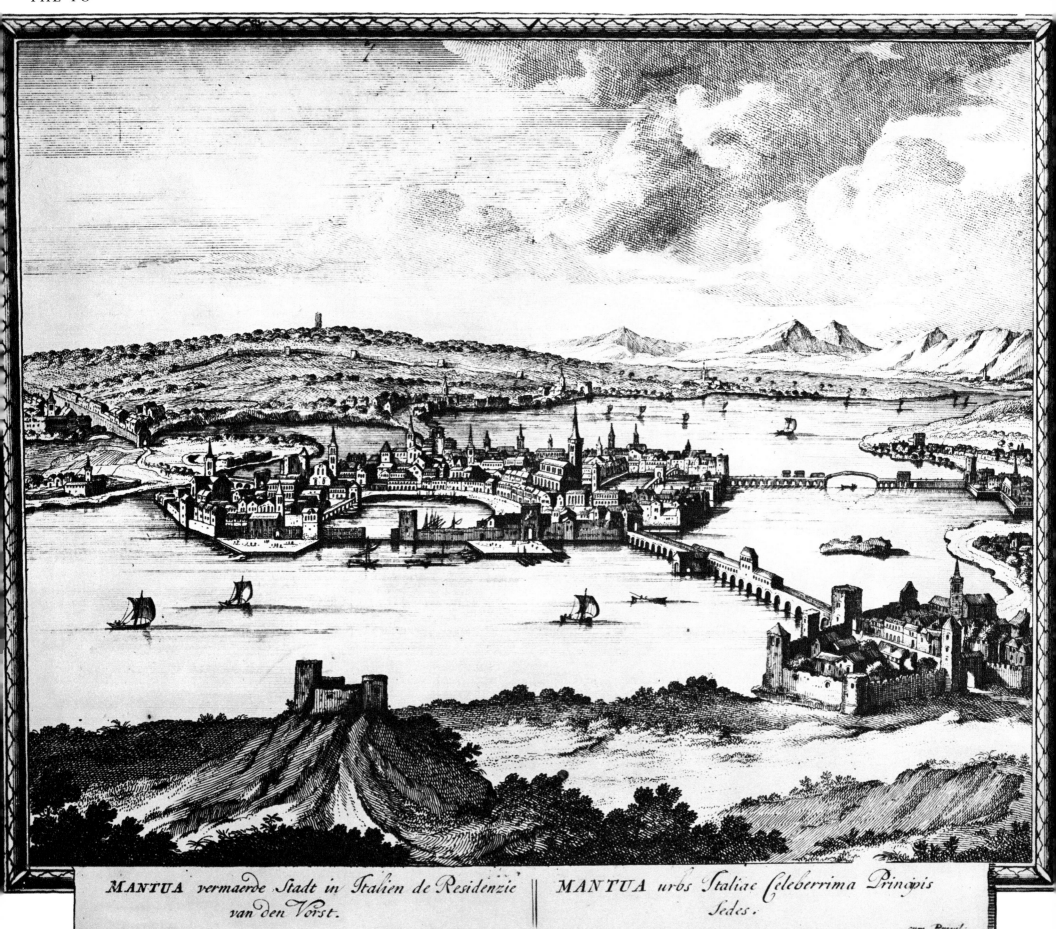

MANTUA vermaerde Stadt in Italien de Residenzie van den Vorst. || MANTUA urbs Italiae Celeberrima Principis Sedes.

P. Schenk exc: Amst:

cum Privil:

on the river banks had inspired Sidonius with these reflections; if so the tree was there long before the Lombards who have given their name to it.

Sidonius' voyage was uneventful, indeed it might have been taking place in Jane Austen's England rather than in Cisalpine Gaul during the decline and fall of the Roman Empire. The writer mentions the tributaries of the Po and the towns as they were passed; he noticed the songs of the birds and the groves of oak and maple, and he mentions that the *cursoria* was manned by rowers. When he stepped ashore at Ravenna he saw a sight which no one could imagine today: he saw the Po, which in Roman times ran south of Ferrara, flowing round, and through, Ravenna.

The surprising thing about this letter – and Sidonius is astonishing in his avoidance of the harsh facts of life – is that were it written, as most scholars believe, in A.D. 467, only fifteen years had passed since Pope Leo the Great, had held his famous meeting with Attila on the banks of the Mincio in the very landscape through which Sidonius had passed. Though he must have met men who were alive at the time, and may even have been present when the Pontiff confronted the ferocious savage and turned him away from Rome, not one word does Sidonius say about it. The Mincio reminds him only of Virgil. It is surely one of the curiosities of literature that a man could write so prettily and affectedly of the trivialities of life while the world was crashing round him; and although Attila had not attacked Rome, he had already destroyed the ring of Adriatic cities whose survivors, at the very moment when Sidonius was making little jokes about the drinking water of Ravenna, were feverishly driving piles into the lagoon and building the refuge which grew into Venice.

Three hundred years after Sidonius had passed along in the *cursoria*, twilight had long fallen on the Roman world and the sixth, and last wave of invaders, the Lombards, had given their name to the great plain of the Po. And Lombardy it remains. As the ambitions of those conquerors involved the whole of Italy, the Pope gave a cry for help which was answered by Charlemagne. He marched into the valley of the Po and laid siege to the Lombard king in his capital of Pavia. The

OPPOSITE *Mantua in the seventeenth century. Built on an outcrop of land jutting out from the bank of the river Mincio, one of the principal tributaries of the Po, Mantua was once an important port and centre of the silk trade. It reached the height of its prosperity in the late fifteenth century during the reign of Isabella d'Este, who married the Duke of Mantua*

ABOVE *The covered bridge at Pavia, a university town near the confluence of the Po and the Ticino. The fourteenth-century bridge has a chapel in the middle dedicated to St John Nepomuk, the patron saint of bridges, and gives a fine view of the town, once called the 'city of a hundred towers'*

BELOW *The Ponte Pietra at Verona, the lovely medieval town on the river Adige, which flows into the gulf of Venice just north of the Po. The Ponte Pietra was built by the Romans, but only two of the original arches remain*

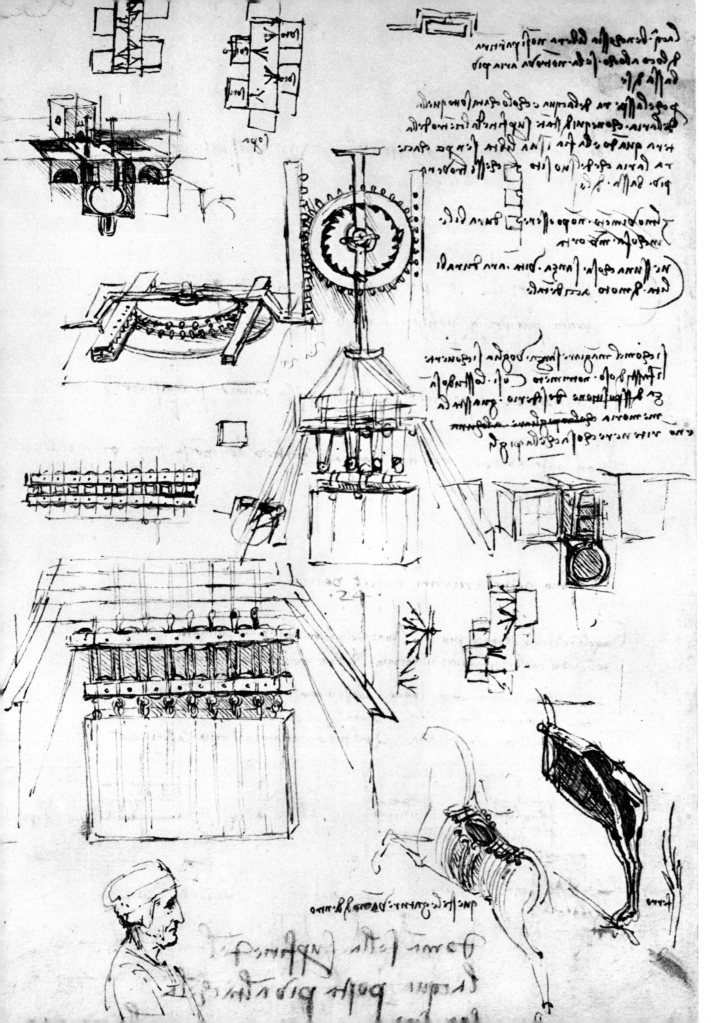

siege was ended only when a supply fleet on its way to the Lombards was intercepted on the river by a Venetian fleet allied to Charlemagne. Therefore, it would appear that the complicated and expert science of river conservation perfected by the Romans did not collapse during the Dark Ages, and the Po in the ninth century was navigable along its entire length. With that surprising glimpse of Venetian war galleys advancing from the Adriatic to the Ticino, the Middle Ages begin.

One should perhaps not exaggerate this achievement. It is known that elsewhere in the valley great areas had returned to waste. Uncontrolled annual floods had covered miles of Lombardy with primeval marsh and forest. In A.D. 589, for example, the Adige at Este moved its channel five miles to the south and many similar disasters probably passed without record. In 1151 the Tanaro in flood diverted the main channel of the Po from the Po di Volano into the more northerly Po Grande channel, and such events caused the communes, now with the assistance of the Cistercians to drain and reclaim the land and rebuild the dykes.

In common with all the great rivers of Europe, the Po revived as a mainstream of traffic during that great

A seventeenth-century engraving of a lock on the canal linking Ferrara and the Po to Bologna. At this time the whole Po valley was criss-crossed by an elaborate canal system joining the many navigable rivers and providing the best means of transport for both people and goods

LEFT *Sketches for sluice gates and drainage systems made by Leonardo da Vinci. Leonardo lived in a great age of canal building and drew up a scheme for draining the Po valley*

era of river travel, the Middle Ages. The freight capacity of a barge was immeasurably greater than that of the pack animals used on the roads, and the roads were always atrocious, often impassable in winter. At sea the sailor, unassisted by the mariners' compass, hugged the coastline and was more scared of pirates and Saracens than the road traveller was of bandits. Only the river offered a pleasant and tolerably safe journey, and under the commerical rule of the Italian communes, the Po once again became a main artery of trade between east and west. While the Crusaders were voyaging down the Danube on their way to Constantinople, the Po barges were bearing in the opposite direction musk and sandalwood, cloth-of-gold and damask, Chinese silk and Byzantine velvet, to brighten the monotony of life in lonely castles all over Europe. Until Venice controlled Verona, which did not occur until 1405, the best route for her treasures was by the Po, then over the Alps to more barges on the Rhine and the Danube.

Whether Chaucer used the waterways of Lombardy can never be known, but it is tempting to imagine that he did so. His two official visits to Italy occurred in 1372 and 1378, and in the Prologue to *The Clerk's Tale*

he describes the course of the Po in detail. After saying that he had heard the story of Griselda from Petrarch at Padua, he goes on, in the modern English version by Mr Nevill Coghill:

But to return to this distinguished man
From whom I learnt the tale, as I began,
Let me say first he starts it by enditing
A preface in the highest style of writing,
Ere coming to the body of his tale,
Describing Piedmont, the Saluzzo vale,
And the high Apennines that one may see
Bounding the lands of western Lombardy;
And he is most particular to tell
Of Monte Viso, where, from a little well,
The river Po springs from its tiny source.
Eastward it runs, increasing on its course,
Towards the Aemilian Way; Ferrara past,
It reaches Venice and the sea at last . . .

Petrarch in his Latin version of Boccaccio's story, from which Chaucer took his tale, never mentioned Ferrara, and some have wondered whether Chaucer's mention of the town was from personal observation.

By the time the medieval communes had merged into the hereditary rule of the great families of northern Italy, the Visconti and Sforza in Milan, the Gonzaga in Mantua, the Bentivoglio in Bologna, and the Estensi in Ferrara, the river map of Lombardy and Emilia began to assume something of the appearance it had borne in Roman times. It delighted the magnates of those days, whose capitals lay some way from the Po, to link their cities with the river by canals. No city of the time could afford to remain land-locked and outside the network of waterways. Both Visconti and Sforza improved ancient channels and made new ones connecting Milan with the Ticino and the Adda, and so with the Po; the Estensi linked Ferrara with the Po by a long canal which still exists, and in the year 1494 Giovanni Bentivoglio opened a three-mile-long canal in a solemn ceremony, which concluded with a Te Deum, that made it possible for ships to sail from the Po and discharge their cargoes and passengers under the walls of Bologna. Whether the river lock was invented in Lombardy or Holland is unknown, though it has been said that Leonardo da Vinci invented it on the Milanese canals when he was in the service of Ludovico Sforza, and those who say so point as evidence to the sketch in Leonardo's notebooks which shows boats passing up a river by way of locks with sluice gates.

French Revolutionary troops crossing the Po at Piacenza in 1796. They defeated the Piedmontese and the Austrians and put the whole of Italy within Napoleon's reach. An engraving taken from a painting by Carle Vernet ·

During the fifteenth and sixteenth centuries the plain of Northern Italy resembled Holland. It was covered everywhere with canals and navigable rivers. The sails of boats moved through the vineyards, and inland towns, whose inhabitants had never seen the sea, possessed docks and harbours. Throughout the Middle Ages and the Renaissance Milan ranked as a naval power and maintained a fleet of warships that often fought the fleets of Venice for command of the three key points on the Po, Piacenza, Cremona and Casalmaggiore. Indeed it is recorded that in 1431 a Milanese fleet defeated a Venetian fleet not far from Cremona. Milan itself in ancient times bore a resemblance to Venice. Ships and barges penetrated the centre of the city along a system of canals, the *Cerchia dei Navigli*, which was filled in only in recent times. How odd it is that some Shakespearean critics should have questioned the poet's accuracy in making Prospero take ship for the Adriatic at the gates of Milan. Shakespeare knew that this was possible, and that a gentleman of Verona could reach Milan by boat by way of the rivers and canals.

The splendour of the Renaissance courts spread itself over the waterways of the plain, such a superb setting for pageantry. Every ruler whose state was linked with the Po owned a showy gilded barge called, after the Doge's state barge in Venice, a bucentaur. When a pope or a prince visited Northern Italy he was met by the local bucentaur and conveyed by river, with the minstrels playing, either to the ruler's capital or to the boundary of his state, where another bucentaur would be waiting to carry him forward on his journey. When a daughter departed to be married she voyaged to her new home in her father's bucentaur, often, oddly enough, in the depth of winter. Some fascinating accounts have been preserved of the ordeals endured by those hardy Renaissance brides. The two famous sisters, Isabella and Beatrice d'Este, were both married in winter and left Ferrara by bucentaur, Isabella, to marry Francesco Gonzaga, Marquis of Mantua, and, in the following year, Beatrice to marry Ludovico Sforza, who became Duke of Milan.

Beatrice, who was not quite sixteen, had the longer

and, as it turned out, the more trying voyage. On Christmas night in the year 1490 snow began to fall over the Po valley and by December 29, the day the bride was due to leave for Milan, it lay three feet deep in the streets of Ferrara. Beatrice's brother, Alfonso d'Este, who was going to Milan not only to attend his sister's wedding but also to bring back his bride, Anna Sforza, drove to the river bank in a sledge. One of the ladies-in-waiting, Beatrice dei Contrari wrote a letter, now in the Mantuan archives, describing this painful experience.

Three bucentaurs and a fleet of boats were waiting at the embarkation point on the Po, and Beatrice, having entered one of the bucentaurs (which were unheated and had no kitchens) and the notabilities the others, the flotilla set off into a blizzard. The boats soon lost contact with one another and the supply ship was lost. After tossing about in the snowstorm all day, darkness fell and it was not until three in the morning that the bride's bucentaur, full of weeping and ravenous young women, tied up at the pier at Torsella. Writing after the event, when she could be

Alessandro Manzoni, considered to be the greatest of Italian novelists for his internationally famous I Promessi Sposi (The Betrothed), *spent most of his long life on his farm in Lombardy. Verdi's magnificent Requiem Mass was written in his memory*

Austrian troops practising a crossing of the Po during manoeuvres in 1833. After the defeat of Napoleon at Waterloo the European powers, meeting at the Congress of Vienna in 1815, ceded Lombardy and Venetia to Austria

OPPOSITE *The Court of Isabella d'Este, an allegory by Lorenzo Costa, court painter at Mantua, showing scenes from Isabella's life (1474–1539). On the left is the bucentaur, or gilded barge, in which she sailed from Ferrara to Mantua to marry Francesco Gonzaga, Marquis of Mantua*

amusing about it, Beatrice dei Contrari said, 'If it had not been for the timely help of Madonna Camilla, who sent us part of her supper from her barge, I, for one, should certainly have been by this time a saint in Paradise.' The bucentaur tossed and rolled all night, making sleep impossible, and while the bride huddled in her furs in the gilded cabin, she was heard to long for death. Several days afterwards a pale and bedraggled Beatrice and attendants with tear-stained faces, disembarked at Piacenza where they were rushed to warm fires, food and comfortable beds. After a day's rest the flotilla set out again, but this time the voyage was a brief one. Late in the frosty afternoon the wedding party saw a gallant company, led by the bridegroom, Ludovico Sforza, waiting for them on the banks of the river at the intersection of the Po with the Ticino. The young women, having repaired the ravages of their voyage at Piacenza and having been revived and uplifted by new gowns, stepped radiantly ashore and were soon restoring their circulation on horseback as they rode the short distance to the Castle of Pavia. The storm continued all through January. It was still raging when Alfonso made the return voyage with Anna Sforza; indeed, as they approached Ferrara the Po was so thickly frozen that hundreds of men had to hack a passage for the bucentaur through the ice.

Happily the bucentaurs made their voyages more often to the sound of lutes and trumpets, moving slowly and heroically between the lines of poplars, towering majestically in their carved and gilded beauty above the mulberry trees in the hush of hot summer days. One can imagine how eagerly the peasant would drop whatever he was doing and run to see them pass, the carved and gilded gods and goddesses gliding smoothly through the vineyards; when the musicians had ceased to play, they must have glided on like a vision, their decks crowded with gaily dressed lords and ladies who still smile at us in the art galleries of Europe.

When Pope Pius II attended the Congress of Mantua in 1460, he described in his *Commentaries* how he sailed to the meeting by river boat, and when it had concluded, took the boat down the Mincio to the Po at Revere, where Borso d'Este, Duke of Ferrara, was waiting in his state barge. Writing in the third person, Pius said: 'He (Pius) spent a night in Revere and the next day

OPPOSITE *A fishing boat and punts in the marshy lagoons of the Po delta*

The Po winding through the plains of Lombardy near Milan

A modern bridge spans the Po at Piacenza, once a thriving port when Italy depended on its many navigable rivers for its trade and wealth

A rescue boat watches over flooded farms and fields. In places silting up has raised the level of the river above the surrounding countryside and increased the danger of flooding

All rivers have their legends – the Po that the many poplars that line its banks are the weeping sisters of Phaethon, who drove the sun chariot headlong into the river

was met on the Po by Borso in the Bucentaur, surrounded by such a throng of smaller craft that there was no part of the river that was not churned by their oars, and the many-coloured standards fluttering in the breeze were a marvellous sight. Trumpets, pipes, and all sorts of instruments made sweet music from the lofty sterns. There were impersonations of various gods and goddesses, giants and virtues; on the dykes, which prevent the river from overflowing, boys and girls were singing and men and women sat there as if at a show. Some shouted "Viva" to the Pope and some to Borso.'

When Lucrezia Borgia travelled from Rome to Ferrara in 1502, to become the second wife of Alfonso d'Este, she went by road to Bologna, then by canal and the river Reno to Malalbergo, a place which took its name from a notoriously bad inn. There Isabella d'Este was awaiting her.

'At Torre della Fossa I changed boats and went on to Malalbergo,' Isabella said later, writing to her husband of the encounter, 'where we met the bride in a ship with Don Ferrante and Don Sigismundo and a few others, and here I found the Duchess of Urbino with them. The boat came alongside, and one bark having

curtsied to the other with joyous haste, I entered the bride's with Madonna Laura, and after exchanging salutes we went on our way and she did not enter the small bucentaur for fear of losing time. About four o'clock we reached Torre della Fossa, where my father (Duke Ercole I) was standing on the shore awaiting us. The archers in their red and white liveries, seventy-five in number, were drawn up in a row, and the whole court gathered round the Duke, who took Madonna Lucrezia by the hand and kissed her, after she had first insisted on kissing his hand. Then we entered the large bucentaur, where all the ambassadors shook hands with us . . . My father and Don Alfonso (the bridegroom) sat on deck, talking and joking together and were much amused by the Spanish clowns, who paid the bride all manner of compliments, and so, amid great cheering and shouting and the sound of trumpets and guns, we reached Casale about five...I will not describe Madonna Lucrezia's appearance, as you have seen her.' (She then proceeded to describe every detail of Lucrezia's dress!)

A sharp contrast to that stately world of courtly voyagers is revealed by Benvenuto Cellini in his *Life*. He tells us how the ordinary person travelled. The

riverside inns were full of tough characters, bargemen, boatmen, men who worked the windlasses that drew boats from canal to canal, men who drove the canal horses and suchlike, a whole now vanished population which served the river with inherited skills and knowledge and no doubt stood in direct descent from the distant Etruscans and Romans who had fulfilled the same functions in earlier centuries. Cellini, who had killed a man in a Roman street fight, thought it prudent to retire to Venice for a time and, arriving at Ferrara, he put up at an inn where he made arrangements to take the Venice barge on the following morning. It was the custom for the bargees to tout for custom in the inns and in that uncrowded world a traveller, by paying an extra sum, as Cellini did, could reserve the boat for himself. As might have been expected wherever Cellini was present, there was a fight in the inn that night. Some exiled Florentines provoked the artist, and Cellini drew his sword. He made a great scene but did no harm. However, in the morning, as he was riding on his way to the river, he was dogged by three of his adversaries, who threatened him and even followed in a skiff for ten miles down the Po, shouting, 'Go thy ways this time, Benvenuto; we shall meet in Venice!'

Such incidents were common though Cellini's atrocious bluster and temper were likely to cause trouble anywhere. On the return journey he took offence when an innkeeper insisted on payment before his guests went to bed instead of in the morning, and Cellini admits without shame that he lay awake in the night wondering how he could get even with the man. In the morning, when seated in the barge with the horses harnessed to the towrope, he suddenly remembered that he had left a pair of slippers in the bedroom and, leaping ashore, ran back to the inn. Entering the bedroom he drew a knife and ripped four beds to tatters 'I had the satisfaction of knowing,' he wrote , 'that I had done a damage of more than fifty crowns. Then I ran down to the boat with some pieces of the bedcovers in my pouch, and bade the bargee start at once without delay.' That violent, picaresque world outlived the stately gatherings upon the decks of bucentaurs, in fact it lingered on in a few places until the coming of the railways.

Since Roman times the Po valley had not known such a golden age as that of the Renaissance. The princes not only made dykes and drained the river and improved irrigation, but they also encouraged farming by their example and introduced new crops. Nothing surprised the French more when they invaded Italy in 1494, than the model farm of the Sforzas, where experiments in stock breeding were carried out and useless land was brought under cultivation by irrigation and scientific treatment. Could one have stood upon the roof of Milan Cathedral, the heights of Bergamo, or the campanile of Parma in the fifteenth century, it is probable that the Po valley would have looked much as we see it today, save for two notable absentees: rice and maize. Though rice now plays such an important part in Italian cooking, it was a late-comer to the north. It is said to have been introduced to Lombardy as an experiment by Galeazzo Maria Sforza, fifth Duke of Milan, in 1475; and he could not have found a more suitable crop. The ease with which large areas of land can be flooded in April – the sowing season – and drained in September, when gangs of harvesters invade the rice fields, is one of the reasons why the provinces of Milan, Vercelli, Pavia and Novara have become the largest rice producing area in Europe.

Maize was an even later arrival in the Po valley. It was believed, like rice, to have an eastern origin, as the Italian word for it, *granturco*, proves; and there is probably hardly a peasant in the north who would not find it hard to believe that a time existed, not so long ago, when *polenta*, the maize porridge of Northern Italy, was unknown.

In 1792 an English visitor who had a sharp eye for a field of corn, Arthur Young, thought the Po valley the 'finest farmer's prospect in Europe' and he was astonished everywhere he went by the fertility of the soil and by the abundance of controlled water. 'Such amazing executions in irrigation,' he exclaimed, 'that we can have in England no idea of it,' and he summed up the Po valley as 'water, clover, cows, cheese, money and music.'

More rice is produced in the paddy fields of Italy than anywhere else in Europe, by methods which have changed little since the fifteenth century. The overseer throws out the shoots from a moving cart for the women labourers to plant in the waterlogged fields. Rice was probably first brought to southern Italy by the Arabs. It was introduced to Lombardy on a large scale in 1475 by the Duke of Milan

The waterways which played so important a part in the history of the northern plain, and from the time of the *cursoria* by way of the bucentaur to the famous Brenta boat to Venice, lent such vividness and colour to the landscape, perished gradually. Political changes in the seventeenth century, the end of the great families, the improvement of roads in the eighteenth century and, above all, the arrival of railways in the nineteenth, had their effect upon the gradual break-up of the ancient system of water communication.

Water, like friendship, demands constant attention. Anyone who has had dealings with a river in mountain country will know that every summer precautions must be taken to persuade it to behave during the winter. Embankments must be strengthened, sandbars removed, and obstacles left over from winter floods eliminated with the tactful intention of collaborating with the flood and not opposing it, since rivers will not be forced. The task of repair is unending and must never be interrupted. One bad flood may sweep away the work of half a century. Unfortunately the capricious and turbulent Po was allowed to get out of hand and the canals and waterways began to fall into disuse. In the seventeenth century many travellers still used them, but the eighteenth-century nobleman preferred to travel by coach. Occasionally, however, one hears of a traveller in the eighteenth century, such as Dr Burney on his musical tour of Europe, who was always ready to take a boat were one available. Goethe, too, delighted in the Brenta boat to Venice. But already many of the main channels had silted up, and Burney noted how thickly some of the canals were clogged by weed. It was not long before cities such as Milan began to fill in their now useless and stagnant canals, and sometimes in a town – one thinks of Modena – the traveller, glancing up at the street signs, will see the word 'canale' instead of the usual 'via'. Thus year by year the river traffic slowed down until at last it came to an end.

Of all the ramifications of the Po navigation system, the only one to survive today is the Brenta boat from Padua to Venice, a craft that features in so many diaries and travel narratives and in the comedies of Goldoni. The Brenta itself is no longer the river 'that reflected the shimmer of barques and echoed to the romantic compositions of Pergolese and Cimarosa'. Nor is the Brenta

Fishing is the main industry of the Po delta. As the fish make their way up the river to spawn they are caught in a screen of nets stretched across the river on poles. RIGHT *Fishermen with a basket of eels which form the chief catch*

boat the same as that which inspired the saying that when the day arrived on which its passengers did not include a monk, a student and a courtesan, it would go to the bottom! Now it is a sleek motor-boat (still called *Il Burchiello*) with a bar and radio, and it may be seen in the season filled with tourists as it passes on its way past the Villas on the river banks.

Two great events in modern times have occurred in the Po valley. One was the introduction of hydro-electric systems. The other was the discovery in recent years of deposits of methane gas. This new activity is worthy to be mentioned among the most important developments in the history of the Po. The first gas field at Caviaga, in the Milan region, was tapped in 1946; since then several others of equal importance have been exploited. The modern traveller is now surprised to come unexpectedly upon some gigantic industrial plant in what until recently was a placid agricultural scene. A network of gas mains now pipes energy into factories and cities, and thousands of Italians who have never known anything but a wood fire now own modern gas cookers.

Strangest of all, Ravenna, having slumbered for centuries, now finds itself in touch with international affairs for the first time since the days of the Exarchs, who governed on behalf of the Eastern Roman Emperor the regions of Italy reconquered from the barbarians in the sixth century. But after the fall of the Exarchate in A.D. 752 Ravenna became a sleepy back-water and only in recent years has it awakened with the arrival there of the State-owned colossus, *Ente Nazionale Idocarburi*, which is said to employ 37,000 people in various parts of the world. It has selected the outskirts of Ravenna for one of its largest plants. Its concern is with gas, petrol and allied products, and a few miles from the site of Classis, where Augustus built a port as the station of the Adriatic fleet, the ENI, the vast state-owned oil company, are constructing a harbour and docks to accommodate the largest oil tankers. So it has happened that a town, which until recently had no industry except the harvesting of pine kernels, now produces annually a hundred thousand tons of synthetic rubber, plastics and fertilisers, and maintains contact by ship with all parts of the world. The works are well hidden; many who go to Ravenna are probably unaware of their existence. The town with its distant memories of the last Emperors of the West, of Byzantine Exarchs, of barbarian kings, of Dante, whose bones lie there, and, in more recent times, of Byron, is still unspoilt. The mosaics glitter upon the walls of its

Byzantine churches, and the sunlight, filtered through biscuit-thin sheets of alabaster, falls upon the little jewel casket where the bones of Galla Placidia, that strange adventurous Empress of the West, were interred fifteen centuries ago.

The discovery of methane gas on both banks of the Po is believed by some to have hastened the sinking of the delta, which has been in progress for some time. Bridges over canals now have insufficient headway, especially when high water and easterly winds bank up the waters of the Adriatic. Though the cause of the subsidence has not been traced to the new gas fields, many a recriminatory finger has been raised by those who say that, as water comes up with the gas, the subterranean structure has been disrupted and the water cushion displaced. Such critics believe that the day will come when the Po in its easterly course to the Adriatic will have to be embanked high above the land, and the delta itself protected from the Adriatic in much the same way that Holland is protected from the North Sea.

The traffic of the Po is now confined to barges, which carry such cargoes as timber and building materials; but once a year in May the river becomes the more lively scene of an international motor-boat race from Pavia to Venice. For one day the Po becomes alive again, and hears the sound of cheering upon its banks, then it returns to its placid retirement. Plans exist, however, though many are still on the drawing board, to rehabilitate the ancient waterway and make it, as it once was, a thriving highway of commerce. An interesting scheme is to link Switzerland with the Po by way of Lake Maggiore and Milan.

Though the Po may appear moribund in comparison with its ancient fame, it is not the Italian habit to forget a feature of such historical interest. An association, 'the Friends of the Po', is in existence, which welcomes those who are interested in the river. The members hold frequent meetings during which literary discussions are sometimes pleasantly varied by a gastronomic excursion to some town or village renowned for its local cooking. An art exhibition was held recently in Piacenza when more than a hundred artists showed pictures of the Po and its scenery.

The modern traveller, as he sees the Po flowing mile upon mile without a single sail upon its waters, must marvel that this river should have been the first and most important of Europe's waterways. It is, however, true that at a time when the Danube and the Rhine, the Seine and the Thames, were beyond the confines of the known world, frequented only by the fisherman in his coracle or by some daring explorer, the Padus, or Po, shone in the full light of civilisation. Emperors sailed upon its waters, poets lived upon its banks, the commerce of the Roman world was passed from town to town, and even across the Alps to the mysterious regions beyond. Virgil saw his river truly when he called it *fluviorum rex*.

Nearly 400 miles from its source at Monte Viso the Po, sluggish and heavy with silt, reaches the Adriatic Sea

THE RHINE

CHRISTOPHER SYKES

A Roman stone effigy of a Rhine river god. To the Romans the Rhine was a shield protecting Gaul from the wild German tribes, and many towns along the Rhine began as Roman settlements.

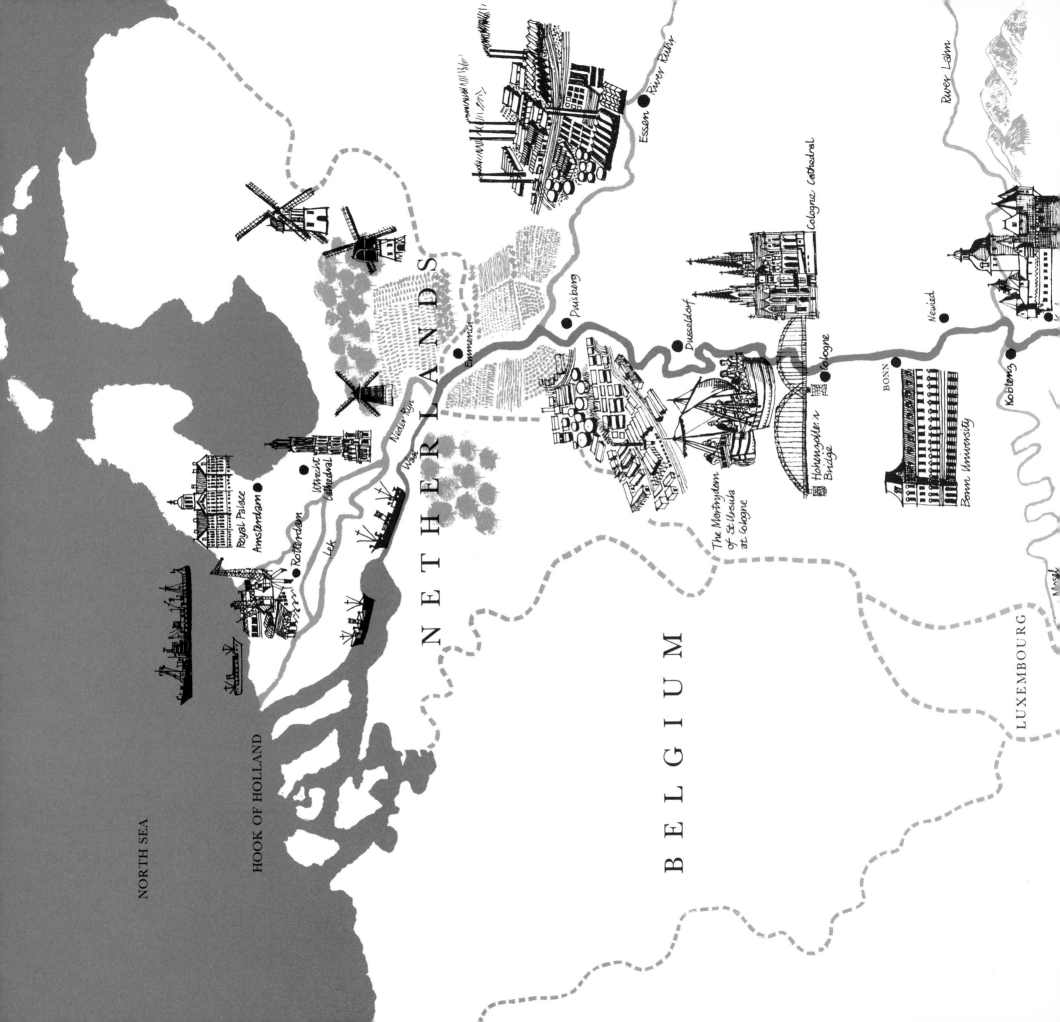

NORTH SEA

HOOK OF HOLLAND

Amsterdam
Royal Palace

Utrecht Cathedral

Rotterdam

Lek

Waal

Neder Rijn

NETHERLANDS

Emmerich

Duisberg

Essen

River Ruhr

Düsseldorf

Cologne
Cologne Cathedral

The Martyrdom
of St Ursula
at Cologne

Hohenzollern
Bridge

BONN
Bonn University

Newied

Koblenz

River Lahn

BELGIUM

LUXEMBOURG

Mosel

Frankfurt

Eschenheim Tower

River Nahe

Bingen

Mainz

Worms

Battle between Romans and Huns 436 AD

Mannheim Siegfried's corpse brought to Worms

River Neckar

Heidelberg

Speyer

Karlsruhe

Baden Baden

Strasbourg

Colmar

BLACK FOREST

Schaffhausen

Der Rheinfall

Lake Constance

Constance Cathedral

River Aaun

Chur

Basel

Basel Cathedral

WEST GERMANY

FRANCE

SWITZERLAND

THE RHINE

Kilometres

Miles

HE RHINE is an intensely political river. You do not need to be a scholar to know that this is the main scene of the long Franco–German conflict from which has come a great part of Europe's ills. In the seventeenth century the growing power of France developed a fixed intention of making the Rhine the French frontier. As the ballad-mongers of the day put it, France would never feel content until Paris was drinking the Rhine:

'Quand Paris boira le Rhin
Toute la France aura sa fin.'

A hundred and fifty years after, in the war of liberation from Napoleon, the Germans used to quote a line written by the patriotic poet Ernst Moritz · Arndt in which he put the other side of the case:

'Der Rhein ein deutscher strom, unsere grenze nicht. – The Rhine is a German river, not our frontier.' Arndt's epigram fell into disuse in the days of German plenty after 1870, but came back into general currency about 1930. Some people took this as an ominous sign.

The Rhine becomes a political and historical river only after its first 230 miles. Its youth is spent innocently in Switzerland where it is born. Like all great rivers it comes from numerous sources and is formed by an accident of nature by which many streams flow into one course. There are two main original streams, the Vorder Rhein and the more southerly Hinter Rhein. The Vorder Rhein is augmented before junction by another smaller stream known as the Medelsrhein, but geographers do not give the poor thing much attention. The foundation members are these two: the Hinter Rhein which begins in the glaciers of the Rheinwaldhorn, and the Vorder Rhein which flows out of Lake Toma very near the course of the early Rhône.

Through the complicated geography of Switzerland the young Rhine takes a wriggling course. It is joined by many mountain torrents; it grows rapidly but, for all that, remains a relatively minor affair until, after taking a more definite north-east course, it receives two major contributions from the Landquart and the Ill. After this increase it turns sharp west and enters Lake

OPPOSITE LEFT *Meltwater from the Rheinwald-fin glacier high up in the Swiss Alps becomes the Hinter Rhein, one of the two headstreams which unite to form the largest, most historically significant and commercially important river in Europe*

OPPOSITE CENTRE *The Vorder Rhein, the Rhine's second source, flows from the Lake of Toma, near the Oberalp Pass, to join the Hinter Rhein at Reichenau*

BELOW *The covered wooden bridge across the Rhine at Sackingen, founded by St Fridolin, the Irish missionary, is a footpath between Switzerland and Germany*

RIGHT *The Rheinfall at Schaffhausen, Switzerland, where the river, one hundred and twenty-six feet wide when it reaches the cliff, thunders down sixty feet to provide one of the most spectacular waterfalls in Europe*

Constance. At this point, when the Rhine is closest to the early Danube, its character is finally determined, for the Rhine leaves the lake as an indisputably great river. It is still flowing due west. After about twenty miles it reaches the old town of Schaffhausen beyond which occurs the famous sixty-foot waterfall, Der Rheinfall, one of the most spectacular episodes in its whole career. Seventy miles or so on it rolls into Basle, and then immediately turns north-east again, leaves Switzerland and enters onto its true and sombre destiny: for the next 120 miles or so it is the dividing line between France and Germany.

It is easy to believe that the Rhine is the natural Franco-German border. The idea has possessed Frenchmen for centuries. It is a case of wishful thinking. It would have improved the map and the peace of Europe enormously if this huge south–north-flowing waterway had been a frontier, but in fact this has rarely been its function. In the last 2000 years men have contrived to use the Rhine as a frontier along its whole length only for some 200 years, and most of those years occurred long before our own age, in the time of the Roman Empire. From the end of the first century BC the Rhine was a main Roman defence manned by the legions against the Teutonic hordes. As a barrier against the barbarian menace to the Empire it was successfully held till around 200 AD (This is to generalise roughly— the story was not at any time a simple one.) By the third century Teutonic pressure had become too great for Roman defensive strength. The point to notice is that after the time of Julius Caesar the pressure and aggression and finally the conquest all tended one way. When Europe pulled herself together again after the Dark Ages this fact most strongly influenced her future shape.

There was little racialism in the ancient world but that is not to say there was none, and there was a lively sense of tradition; of the tradition of Roman citizenship in Gaul and of tribal and racial loyalties among the Teutons. Both traditions were strong but the Teuton one shaped the map more than the Gallic. Charlemagne's Empire had no Rhine frontier. For 27 years after his death the river frontier reappeared on more or less the same short stretch as at present, but when it vanished it did not reappear again until the Peace of Westphalia in 1648. From then till now, with a half-century gap from 1870 to 1918 and a four year gap from 1940 to 1944, the Alsatian Rhine border has been a Franco–German frontier. But this again is to simplify. There was one anomalous interregnum.

At the beginning of the nineteenth century there was a reversion to Roman political geography when for 13 years under Napoleon, from 1801 to 1814, the whole left bank of the Rhine, from Switzerland to the sea, formed the French frontier. This Napoleonic achievement was dazzling enough, but could never be durable. It aroused a rebellious spirit to which Arndt gave expression in his famous line about the Rhine being a German river. Modern nationalism was already on the march and, thanks to the distribution of population which had been left at the end of the Roman Empire, there were too many Germans on the left bank to allow a Rhine frontier to leave modern France with an easily united population. Even today with only the short Alsace frontier there is a large German-speaking population in France, but no French-speaking population in Germany.

The first great city of the Rhine after Basle is the Alsatian capital, Strasbourg. It is not built on the river but near it, on the left bank tributary, the Ill (not to be confused with the Swiss Ill). From the Alsatian or the Baden side the spire of the cathedral points high over the town, visible from a long way off in the plain through which the Rhine wanders. It is the great landmark.

There is no church in the world like Strasbourg cathedral. It is very different from our idea of a Gothic cathedral, more elaborate and fantastic as a whole, and its sculpture is much more realistic. The colour of the stone is typical of this country, a vivid red. The single spire, rising to an enormous height from the twin towers of the Western façade, makes one think of the dominating North spire of Chartres, but again there is a vast difference between Strasbourg and the greatest and most classic of all Gothic cathedrals. Strasbourg is markedly unclassic; it is Germanic, riotous, enthusiastic. The whole town, in its beauties and in its ugly things, is extremely German in aspect. One can see why Germans thought that it should belong to Germany, as it might still do today if the Germans had been wise.

The outline of the later story is also worth remembering here. The only reason that the Alsatians were apportioned to the French rather than to Imperial Austria in 1648 was that these territories had been so ravaged, so subject to burning, slaughtering and plundering by French and Swedish troops in the Thirty Years War that the Emperor was quite unable to maintain an army there. So the Treaty ordained that the German-speaking Alsatians were delivered over to the people who had turned their fertile country into a desert.

The peace of Westphalia was generous to France but failed to satisfy the appetite of Louis XIV. He wanted one thing above all: the great prize of Strasbourg which remained outside French rule as a 'free city'. In 1681, not even bothering to invent a cause of war, Louis XIV attacked Strasbourg and its neighbourhood. His brutal annexation was not recognised till 1679, and in the meantime Alsace had again been forced to endure murderous warfare as horrible as that she had undergone in the Thirty Years' War. For more than 200 years after men remembered with horror the massacres which accompanied Louis' campaigns, and the name of The Grand Monarch is still held in these lands, and the Rhineland beyond, in utter execration.

But the French crown in the next generations pursued a policy of some astuteness and magnanimity. Louis XV played his cards well. His appearance on the battlefield at Metz at the moment of French victory excited, strange to say, national French pride in the Rhine provinces of the east. In the next year, 1745, when he recovered from his nearly fatal illness, and the French, in a delirium of loyalty, named him 'Louis le Bien Aimé', the King organised special celebrations in Strasbourg. Accounts and illustrations of the time indicate that the succession of fêtes and receptions arranged for the Most Christian King's visit to the Cathedral City were beyond belief in their splendour and extravagance. Today such junketings might worry the social conscience. In the cruder eighteenth century they only made a popular ruler more wildly popular than before. Louis XV's success endured.

The goodwill which the monarchy had fostered and obtained in Strasbourg and Alsace was carefully jeopardised by the doctrinaires of the Revolution. The Republican Government hastened to close the ancient University as the teaching was in German and the place was feared as a hotbed of German counter-revolution. Under the monarchy the city had preserved some of its former Imperial 'free city' privileges. These were all swept away by the intellectuals in power. They suppressed the very name of Alsace and for official purposes transformed the province into the departments of the Haut Rhin and the Bas Rhin. They proposed and were narrowly prevented from pulling down Strasbourg Cathedral. Yet these bone-headed idealists failed to do the damage one might expect of them. Strasbourg never became a centre of German anti-French activity.

This loyalty was not changed when the German Empire acquired Alsace in 1870. The Germans lacked

OPPOSITE *At the foot of the Alps the fast-flowing mountain stream begins to gather strength, and timber cut on its banks must be manhandled past rocks and shoals*

the necessary statecraft. After a career of unscrupulous but brilliant success under Bismarck, they entered now onto that career of crass victory-drunk blundering which became their national weakness. The first blunder was to take more than half of Lorraine as well. The claim for Lorraine was non-existent, whereas that for Alsace was at least arguable. This put the whole German action in a gross light.

The Germans did a fine thing for Alsace: they re-opened the University of Strasbourg. This was much appreciated, but it remained a single act of liberal statesmanship, and during most of the occupation the Germans of Bismarck's Empire proved abundantly that they were incapable of rule outside their own borders. They made no endeavour to conciliate their new subjects.

In Paris the statue representing Strasbourg in the Place de la Concorde was covered by black veils from 1870 to 1918. All France mourned the loss of the two Eastern provinces, and the Alsatians and Lorrainers mourned with them. Wilhelmine Germany, faced by this spirit of patriotism, had only increased it by repression. Hitler, who had no statesmanship at all beyond political cunning, followed the same policy in a viler form, and brought the same result in a more terrible degree upon himself and his people.

Here then is the Rhine as the immediate scene of that terrible conflict between two great peoples. No place in Europe, not even Belgium, has had such a long history of warfare and suffering. But as often happens, nothing of this is visible on the surface. The Strasbourg countryside which has been ravaged heaven knows how many times is beautiful. The impression everywhere is of smiling, peaceful, prosperous rusticity. There is wonderful landscape in the Vosges mountains to the West and in the hills and valleys of the Black Forest to the East. In the plain between the two ranges the Rhine flows North, and no frontier could look more benign, happy and majestic. Where is the reality? In the captivating loveliness of the scene, or

in the horrors hidden away in the memory of men?

At Strasbourg the Rhine increases in volume from its junction with the French Ill. Five miles beyond the Alsatian town of Lauterbourg the river leaves France, and after the little frontier town of Berg both banks are German for the next 350 miles.

The first great German Rhine city is Speyer, or as it used to be called in English: Spires. There is only one thing to be seen here and that is the Kaiserdom, the venerable cathedral. It was founded in 1030 by the Emperor Conrad II and added to in succeeding centuries, sometimes in order to repair the damage of war, and sometimes to add to its glory. Speyer is for those who like to feel that they are treading the soil where great events of history took place. The town was a residence of the Holy Roman Emperors in the early Middle Ages and a seat of the Imperial Legislative Court. It was here that the term 'Protestant' was invented at the Imperial Diet of 1529. Five Emperors and the ancestor of Emperors, Rudolph of Hapsburg, are buried in the cathedral. But unfortunately Speyer does not give those pleasures to the eye that ought to accompany

historical eminence. The town and cathedral were twice utterly ravaged by the French, under Louis XIV in 1689 and by the French republican army in 1793. King Ludwig I of Bavaria undertook the restoration of the cathedral in the mid-nineteenth century. What one sees today is the Kaiserdom as it would have looked when brand new if the architects and artists of the Middle Ages had been as tasteless as those of good King Ludwig's time. So onwards to Mannheim, the next great Rhine city.

The conjoined cities of Ludwigshafen and Mannheim mark a new phase in the course of the Rhine. From here on it is a great industrial river, and for practical purposes Mannheim can be described as the terminus of Rhine industrial navigation. It is the second largest inland port in Europe and there is no other of this size at such a distance from the sea. After Mannheim the Rhine is not only a potential frontier and an abundant source of irrigation, but a major factor in Germany's industrial economy.

For a long time Mannheim was part of the Bavarian Electorate and used as the Electoral capital city. It rose

OPPOSITE TOP LEFT *Bachrach, Germany, where wine has been made for centuries, and was once so highly prized that Pope Pius II had a cask sent to Rome every year and the town of Nuremberg paid an annual tribute of four tons to the Emperor Wenzel*

OPPOSITE TOP RIGHT *The once impregnable fortress of Gutenfels ('Good Rock') looks down on the little town of Caub and the Pfalz castle, with its jutting turrets and watchtowers. From Caub, in 1814, Marshal Blücher launched his Silesian army across the Rhine in pursuit of Napoleon*

OPPOSITE BOTTOM LEFT *A raft built of cut timber being worked down river past the island of Nonnenwerth and the towering castle of Drachenfels ('Dragon's Rock'). These floating islands, complete with huts and lookout towers, were as much as 1,000 feet long and needed eighty men to handle them*

OPPOSITE BOTTOM RIGHT *The town of St Goarhausen, founded by St Goar, a priest of Aquitaine. Perched high above the village is Burg Katz, built in 1393 by Count John III, destroyed in 1804 during the Napoleonic Wars, and recently restored*

TOP LEFT *Across the river from St Goarhausen is the thirteenth-century Rheinfels castle, the most imposing ruin on the Rhine. It stood firm against the combined attacks of the Rhenish towns up in arms against its river tolls, and repulsed the French under Marshal Tallard (1652–1728), but was taken — and later blown up — by the French Revolutionary army in 1794*

TOP RIGHT *Coblenz in the seventeenth century, when it was one of the wealthiest cities in the Hanseatic League, with an army of 30,000 men. It began as a Roman station built to guard the junction of the Rhine with the Moselle and the Lahn*

LEFT *Napoleon's meeting with Karl Theodor von Dalberg, newly elected Prince Primate of the Confederation of the Rhine, at Mainz in October 1806. The French victory at Austerlitz six months earlier had finally brought to an end the one thousand year old German Empire. Napoleon's reorganization of the German states, many of which were surprisingly loyal to him, laid the foundations of modern Germany*

to great prominence as a musical centre in the second half of the eighteenth century. Dr Burney, the eminent British musical scholar of George III's reign, declared the Electoral orchestra to be the finest in the world. He described it as 'an army of generals fit not only to plan but to fight a battle!' Mozart came here as a very young man fired with ambition to write a tragic opera. But before he could do so, the Electoral Court, and most of the orchestra, had left for Munich, and so '*Idomeneo*' was first played there. Mannheim fell into decay, and its gigantic baroque palace was unused, to the delight, one may suppose, of art critics of 100 years ago, who despised the baroque style. It became the habitation of rats, mice, bats, and the little beasts that slowly devour wood. But not long after the remove of the Elector's court, the Industrial Revolution began to transform the German economy, and with it German life, and incidentally the Rhine and Mannheim.

Before the Second World War, Mannheim was an instructive sight. The enormous Electoral palace, which, compared to the residence and gardens of nearby Schwetzingen, is not a very inspired work of classical architecture, and the lovely theatre where the orchestra used to play, stood in mournful aesthetic contrast to the monuments of the Bismarckian age and the functional building of contemporary manufacturing progress. Today the scene is much the same, but, so to speak, a bit more so. The Bismarck-era buildings and monuments remain in large part, but there is a great deal of new style concrete-steel-glass-box-architecture on the site of recent destruction.

The Rhine at Mannheim is nearly 500 yards wide, and from here on until it reaches Bingen, it grows steadily in size, achieving as early as this its greatest width in Germany. The next famous place is Worms with another great cathedral, also much over-restored, and then comes Mainz where the river changes course as it meets the Taunus range of hills and flows south-west for about twenty miles. Mainz is extraordinarily beautiful and its cathedral, though subject to all the ravages of the Thirty Years' War and the aggressions of Louis XIV, like almost every other great building in the Rhineland, has not been subject to such excessive restoration zeal as others.

OPPOSITE LEFT *Grape pickers at Nierstein look over some of the world's most famous vineyards, where vines were first cultivated by the wine-loving Romans*

OPPOSITE RIGHT *At Diedesheim, oxen wait patiently while the grapes are pressed. Hock, the white wine produced in Rhine vineyards, gets its name from Hochheimer near Mainz*

LEFT *The grape harvest at Johannesburg, whose celebrated Hock was developed by the monks of a nearby monastery seven hundred years ago*

BELOW *A Roman sandstone carving which shows how barrels were transported from the vineyards in Roman times. The barge has a wolf's head at the prow and a ram's head at the stern*

At the little town of Bingen the Rhine turns north again and quickly enters the type of landscape for which it is most famous: steep hills on either side, massively wooded or planted with vineyards, and plentifully stocked with ruined watch-towers and strongholds. This is the 'romantic Rhine' which has inspired more bad pictures than can be counted and which, in old-fashioned performances of Wagner's *Ring der Nibelungen*, was represented in the backcloth to several scenes. When Byron wrote:

'The castled crag of Drachenfels
Frowns o'er the wide and winding Rhine,'

this is the picture he had in mind.

The German, French and English romantic writers 'discovered' the beauties of the Rhine and its medieval past at about the same time. The excitement went to all their heads to about the same degree. Like the mountains of Switzerland this great spectacle was not productive of valuable literary or pictorial art. It led many astray. Thackeray's now forgotten story '*A Legend of the Rhine*' may have had the salutary effect of putting an end to the English literary side of the nonsense. This masterpiece of parody; written supposedly at the expense of Sir Walter Scott but more pointedly of his imitators, is a superb work of fantasy and caricature. The hero, 'The Childe of Godesberg' with his long golden ringlets and almost pathological chivalry, is capable of any physical feat, and when fleeing from the wrath of his father the Margrave, he swims under the Rhine for 25 miles, from Godesberg to Cologne. It is one of those comic tours de force that make you laugh aloud. It must have been difficult after its appearance for an English literary man or woman (for much of the romantic Rhine literature was written by women) to write in the strain of Scott's worst novel, *Anne of Geierstein*.

But the cult is still alive. Every healthy adolescent boy and girl in Germany still goes through a severe attack of *schwermerei* about the romantic Rhine, and is apt to read Max Schweckenburger's famous poem 'Die Wacht am Rhein' in floods of tears. But then, today, he or she grows out of it and feels faintly embarrassed. As a result the river between Bingen and Bonn, has come to have a bad reputation among more sophisticated people, especially Germans. They stress the absurdities: the medieval background contrasting with the artificial tourism, the 'castled crags' frowning on vulgar little puffing steamers, and on the puffing little cigar-smokers on board who have come to satisfy a petit bourgeois craving for the romantic agony. An anti-Rhine snobbery

has developed and many smart people think it rather wrong to go there at all. This is all rather silly, for no amount of reaction against the romantic cult can alter the fact that this landscape is of utterly unimaginable grandeur, and the castles on the crags on either side of the river indicate its fierce and tangled history with the most marvellous precision. The proportions of the scene are perfect. Before entering the gorge the Rhine is over 2500 feet wide, but within it narrows in places to less than 400 feet in width, sometimes achieving 75 feet in depth. This relative narrowness of the river, with the lofty precipitous hills on either side are the essence of Rhine magnificence. To deny such beauty is to be befuddled with fashion. Advice to tourists: surrender to the tremendous scene before you; read Thackeray's legend after, to restore your sanity; on no account take out your paints.

The gorge is interrupted at the point where the Moselle and the Lahn both flow into the Rhine at Coblenz. The river valley widens out in a plain ringed by the now more distant hills: then, after Neuwied, the hills close in again and the river enters a second gorge. Coblenz was once a scene of the classic Franco-German quarrel on the Rhine but with a difference. Here were the royalist headquarters after the Revolution, and here was cemented the alliance of the emigrated nobility, the Austrians and Prussians. But the war that resulted has grown rather dim in the shadow of Napoleon's wars. Today the town is famous for its wine market and the delights of drinking deep of untravelled Rhine wine and Moselle. It is also famous for the beautiful and ancient Church of St Castro, and for two extremely ugly and gigantic memorials. One is the statue of the Emperor William I, which the French over-turned in the intoxication of the 1918 victory. (It was put back.) The other is equally hideous but genuinely impressive: the vast bronze statue of Germania which dominates one of the first hills when the river once again enters a gorge.

The Rhine in the second gorge, after Neuwied, flows past the famous island convent of Nonnenwerth, a beautiful building of the eighteenth century, past the Drachenfels on the right, at which point the guides on the steamers remember Byron of course, (and since the invention of radio there is no escaping the lecture even from the shore), past Godesberg where Neville Chamberlain met Hitler during the Munich Crisis in 1938, a place of evil memory. A little beyond Godesberg the river finally leaves the gorge. The Romantic Rhine is over. The first city beyond is Bonn.

OPPOSITE *On a rock in the middle of the river at Caub stands the Pfalz, a six-sided fortress built by the Emperor Lewis the Bavarian (1314–47) to exact tolls from passing boats*

OVERLEAF LEFT *Just below the Burg Katz, seen here with its single turret silhouetted against the river five hundred feet below, is the famous Lorelei, the cliff where according to legend the Nibelungenlied treasure is buried and where the siren lived who lured boatmen to death by her song*

OVERLEAF RIGHT *The river cuts a deep and narrow gorge, noted for its echo and feared by boatmen, round the Lorelei, pictured from the hills above St Goarhausen*

ABOVE *At St Goarhausen, now a popular resort, a modern riverside town has taken the place of the medieval walls and watchtowers, but the Burg Katz still dominates the river*

RIGHT *Rhine barges near St Goarhausen. Their principal cargoes are coal from the Ruhr, fuels, ore and cereals to Switzerland and Italy*

OPPOSITE *Traffic on the river is controlled from signal stations, either specially built like this one or set up in converted castles*

It is a cosy, lovable, unspectacular little eighteenth-century town, with its famous university housed in what used to be the Electoral palace when Bonn was part of the Archepiscopal principate of Cologne. Its cathedral, the 'Munster', must once have been among the finest examples of the early Gothic style in Europe, but the old sad tale was re-enacted here as elsewhere: the wars ravaged the building and the restorers hastened to add their own touch of ugliness. The main structure is intact, but the restorers have succeeded in making the interior of the church humdrum and quite remarkably un-interesting. Strangely enough, the best things in the medieval church today are the baroque ornaments, notably a marvellous bronze statue of Saint Helena.

The people of Bonn, or rather their tourist trade, have succeeded in establishing a myth that this is where Beethoven spent his life. He was in fact born here but left as a very young man, after which his interest in Bonn seems to have been of the most slender kind. He is decidedly not the composer who immortalised the Rhine. Everyone knows who *that* was. A word on him and his work. In so far as the story of Siegfried, Brun-hilde, Hagen and Gunther can be said to have had any historical basis, (and it probably had none at all), the events celebrated in *Die Götterdämmerung* took place at Worms, but Wagner gives the impression in the Ring that they occurred in the dark valleys where the Rhine flows between hills. Certainly the tremendous E flat chord with which he opens *Das Rheingold* is in the Drach-enfels mood. Wagner allowed himself many freedoms. His version of the Rhineland Nibelung myth bears little resemblance to the ancient originals. They are far more crazy, and as Wagner's libretti are among the most fantastic hitherto devised, the reader may imagine

Rudolph I (1218–91)

Johann Wolfgang von Goethe (1749–1832)

Johann Christoph Friedrich von Schiller (1759–1805)

Gebhard Leberecht von Blücher (1742–1819)

Heinrich Heine (1797–1856)

Some of the great names associated with the Rhine:

Rudolph I, elected German king and Holy Roman emperor in 1273, was born on the Aas near its junction with the Rhine. The expansion of German power during his reign established the basis for the rule of the Hapsburg family

Johann Christoph Friedrich von Schiller escaped a military education to become a poet and dramatist. His first play The Robbers *was produced in Mannheim, where he was later appointed 'poet-dramatist' and where he began writing his famous tragedy* Don Carlos

Heinrich Heine, the German lyric poet and writer whose romantic ballad, Die Lorelei, *depicted the Siren of the Rhine as a beautiful golden-haired, bejewelled maiden. It was set to music by Silcher and became world famous*

Johann von Goethe, the 'universal man' and the greatest of all German writers and poets. He met J. G. von Herder, the writer who influenced him most, in Strasbourg, and there he planned his great drama Götz von Berlichingen, *based on a real life robber baron with an iron hand*

LEFT *Field Marshal von Blücher, the Prussian Commander who played a decisive part in Napoleon's defeat at Leipzig, helped most to persuade the allies to pursue Napoleon across the Rhine and into France in 1814. Although badly wounded during the Hundred Days, he helped to win the battle of Waterloo*

Richard Wagner (1813–83)

Klemens Brentano (1778–1842)

Alfred Krupp (1812–87)

LEFT *Ludwig van Beethoven (1770–1827)*

Ludwig van Beethoven, who in spite of becoming deaf at the age of thirty, produced some of the greatest music ever written. A true Rhinelander, he was born at Bonn in the garret of a house now kept as a national museum

Richard Wagner, the dramatic composer, poet and essay writer, who revolutionized the art of opera. Many scenes of The Ring, *the famous operatic tetralogy in which the gods and heroes of mythology are brought to life, are set around the waters of the Rhine*

Klemens Brentano, poet and propagandist, was born on the Rhine at Ehrenbreitsen. Except for a monastic six years recording the revelations of the Nun of Dulmen, he led a restless life, and is best remembered for his editorship of Der Knabe Wunderhorn, *which became the mouthpiece of the young romantics and helped propagate the many legends about the Rhine*

Alfred Krupp, the 'Cannon King', who founded the great gun factories at Essen, where he was born. He introduced the Bessemer process and the steam hammer into Germany, and caused a sensation at the Great Exhibition in London in 1851 with a solid, flawless ingot of cast steel weighing two tons

OVERLEAF *On New Year's Eve, 1814, Blücher's victorious troops crossed the Rhine from the village of Caub in a pursuit of Napoleon that was to end at Waterloo*

LEFT *Troops of the US 7th Army aboard a raft during the Allied crossings of the Rhine in 1945*

BELOW LEFT *Troops of the German army at Ehrenbreitstein on the Rhine during Hitler's reoccupation of the Rhineland in March 1936*

BELOW RIGHT *In Cologne war victims cart their belongings along streets flattened by Allied saturation bombing, which nevertheless failed to destroy the vital target, the Hohenzollern railway bridge, or Cologne's chief glory, its six hundred years old cathedral*

ABOVE *A medieval picture which tells the story of St Ursula, patron saint of Cologne. According to the legend, St Ursula and her 11,000 virgin handmaidens were martyred in Cologne by the Huns, and were buried in and around the Tomb of the Virgins. The tomb owes its existence to a vision seen by Clematius, a Roman official*

LEFT *The value and volume of trade carried on the Rhine in the sixteenth century is shown by the size and strength of the river craft in this engraving by Anton von Worms*

what the raw material is like. If one is a Wagnerite, one instinctively remembers the E flat chord at a first sight of the Rhine. There is no river music comparable to Wagner's, not even the *Blue Danube*.

After Bonn there comes a great Rhine moment. About thirty miles north there stands Cologne, the most famous German city of the whole river.

In the nineteenth century German restorers did as much damage to the Gothic heritage of Europe as their brethren in England did, but in Cologne Cathedral there exists an exception which is their defence before history. The exception is of immense beauty. It is a truism that the great Gothic cathedrals were rarely if ever built to a single plan but were the work of several generations reflecting different periods, ideas and tastes.

In the case of Cologne this principle was carried to a final, extravagant and logical conclusion. The building was begun in 1248 and from there was continued until 1508, when it was still far from being finished. Cologne suffered as fearfully as anywhere in the Rhineland from the religious wars of the sixteenth century, and from the Thirty Years War. Throughout that period and

throughout the eighteenth century the cathedral remained unfinished, partly through the decline of this great city which had been, but after the Thirty Years War was no longer, an industrial navigation terminus, as Mannheim is today, and partly because the spirit had gone out of Gothic art. Desecration came to add further affliction. The cathedral was degraded to being used as a barn under French rule from 1796 to the fall of Napoleon. But in 1816 the venture was taken up again under the impetus of Prussian rule, and as a result (a thing that those anti-Prussian enthusiasts Belloc and Chesterton must have found hard to understand) this great Catholic cathedral was completed under the patronage of Prussian sovereigns in the nineteenth century. The work of the Middle Ages was magnificently continued. An important point to note is that the last architects had considerable documentary evidence of the fifteenth-century plans for the completion of the cathedral, but one must always remember that they were not merely restoring but continuing. As a result, Cologne Cathedral, for all its modern content, which includes the two famous spires, is not only a superb example but an unself-conscious example of medieval architecture at its most glorious.

One of the modern splendours of Cologne is the Hohenzollern Brücke, built between 1907 and 1911. This bridge carries the railway across the Rhine which is 1500 feet wide at this point. For that reason it is of the highest industrial and strategic importance. With the object of putting it out of use Cologne was mercilessly bombed during the Second World War. The city was subjected to what was called pattern–or saturation-bombing, agreeable euphemisms for the policy of destroying a whole inhabited area for the sake of some intended target. The cathedral was struck many times in the course of these enterprises, worthy of the wars of old in which no effort was spared to exterminate whole cities. During months, even years, of bombing the bridge eluded the skill of Allied airmen. Almost to the end of the war trains clanked across the Rhine along its four tracks of railway. At last, in March 1945, two months before the German surrender, the central arch

LEFT *Through Duisburg the vast production of the Ruhr, the most concentrated industrial centre in Europe, makes its way south into Germany and Switzerland and north through Holland to the North Sea*

OPPOSITE *The bridge spanning the Rhine at Duisburg, which, with its neighbour Ruhrort, forms one of the largest river harbours in the world. Almost totally destroyed in World War II, Duisburg is the centre of Germany's 'economic miracle'*

was struck. By this time the whole of the mid-city area of Cologne had been shattered and presented an utterly horrifying sight: acre upon acre of ruined houses from which the cathedral, for all the bashing by Allied air forces, still stood forth with its majestic outline intact. Even ten years after 1945 Cologne was still a scene of ghastly desolation, an appalling reminder of the folly of the hate of nations.

The bridge was temporarily repaired between 1946 and 1948, but its restoration was not finally completed until ten years later, in 1958. Ironically enough the equestrian statues at each end, representing the last four Prussian sovereigns had remained unharmed throughout. Even the iron plumes on their helmets and the iron spikes of Wilhelm II's moustaches had survived with hardly a scratch.

Since the war the great majority of Germans have shown remarkable restraint and balance of judgement towards those who wreaked destruction on their country. They put the blame where it belongs, to the account of the semi-lunatic who ruled Germany from 1933 to 1945. But in Cologne there is a different spirit. An Englishman or American there is likely to meet with angry looks. It would be strange if it were otherwise.

North of Cologne the Rhine enters Westphalia. Düsseldorf is the next great river town. It is often spoken of in Germany as a place of much elegance, but precisely why it should enjoy this reputation is puzzling. It has for the most part a heavy, solid, late nineteenth-century, respectably dull look. It might be worse, of course, and it has some good museums and a worthy opera, but so have many other German towns. Possibly it is more enjoyable in summer than in winter. North of Düsseldorf come Duisburg and the industrial centres of the lower Rhineland and the Ruhr country. All these towns were the scene of frightful devastation in the last three years of the war and it was in this country (though not on the Rhine itself) that the dam-busting raids took place in May 1943. The recovery of this industrial centre is the principal feature of the 'economic miracle', that *Wirtschaftswunder* which has rescued West Germany from disaster and which is, all the same, mysteriously resented and mocked at by modern Germans, especially of the younger generations.

In the midst of the industrial North German Rhine there is one ancient city of considerable beauty, and that is Cleves. It has one of the finest of medieval gateways and the cathedral of St Victor with its twin spires is a most beautiful and attractive church in the Romanesque style. It provides relief from the harshness of the in-

dustrial area, but the grim beauties of the lower Rhine manufactures are an unforgettable sight, especially on a winter evening when the riverside factories are glowing and their fires reflected in the wide barge-crammed river. The scene has all the sinister colouring of a real-life Nibelheim.

As the Rhine reaches its last stages its course becomes wildly irregular. The drop of the land towards the sea is slight, and so the river's width increases while its pace diminishes in inverse proportion. In a wet winter the flat lower Rhineland is in continual danger of flooding. The last German town is Emmerich and when the Rhine

OPPOSITE *A barge on the river Waal, the southern arm of the Rhine in Holland, approaching Rotterdam and the North Sea*

A barge basin at Herne, a Ruhr river port and mining centre north of Duisburg, which is connected to the Rhine by a canal

The Niederrhein (Lower Rhine) flows through flat, peaceful countryside as it leaves Germany at Emmerich and, in Holland, branches out into many, lesser streams

OPPOSITE LEFT *Eight hundred miles from a log manhandled in a mountain stream, the mighty prow of an oceangoing ship in Rotterdam marks the end of the Rhine's voyage to the sea*

OPPOSITE CENTRE *The railway bridge over the Lek at Rhenen, Holland. The sixteenth-century church was destroyed during the Second World War but is now rebuilt*

OPPOSITE RIGHT *A river's symbols of wealth and beauty: a seagoing merchant ship and one of the fleet of small pleasure steamers which carry sightseers from all over the world*

BELOW *A Dutch herdsman looks out across the river and the watery maze of canals it feeds*

leaves Germany it leaves its former character behind. No more E flat chords. No more Wacht am Rhein. No more legends.

This is not to say that the magic has been lost. Far from it, but the new magic is of a quite different kind. It is not Rhine magic, and the Rhine, as a great river flowing under its own name, slowly vanishes while different identities take over. The first thing that happens is that one branch flows due north to the Zuider Zee under the name of the Yssel. At this same moment the main west-flowing stream becomes the Waal, and after confluence with the Maas flows under the name of the Waal to the final delta. Only a far lesser stream, also flowing west, above the Waal, keeps the name of the Rhine. As such, and still as a navigable river, it flows through Arnhem, but about thirty miles north of that town (long to be remembered as the scene of the famous battle in 1944), further misfortune awaits the Rhine. There is another bifurcation and again the main stream discards the original name and flows to Rotterdam and the sea as the Lek. The lesser stream, north of the Lek, is now called the Oude Rijn, meaning the Old Rhine. Poor old thing, it keeps on bravely, flowing through Utrecht, but beyond this town there is another last bifurcation, and this time a fatal one for Rhine worshippers. Again the main stream takes a different name, the Vecht, and again the lesser northern stream retains the original name; but by now, the Oude Rijn is such a pathetic little trickle that it would not in fact reach the sea at all without the artificial aid of canals and sluices. If this thing is really that mighty river which flows by the Drachenfels, then T. S. Eliot is proved right again, and the Rhine certainly ends with a whimper.

But in fact this is to look at the matter quite wrongly. It is to attach ridiculous importance to the power of names. We should forget the name altogether and look for the magic, and the new magic is, in fact, of the utmost potency. For the Rhine is one of the main river supplies of Holland and is thereby a chief formative influence in the incomparable watery Dutch scene. This is the subject of the great Dutch landscape painters of the seventeenth century, and the water is more than half Rhine water in origin. Those who have enjoyed the romantic Rhine, can now enjoy a second and greater gift, the classic Dutch painters.

Since the emergence of the Rhine from innocent Switzerland to the Franco–German frontier in Alsace, the great river is one that has nowhere been free from the splendours and curses of history. Of no place is this more true than of Holland. In the numerous wars

fought in Holland, between Dutch and Austrian, Dutch and Spanish, Dutch and French, and – as they say in sporting chronicles – others, the thousand criss-cross waterways of Holland supplied impregnable defence lines or places to be seized by courage or craft. In the Second World War, for the first time in Holland's long and troubled history, the canals and even the rivers proved of no avail against modern technique, and modern treachery. It may be said that in the Second World War, for the first time in European history, the Rhine, along its whole huge length, proved of no avail as a defence to either side. For all that the memory of the old wars lingers here as it does along the German

Rhine. It will be yet many years before the memory of Louis XIV is forgotten in Holland, though the recent memory of Hitler may help it towards oblivion, as the greater cancels the lesser atrocity in men's minds. There comes the point where every one has 'supp'd full with horrors'.

The Rhine ends happily nonetheless, in the Dutch landscape which has enriched the world as the scene of an eminently and progressively civilised way of life, and the inspiration of an immense enlargement of man's sense of the beauty of nature. What matter that under its own name the river is lost at the end, like the Nile, in a watery maze.

Rotterdam, which owes its great prosperity to the Rhine and Germany's 'economic miracle', is the largest port in Europe, with more than twelve miles of quays for seagoing ships and nearly nine for inland shipping

THE SEINE

JAMES CAMPBELL

Paris, which began as a sprawl of wooden huts on an island in the Seine, proclaims its origins in its coat of arms, a ship surmounted by the royal fleur-de-lis with the motto Fluctuat nec Mergitur — *it floats and does not founder. This was originally the seal of the merchant guild of the* Marchands de l'Eau, *who traded up and down the Seine and on whose commercial enterprise the prosperity of Paris was founded*

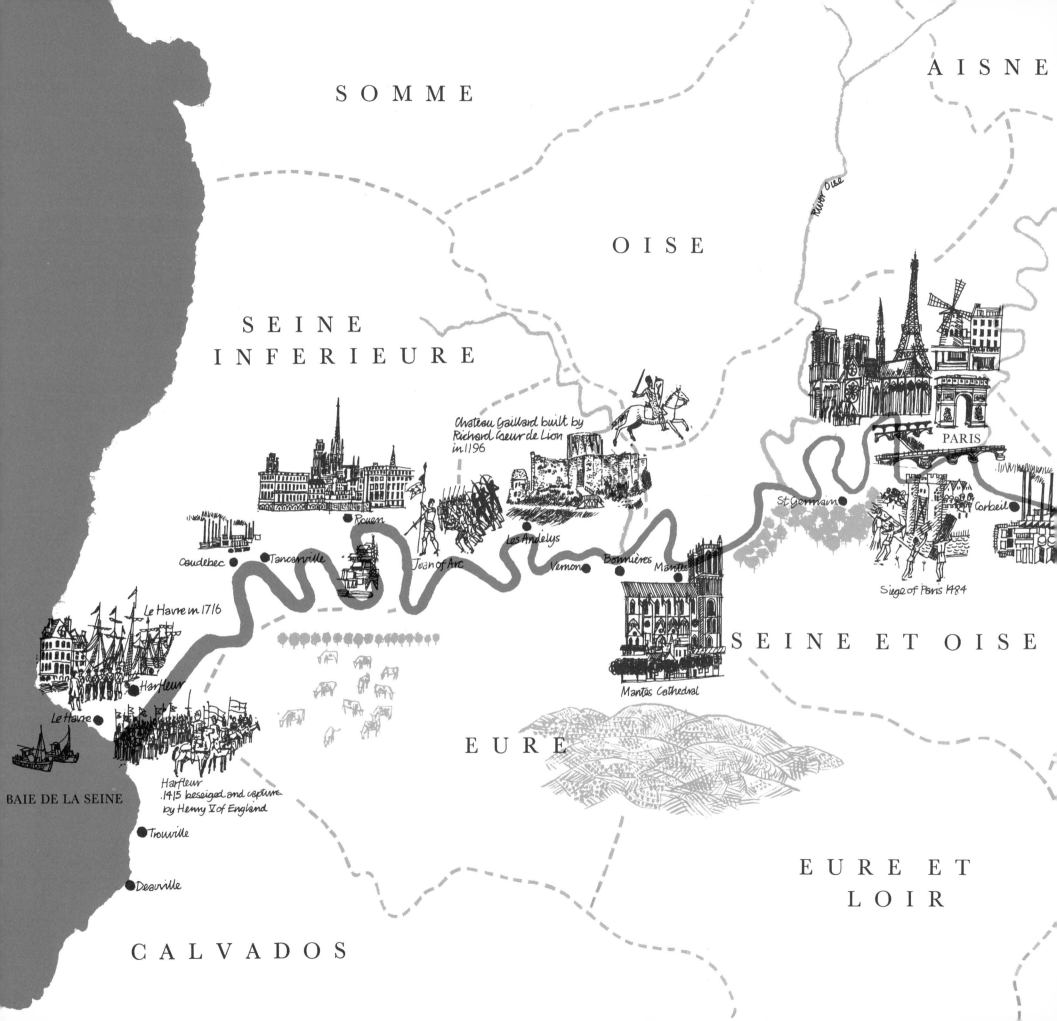

SOMME

AISNE

OISE

River Oise

SEINE
INFERIEURE

PARIS

Chateau Gaillard built by
Richard Coeur de Lion
in 1196

Rouen

St Germain

Corbeil

Les Andelys

Coudebec

Tancarville

Jean of Arc

Vernon

Bonnières

Mantes

Siege of Paris 1484

Le Havre in 1716

SEINE ET OISE

Harfleur

Mantes Cathedral

Le Havre

EURE

BAIE DE LA SEINE

Harfleur
.1415 beseiged and capture
by Henry V of England

Trouville

Deauville

EURE ET
LOIR

CALVADOS

HAUTE MARNE

MARNE

River Aube

Nogent

SEINE ET
MARNE

Troyes

AUBE

Vix

The Great Vase of Vix

Châtillon

CÔTE D'OR

Melun

Montereau

River Yonne

Fontainebleau

Moret

La Cour des Adieux

River Loing

LOIRET

THE SEINE

NIEVRE

Kilometres 0   10   20   30   40

Miles 0   10   20   25

To the Loire Canal d'Orléans

Canal de Briare

Shorter than the Rhône or the Loire, more placid and less spectacular in its course, the Seine is nevertheless the greatest river of France. Its source, as recognized by the Paris Municipality, may only be hallowed by a Second Empire goddess from the Paris Exhibition of 1867 and its upper course be dominated more by a canal system than by geography, but throughout history its banks from mouth to source have been the scene of great events –'C'est l'histoire qui consacre la géographie.' Henry Richmond sailing from Le Havre for Milford Haven to become the first Tudor king; Lafayette preparing his expedition there in 1779 to support the American colonists' struggle for independence; ten years later the young Wordsworth responding to the first events of the Revolution and writing: 'Bliss was it in that dawn to be alive, But to be young was very heaven!'; Henry V before the breached walls of Harfleur; Joan of Arc burnt at Rouen and her ashes thrown into the Seine; Monet painting Rouen cathedral at least twenty times; William the Conqueror thrown from his horse at Mantes in 1087 and fatally injured; Henry VI of England and Napoleon the only two sovereigns to be crowned in Notre Dame; German snipers firing inside the cathedral during de Gaulle's triumphal entry in 1944; Wagner, in exile, conducting a band on the Champs Elysées; Renoir painting at Chatou, and Seurat at Asnières; Mallarmé meditating on the bridge at Valvins; Attila and the Huns defeated at Troyes in 451 by the Bishop, Saint-Loup; Henry V married at Troyes to Catherine of France; Châtillon, the birthplace of St Bernard . . . the index to the Seine is as endless as the smile on the face of *l'inconnue de la Seine* herself.

In his garden on the Île de la Cité, in the middle of the Seine, Louis IX (St Louis) used to dispense justice in the thirteenth century. The fact is symbolic of the history of the Seine, of Paris and of France, for it was from this minute fortified island, originally a Celtic settlement in the swampy alluvial deposits of the Seine basin that

Paris and the French state have grown. Julius Caesar first described the Île de la Cité in 52 BC: '*Id est oppidum Parisiorum quod positum est in insula fluminis Sequanae.*' Used by navigators and fishermen from the earliest times, it was a natural defensive site, protected by the river and the surrounding marshes (Lutetia, the Roman name for Paris, means a marsh) but it was high enough, particularly at the end where Notre Dame now stands, to be above flood level. It was on this site that a roughly inscribed Celtic stone – the Sailors' Altar – was found.

This was the nodal point of the whole Seine and Paris basins, formed thirty or forty thousand years ago by the vast quantities of mud and gravel washed down by the Seine, then a river of Mississippian size, at a time when rainfall was heavier than today, when there were heavy snowfalls on the uneroded mountains, and before the Seine was divorced from its original consort, the Loire.

The primeval cataclysm which separated these two rivers determined the placid character of the Seine.

RIGHT *Tranquillity and peace on the banks of the river near Melun*

BELOW *Skirting the forest of Fontainbleau the Seine turns north to Melun. Scenes like this, with their subtle tones and changing moods, have inspired some of the world's greatest landscape painting*

Monet at work in his floating studio at Argenteuil by Manet. Now a suburb of Paris, Argenteuil was once a meeting place for the Impressionists and often figures in their paintings

LEFT *The cathedral at Mantes-la-Jolie by Jean Corot, one of the forerunners of the Impressionists. The cathedral was built with money bequeathed by William the Conqueror to replace the church burned down during his attack on the city in 1087*

OPPOSITE Les Demoiselles au bord de la Seine *painted in 1856 by Gustave Courbet, who was probably the most important single influence on the Impressionists and introduced a new realism in both subject matter and treatment. This painting was regarded by his contemporaries as vulgar and shocking because the young women obviously did not belong to society*

Their common watershed heaved towards the Atlantic leaving only one main tributary from the Massif Central to enter the Seine before Paris–the Yonne, whose torrential sources are in the solid granite mountains of the Morvan region. In times of flood this water flows through Paris four or five days before that of the Seine itself and the upper Marne, and its influence on the main stream has often been disastrous. In 1176 the city's two bridges were swept away with mills, houses and livestock and, according to tradition, the flood was only halted by the Bishop of Paris leading a procession carrying a nail from the True Cross. In 1658 the newly built Pont Marie, joining the Île Saint Louis to the right bank, collapsed with its twenty-two houses and 120 people were drowned. In 1910 the left bank was under water, the wood blocks forced up from the streets, and even in 1955 the quais of the Île Saint Louis were submerged. In contrast, the tributaries flowing into the right bank of the Seine–the Aube, Marne, Oise and Epte–are stable, slow-moving rivers of the plain, flowing over chalk and clay, their levels largely regulated by natural underground reservoirs.

The sources of the Seine itself are at the northern foot of the wooded slopes of the Côte d'Or, about 1,500 feet above sea level, twenty miles north-west of Dijon. The upper stretches of the river have a quiet pastoral quality, with grazing for horses and cattle where the chalk is near the surface, and arable where the alluvial deposits are deep enough to take the plough. At Commeville and Mussy, north of Châtillon, the mill-stream still grinds wheat and mustard seed. This was the *Valles Bernardus amabat*, and it was here in the water meadows that St Bernard chose a site for the Abbey of Fontenay.

It was the country of the Sequanae, a Celtic tribe whose goddess Sequana was the deity of the Seine. Until 1953, excavations near the river's sources had produced only a moderate Gallo-Roman haul–a bronze galley with its prow in the shape of a duck's head (a conceit common to most Roman votive ships); another votive ship with a fine bronze statuette, eighteen inches high, of a crowned goddess, perhaps Sequana herself; a large vase inscribed *Arae Sequana Rufus Donavit* containing a hundred silver and bronze ex-votoes; and the ruins of a Gallo-Roman temple. Not surprisingly the peasants of this countryside discouraged the early archaeologists of the 1840s; stones were for farm buildings and not museums. But times change and it was a farmer who, during the winter of 1953 when frost made farm work impossible, started digging in a dip in his field at Vix, a small village on a bluff overlooking Châtillon, about

forty miles from the source, and found the incomparable Treasure of Vix. Here in the tomb of a Celtic princess of the sixth century BC was a hoard of treasure (now in the museum at Châtillon) of remarkable beauty. Crowned with a golden diadem, the princess was found lying on a chariot, by her side a bronze urn over five feet high with a frieze of warriors, naked but for their armour. It is clear that there was a highly developed civilization in the Seine valley before the Roman occupation.

It is at Vix that the Seine first becomes navigable for small boats and the quality of the treasure seems directly related to the importance of the site on the ancient trade route from Marseilles to the channel, via the Rhône, the Saône and the Seine. The system of waterways, based on

the rivers, is of fundamental importance to the history of the Seine and of Paris. Within a radius of less than sixty miles from Notre Dame, the Seine is met by the Oise, the Marne, the Aube, the Yonne and the Loing. So placed, and also on the direct overland route from Flanders to the Pyrenees, Paris developed as a naturally important link in the Roman Imperial system.

It was in the aftermath of the decline and fall of the western Roman Empire that Clovis, leader of the Franks, established his capital at Paris. Having defeated both the Huns and Siagrius, the local legatee of Roman military power, Clovis was converted to Christianity and was baptised at Rheims on Christmas Day 506. His establishment of a royal Frankish line at Paris, marks the beginning of modern French history.

159

Alfred Sisley (1839–99) by Renoir

Edouard Manet (1832–83)

Some of the most important Impressionist painters, the group of late nineteenth-century French artists who rebelled against traditional ideas of composition and drawing and the posed emotions of the orthodox art of their day. Their aim was to achieve a greater naturalism by the exact analysis of tone and colour. They worked out of doors, frequently on the banks of the Seine, fascinated by the interplay of light on water and their paintings comprise a unique record of the river in all its moods

OPPOSITE *An evening scene by Alfred Sisley, one of a series of works painted near Rouen*

Jean Corot (1796–1875) a forerunner of the Impressionists

Claude Monet (1840–1926)

Camille Pissarro (1830–1903) A self portrait

Pierre Renoir (1841–1919)

But the final domination of France by Paris and the Seine was not in fact the direct product of the Merovingian dynasty established by Clovis, whose authority remained local. It was also a result of the Arab invasion of Europe in the eighth century. Having conquered the Middle East – and so Byzantium and the north African coast – in the last fifty years of the seventh century, the Arabs crossed the Straits of Gibraltar in 711. By the end of the next year they had occupied the whole of the Spanish peninsula and begun to push north into France. They were finally halted by Charles Martel at the battle of Poitiers in 732. This was a definitive victory for the Frankish Empire as a north European military power, but the results of the Arab invasion were no less decisive. Trade in the western Mediterranean was seriously affected and there was a decline in the wealth of towns in southern France. The north, where society tended to be based on landed property, held its own. As a result the centre of Western Europe shifted away from the Mediterranean countries with their flourishing commercial life to the poorer, agrarian, Frankish territories of the north. This shift was as important for the history of the Seine and of Paris as the primeval separation of the Seine from the Loire.

Although the Vikings held islands in the Seine from which they raided Paris, the Île de la Cité, protected by the river, was able to survive the Viking invasions of the eighth and ninth centuries. The situation was stabilized by Charles the Simple's recognition of Rollo, a Viking, as Duke of Normandy at Clair-sur-Epte in 911. As the political and social structure of northern France developed round the geographical units of Normandy, Burgundy and Champagne, so the importance of the Seine grew as the common frontier of all three. The original trading posts on the river, Troyes, Montereau, Mantes, Rouen, developed as provincial capitals and it was at these towns that the central power of Paris, expressed along the Seine, came into conflict with

ABOVE *The Sailors' Altar, a votive pillar representing the Gallic guardians of the Seine, excavated on the Île de la Cité. This is the earliest known representation of the original Gallic settlers, mentioned by Caesar in his* Gallic Wars *as the 'Parisii'*

OPPOSITE *A peaceful backwater near Paris – the camera records the scenery which inspired the Impressionist painters*

BELOW *The Tour de Neslé, one of the hundred towers built by King Philippe-Auguste in the thirteenth century to protect the city. A seventeenth-century engraving by Jacque Callot. According to legend it was from this tower that Marguerite of Burgundy flung the bodies of her discarded lovers into the Seine. The tower stood on the site of what is now the Institut de France*

ABOVE *A seventeenth-century painting of fishmongers' and laundry women's barges moored on the Quai de la Megisserie near the Pont Neuf*

Promenade du Pont Ponpons. (Pont des Arts.)
Dédié au beau Sexe, par un Amateur.   A Paris chez Martinet rue du Coq. N°15.

the rival powers of Burgundy at Montereau, and of Normandy at Mantes and Rouen.

Throughout the Middle Ages Paris was, above all, the fortified centre of a dynasty extending its perimeter to increase its self-sufficiency and military power. As the town grew it was the *Marchands de l'Eau*, the merchant guild which traded up and down the Seine, who dominated the commercial life of Paris from their quai on the site of the Hôtel de Ville. By the time of Saint Louis their Provost had been made a royal official, and the seal of their guild, a Gallo-Roman ship with the motto *Fluctuat nec mergitur* (It floats and so does not founder) had become that of the city of Paris itself.

The security and prosperity of Paris have always depended on the Seine. Downstream, the prerogatives of the *Marchands de l'Eau* ended at Mantes and control of the river therefore depended on the balance of French and Anglo-Norman relations. The great castle of Château Gaillard, on the bluff above Les Andelys, built by Richard Coeur-de-Lion in 1196 to block the route from Paris to Rouen, was testimony to the vital importance of the control of the Seine, and its capture by Philippe-Auguste in 1204 after Richard's death contributed greatly to the effective ending of the military power of England in Normandy.

Upstream from Paris, the canal system developed with the city's need for food and raw material. The Briare canal, begun by Henri IV and the Orléans canal, opened by Louis XIV, reunited the Loire with the river system of Paris. This was the prerequisite for the great expansion of Paris in the eighteenth century. Later, in 1810, the need for coal led to an underground canal being

ABOVE *Preening society on the Pont des Arts during the First Empire. Built in 1804 for pedestrians only, this bridge used to be lined with orange trees and rose bushes and was a favourite meeting place for fashionable people in the early nineteenth century*

BELOW *A famous incident during the revolution of 1830 against the reactionary King Charles X, when a young revolutionary was killed as he rushed across the bridge and planted the tricolour above the central arch. As he fell he cried 'Arcole', the scene of a famous French victory in 1796, when Napoleon led his troops across a bridge over the Adige in northern Italy. The bridge is called the Pont d'Arcole in memory of the episode*

OPPOSITE *A view of Notre Dame and the Quai St Michel by Honoré Daumier, a nineteenth-century painter more usually known for his political caricatures and paintings of the common people*

built to join the Escaut and the Oise, and in 1832 to the Sombre and Oise canal. In 1832, also, the Burgundy canal was completed in response to the growing demand for wine, and the need for wood led to the building of the Ardennes canal in 1833. When the Railway Act of 1842 made Paris the central terminus for the whole of France so that it could be easily supplied with perishable food by rail, engineers began to deepen the existing canal routes and make new ones for the transport of the heavy raw materials needed for building and industry–the Nivernais canal in 1852, the Rhine-Marne canal in 1853. Eventually in 1879 the plan was completed so that barges could circulate among all the rivers and canals, and, today, a barge can sail from Le Havre via the Seine, the Rhône, the Rhine and the Danube to the Black Sea.

The most obvious effect of this system of canals on

TOP Dog clippers on the banks of the Seine in about 1900. A photograph taken by Atget, one of the greatest of the early photographers, who made a unique record of everyday life in Paris at the turn of the century

This nineteenth-century engraving shows a Parisian from the suburb of Alfort climbing into his flooded home. Because Paris has always been subject to flooding the banks of the Seine often have to be reinforced

RIGHT *An early photograph of the Pont Alexandre III, looking west towards the Pont des Invalides. Moulded in steel and balustraded in white stone with gilded statues, it is the most flamboyant of the Paris bridges. Built between 1897 and 1900, it was named after Czar Alexander III (1845–94), whose reign was marked by a growing friendship between France and Russia*

OPPOSITE *Notre Dame and the Pont St Michel by Matisse*

the Seine itself is that, below Montereau and the junction with the Yonne as far as Paris, the Seine is a waterway rather than a river: the flow is controlled by vast locks and the river's character is determined by the expanding industrialisation of Paris. It is as though the upper Seine has reverted to its original function as a trade route. Troyes, once the greatest trade centre of northern France with its 'Hot Fair' and 'Cold Fair' in summer and autumn, where Henry V was granted the hand of Catherine of France by the treaty of Troyes in 1420, and where nine years later Joan of Arc drove the English and their Burgundian allies from the walls and set up her standard, is now the centre of the hosiery trade. Sens is only known now for its fine cathedral, the model for Canterbury, and for its treasury, one of the richest in France. The importance and original character of these towns have been subordinated to Paris. No one complains, for since the time of Clovis Paris has been the magnet to which all Frenchmen have been drawn.

The establishment of an unchallenged central authority – both military and ideological – had been the main problem for Clovis and his successors in the Middle Ages. It was not until the thirteenth century when Philippe-Auguste and Philippe-le-Bel united Normandy and Champagne to the crown that Paris could become a great city. Philippe-Auguste's extension of the city walls, the first real expansion of the city from the Île de la Cité, was a symbol of this new stability. On the island itself, Notre Dame was begun in 1163 and the Sainte Chapelle in 1248 to be a shrine for the Crown of Thorns brought back from the Holy Land by St Louis. But these were the more sophisticated expressions of the central power. The Louvre remained no more than a fortified tower outside the city walls and the bridges crossing the river from the Île de la Cité were still made of wood.

If the buildings on the Île de la Cité expressed the prestige of central religious authority, the foundation of the University in 1200 on the left bank was as significant an expression of intellectual development as the new Gothic architecture of the Sainte Chapelle. The humanist renaissance of the twelfth and thirteenth centuries in France is as important as the original Roman settlement to which it was the heir. Paris, for the first time,

An aerial view of Paris showing the Seine dividing round the Île de la Cité and the Île Saint Louis

became the *patria* of the mind, and the rival in men's
hearts of Rome. It is as well to remember in our non-
heroic, Freudian age, that Abelard was the intellectual
hero of Europe in the twelfth century. Even Peter the
Venerable, the severe Abbot of Cluny, where Abelard
–a heretic, hounded by two councils–had retired to
die, could write 'by so coming he enriched us with a
wealth beyond all gold'. Abelard's personality, no less
than his claim for reason against authority, was an en-
franchisement of the human mind which has perman-
ently affected French thought. Teilhard de Chardin is,
perhaps, its most modern scholastic example.

'Paris,' wrote Guido de Basoches, a scholar from the
Seine valley, in 1250, 'Queen of cities, moon among
stars, so gracious a valley, an island of royal palaces . . .
And on that island hath Philosophy her royal and
ancient seat: who alone, with Study her sole comrade,
holding the eternal citadel of light and immortality,
hath set her foot on the withering flower of the fast
ageing world.' So the university, as the 'fille ainée'
of the sovereign, became part of what Michelet called
the unique equilibrium of Paris–on the south bank of
the Seine the intellectual centre; on the north bank,
commerce; in the centre of the Île itself, Notre Dame–
the symbol of authority. A sense of order is created by
this equilibrium, as though Notre Dame, the Pont Neuf,
the Louvre, the Place de la Concorde, the quais, the
bouquinistes and even the clochards are the results of
the deliberate application of French genius.

In fact the quais only date from the reign of Henry
IV, as does the Pont Neuf. After its completion in 1607,
the Pont Neuf being the only bridge uncluttered by
houses became one of the great public meeting points
of Paris and remained so for two centuries. On it were

BELOW *A* clochard, *one of the tramps that are a familiar part
of Paris life, asleep on the embankment*

LEFT *Fishermen on the point of the Île Saint Louis*

RIGHT *Parisians with their families fishing from the quai, shadowed by the huge barges which ply up and down the Seine*

stalls, quacks, ballad singers, pimps, hawkers of pamphlets, dentists. It was from Mondor, a seller of patent medicines on the Pont Neuf, and his comic feed, Tabarin, that Molière derived much of his dialogue for *Le Médecin Malgré Lui*. And it was from the Pont Neuf that the itinerant booksellers were expelled in 1649 to their familiar sites on the quais.

There are thirty-two bridges over the Seine in Paris and from the quais between them France is governed and Paris victualled, the prices at Les Halles affecting every farm in France. These bridges give a sense of unity and coherence to Paris, which is not altogether merited. Apart from the Île Saint Louis and the Place des Vosges (originally the Place Royale, designed by Henri IV as a model housing estate for artisans, but occupied when finished by many famous people including Richelieu, Corneille, Molière, the Prince de Condé and Ninon de Lenclos), the only serious attempt at planning was made in the mid-nineteenth century by Baron Haussman, the famous Prefect of the Seine, who was responsible for the present pattern of the boulevards.

The Louvre, dominating the Seine and centre of Paris, its monumental grandeur best approached over the clattering, wooden Pont des Arts, is the perfect example of the haphazard growth of a great Parisian building. Originally the right bank tower at the end of Phillippe-Auguste's city wall of 1190, the Louvre faced the Tour de Neslé on the left bank. It was included within Charles V's city wall of 1364 but stood neglected until François I returned from his disastrous Italian campaign and, inspired by the ideas of Leonardo da Vinci, Andrea del Sarto and Benvenuto Cellini, began to transform the old fortress into a modern Renaissance palace. In 1564 Catherine de Medicis began her own palace, the Tuileries which was later joined to the Louvre by Henri IV's addition of the Pavillon de Flore. Even Perrault's monumental façades, which have had such a lasting effect on official civic architecture, could give no more than a superficial unity to the constantly developing building and, when Louis XIV moved his court to Versailles in 1680, the north and east wings of the Cour Carrée were unfinished and unroofed. By 1750 the Louvre had become such a warren of improvised dwellings, shops, stills, and factories that Louis XV was only prevented from demolishing the whole building by the intervention of Madame de Pompadour's brother, Marigny, the superintendent of royal buildings.

Louis XVI opened an entrance to the Seine through the south wing and Napoleon exposed the northern

ABOVE *A bouquiniste's stand on the quai de Conti, one of the 230 on the Left Bank which for hundreds of years have sold second-hand books and prints*

RIGHT *A clochard leaves his possessions at the kerbside to talk to a painter on the Pont de l'Archevèché. On the left are the stands of the bouquinistes*

OPPOSITE LEFT *The shadow of the cupola of the Institut de France, the home of the Académie Française, reflected in the trees overhanging the quai de Conti*

OPPOSITE RIGHT *A view up the Seine towards Notre Dame and the Ile de la Cité taken from the Petit Palais, built for the international exhibition of 1900. In the far distance can be seen the dome of the Sacré Coeur*

OPPOSITE *A view up the Seine towards the twin towers of Notre Dame and the spire of the Sainte Chapelle. In the foreground is the Pont de la Concorde, followed by the Pont Solférino, a temporary metal footbridge replacing Napoleon's original structure due to be rebuilt in 1966. Beyond it are the Pont Royal, the Pont du Carrousel, the Pont des Arts and, just visible between the trees, the Pont Neuf*

RIGHT *The Seine near the Pont Neuf, the oldest bridge in Paris, completed in 1598 by Henry IV. For centuries it was the favourite pitch of ballad mongers, jugglers, showmen and thieves*

OVERLEAF LEFT *The quais of the Seine, once the haunt of pickpockets and robbers. To-day their tranquillity is threatened by plans to replace them with through motorways, some of which have already been completed*

OVERLEAF RIGHT *The arches of the Pont Neuf seen from the quai of the Ile de la Cité*

side by driving the Rue de Rivoli through from the Place de la Concorde. The completion of the interior was continued after the Restoration by Louis XVIII and Louis-Philippe, and in 1852 Napoleon III began the final completion of the rectangle of buildings by commissioning what is now the Musée des Arts Decoratifs.

It took nearly seven hundred years to build the Louvre and the Tuileries. But in the night of 23 May 1871 the Communards set fire to the Tuileries, the library of the Louvre, the Hôtel de Ville, the Quai d'Orsay, the Palais de la Légion d'Honneur and the Palais de Justice and the Seine, reflecting the fires, flowed like a river of blood. For ten years the Tuileries stood gutted, before being demolished in 1882–4, so that now the courtyard of the Louvre opens directly onto the gardens of the Tuileries.

The buildings of Paris tell their own story of the city's history. But perhaps the most amazing record of the Seine itself is of an entirely different kind. It is found in the work of the great Impressionist painters. Rebelling against the sterile academicism and posed emotions of orthodox art, this group, led by Monet, Sisley, Pissarro and Renoir – to mention only a few of the painters whose names have become household words – took their canvases out of doors into the fields and woods of the Seine valley. They were fascinated above all by the analysis of light and the refraction and reflection of sun on water. The result was a unique portrayal of the river, its tributaries, its canals, barges and forests. Marlotte in the Forest of Fontainebleau, the Grenouillère restaurant at Chatou – the scene of Renoir's *The Boatmen's Luncheon* – Argenteuil, St Mammes, Marly have all become familiar through the work of the Impressionists.

Never has a countryside been recorded with such vision. As Marcel Proust wrote:

A picture by Monet makes us love the landscapes which please us in it. He often painted the banks of the Seine at Vernon. No doubt we can be of the opinion that he would have seen things as lovely elsewhere and that perhaps it was his personal circumstances that took him there. Never mind. To draw out the truth and beauty of a place we must know that they are there to be drawn out, that Gods are everywhere latent in its soil . . . Monet's pictures show us the magic vein in Argenteuil, in Vetheuil, in Epte, in Giverny. They show us, too, the heavenly pasturage our imagination can find in things less localized, islet dotted rivers during those motionless hours of afternoon when the river is blue and white with sky and clouds, and green with trees and lawns and pink with sunbeams already sloping on tree trunks, and splashed with scarlet in the shadow of the garden hedges where the tall dahlias push through. The pictures make us adore a field, a sky, a beach, a river, as though these were shrines which we long to visit.

From the terrace of the château of Saint-Germain-en-Laye, four hundred feet above the Seine, where Louis XIII died, Louis XIV was born and the exiled Stuarts lived for a time after the Revolution of 1688, one can look out over the whole area of the Île de France. The haze over Paris, visible even on clear days, is quite different from the brown bowler hat of smog which sits on London. It is the result of the evaporation of water in the porous chalky soil of the Paris basin and it was, in particular, the effects of light on this haze which so enthralled the Impressionists. Away from the Île de France, downstream from Paris, the character of the river changes. Swollen by the Marne, the Oise, the Yonne and the Loing, the Seine becomes a great river in the natural sense. No longer part of the complicated river and canal system centred at Paris, it winds along the north-east edge of the chalk cliffs of Normandy, doubling the distance between Paris and Le Havre with great loops, which enclose large areas of alluvial arable land and forest.

The strategic importance as well as the wealth of Normandy is evident. Vernon, Rouen, Caudebec and Le Havre were all nearly obliterated in the last war and have now been rebuilt. Normandy has been laid waste by invading armies many times. After the Hundred Years' War it was the most devastated province of France, but within the next century it had completely recovered and the merchants of Rouen and Le Havre were financing expeditions to the New World. Then, Normandy was rich in iron and had an advanced technology, producing enormous quantities of armour, besides tanning, glass and textiles. Rouen 'la grande ville drapante' of the west was also 'la ville aux cent clochers'. After the Second World War there were more than five hundred wrecks in the harbour. Today, the whole harbour area has been rebuilt so that, from the *corniche* above Rouen the city lies below like an architect's dream town. Along the quais, and towards the cathedral, one has the impression of looking down on great horizontal slabs of pitted concrete – the offices, flats and warehouses of the new Rouen. Beyond and above the concrete soar the spires of the great cathedral and the churches, once white themselves, while in the centre of the town the Place du Vieux-Marché where Joan of Arc was burnt in 1431 still remains.

Between Mantes, the old limit of the sphere of

Richard Coeur-de-Lion (1157–99), king of England and Normandy, the champion of Christendom, and the greatest warrior of his day. He built the Château Gaillard during his campaign of 1194–98 against Philippe-Auguste of France

179

ABOVE *The new suspension bridge at Tancarville, the only bridge across the Seine between Le Havre and Rouen*

LEFT *A prospect of Rouen from the hills above the Seine. The spire of the cathedral rises above the city in which William the Conqueror died, Richard Coeur-de-Lion received his crusader's banner and sword, Joan of Arc was burned at the stake, and Henry VIII and François I met at the Field of the Cloth of Gold. The city was badly damaged during the Second World War and has been extensively rebuilt*

181

The Seine completes its journey to the sea at Le Havre, France's second greatest seaport, a naval base, and an important commercial and shipbuilding centre

Parisian influence, and Rouen the Seine becomes as broad as the Loire. For historians the Château Gaillard remains one of the most important sites in northern France but in reality the scene is as Signac painted it in 1886 – one of mature domesticity, with the Seine flowing past a group of waterside houses and a man sitting watching a barge, his back to the great ruin.

Abandoned, also, in a forest practically encircled by the Seine is the magnificent ruin of Jumièges, where Edward the Confessor was educated. But the Benedictine Abbey of Saint Wandrille, a few miles east of Caudebec, which was dissolved during the Revolution, but to which the Order returned in the 1930s, still stands. It lies in its own hamlet, by its own stream, a minute tributary of the Seine. Founded in the eighth century, a great religious centre in the eleventh, and converted into a manor house after the Revolution, the abbey is now a mixture of Norman and eighteenth-

century styles. The sense of peace and seclusion at Saint Wandrille is a remarkable fact in modern, secular, technological France. Nevertheless, perhaps because it is so professional, the peace at Saint Wandrille does not seem an escape, but a natural complement to the great new suspension bridge at Tancarville and the new model town of Le Havre.

France suffered appallingly during the two World Wars, not only in terms of the destruction of buildings and communications but in the tragic loss of life. But the springs of French intellectual life have remained unaffected. The wars and revolutions of the last two hundred years have cross-fertilized, not sapped, the intellectual life of Paris. Since 1918 the *quartier latin*, the centre of French thought and culture, has become the Left Bank, a great meeting ground for writers, artists and philosophers of all nations, drawn to Paris by the great traditions of French culture and independent

thought. Here was the context for James Joyce to write and publish *Ulysses*, for Stravinsky and Diaghilev to revolutionize the ballet, and for Picasso and the painters of the École de Paris to create the idioms of twentieth-century painting. Here, also, on the Left Bank of the Seine at St Germain des Prés, the oldest intellectual forum of Paris, Sartre expounded his new philosophy of existentialism. From Abelard to Sartre the converging flow of men and ideas on Paris has been part of the essential life of the city and has given it a unique cosmopolitan character and authority.

Paris without the Seine is inconceivable. The river is too closely interwoven with the diverse and intricate strands which make up the city's character. Moreover, it is a great artery stretching across France, a constant reminder of Napoleon's famous statement: 'Paris, Rouen and Le Havre are all the same city and the Seine is their main street.'

THE TAGUS

THOMAS HINDE

This monument to Henry the Navigator and the men who discovered Portugal's New World empire stands near the Tower of Belem on the Tagus at Lisbon, the starting point of many of their expeditions

THE TAGUS

ATLANTIC

River Zezere

River Alagon

Lines of Torres Vedras 1809-10

Santarém
Bull breeding region

Abrantes
Boat Building

Almoural Castle

Alcantara: Roman Bridge

Tower of Belem

LISBON

PORTUGAL

SPAIN

River Salor

LISBON BAY

Kilometres 0   25   50

Miles 0   10   20   30   40

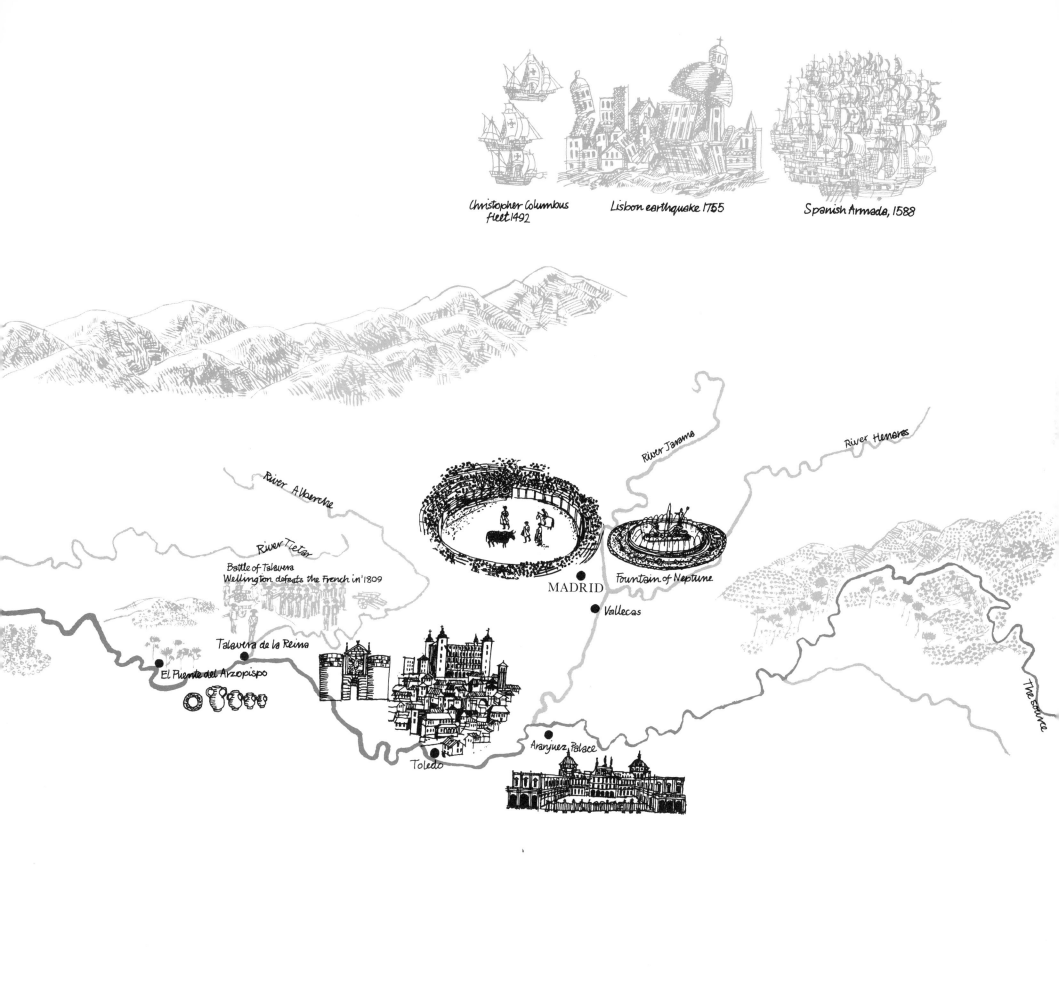

Christopher Columbus
fleet 1492

Lisbon earthquake 1755

Spanish Armada, 1588

River Alberche

River Tietar

River Jarama

River Henares

Battle of Talavera
Wellington defeats the French in 1809

Fountain of Neptune

MADRID

Vallecas

Talavera de la Reina

El Puente del Arzopispo

The Source

Toledo

Aranjuez Palace

N SPAIN and Portugal all but the largest rivers dry in summer into bare beds of rock and shingle, mere scars in the landscape. Across this arid landscape the Tagus flows, winter and summer, with gathering assurance. Rising in Aragon, less than 100 miles from the Mediterranean, it crosses three-quarters of Spain and the whole of Portugal before reaching the Atlantic. At Toledo it flowed past the city which was the capital of Spain till 1560 when Philip II moved his government up that unworthy tributary the Manzanares, to Madrid. At Lisbon it provides a totally contrasted but equally impressive setting for the Portuguese capital.

The crease in the map of Spain, the Tagus has been called, and certainly it suggests the crease of a folded map in its deep granite gorges. Its gorges are most memorable and there seems no need to look for a more devious derivation for its name when *Tajo* means 'gorge' in Spanish. Such flamboyance is less typical even of the Spanish parts of the river than the visitor who remembers it chiefly at Toledo might believe. Of all European rivers the Tagus defies summary most successfully and changes its personality most abruptly from mile to mile. At Peralejos, close to its source 5000 feet up in the Montes Universales, it is wild and dramatic enough. Here orange cliffs tower vertically on either side, in such unnatural shapes that they seem to be the work of giants and suggest the massed pieces of some vast chess set. Far below, the river is a mountain stream in a green bed of poplars, hurrying over rapids of grey rock.

North-west, through the Sierra de Cuenca, the Tagus makes a sixty-mile loop to reach the lake of Entrepeñas, a huge resevoir as blue as the summer Mediterranean held up by the tall dam below Sacedón. Mountains slope down to its deserted sandy shores and only an occasional advertisement for water skiing suggests the inland resort it may become. Through a lower lake, as green and weed-filled as Entrepeñas is clear and blue, across a bare and treeless countryside of wheat fields and white sided hills, it comes to its first important site, the small town of Aranjuez.

Aranjuez was created by the Tagus. The river here falls over rapids which with a little improvement made the surrounding *vega* easy to irrigate. Cool, fertile and central, it was a natural escape for Spanish royalty from the fierce heat of Toledo or Madrid, and Philip II made it a royal residence. To improve the gardens he imported English elms which, with giant plane trees, still shade its imposing avenues. But the palace as it now stands is a Bourbon creation, a symbol of the homesickness for France felt by that line of foreign kings, who succeeded the Hapsburgs in 1701, among their barbarous southern subjects.

Two fires had destroyed most of the earlier building when Philip V began work on it in 1727. (He had already built the palace at La Granja – of whose giant waterworks he said that they had cost him three million

186

The infant stream of the Tagus near its source on the slopes of the Muela de San Juan in the Montes Universales, eighty-eight miles east of Madrid. The Tagus, 565 miles long, is the largest river in the Iberian peninsula

PHILIPPVS V.

PHILIPPVS V. *Ludovici Delphini Franciæ ex Mariâ Annâ Victoriâ è Bavariæ Ducibus secundogenitus, ac Nepos LUDOVICI MAGNI Galliarum Regis et MARIÆ THERESIÆ Caroli II. Hispaniarum Regis disjuncti ururoris, ejusdem nuncupatus Dux Andegavensis, ad Hispaniæ Monarchiæ successionem vocatus. Parisiique primu ab Auo Ludouico Rege salutatus die 16. Nouemb. 1700. egregiæ indolis, prudentiæ, ac pietatis specimina illustria statim edidit, quibus Hispaniæ ueterem splendorem se restituturum, Christianoque Orbi maiora semper prosperitatum incrementa se tributurum spopondit. . . . .*

The Palace at Aranjuez as it was in 1773, when it was drawn by an army officer, Domingo de Aguirre, and as it is to-day (right). Aranjuez was the scene of Charles IV's abdication in 1808 and the setting for Schiller's famous play Don Carlos

OPPOSITE LEFT *A contemporary portrait of the four-times-married Spanish King Philip II (1527–98), who launched the Armada against England in 1588, with his heretic-hunting wife Mary, daughter of King Henry VIII. It was Philip II who first made Aranjuez, a small town on the banks of the Tagus near Madrid, a royal residence and planned its beautiful gardens*

OPPOSITE TOP *A portrait by Goya of Charles IV (1748–1819), the weak king whose surrender to Napoleon, in the guise of an alliance, so enraged his subjects that they forced him to flee the capital to Aranjuez, and to abdicate the throne in 1808*

OPPOSITE BOTTOM *An engraving of Philip V (1683–1746), the founder of the Bourbon dynasty in Spain, whose accession upset the European balance of power and brought about the thirteen years' long War of the Spanish Succession, Philip V was responsible for restoring the beauty of Aranjuez after two fires had razed most of the earlier buildings*

pesetas and amused him for three minutes.) At Aranjuez, on the banks of La Ria – an artificial cut made across the gardens – he created a splendid alien building to which his two successors, Ferdinand VI and Charles III added.

Here, in Ferdinand's time, the court would take to the river and cruise on its milky green waters between banks of rush and willow herb in the decorated barges known as the toy 'fleet of the Tagus'. Charles had more important plans for the river. It was the age of inland waterways and he planned not only to make it navigable from Aranjuez 340 miles to the Atlantic but to link it by its tributary the Xarama and a canal to Madrid. The first was an idea which an Italian had persuaded Philip II to adopt, proving his point by arriving at Toledo in a 'sloop of four oars', to the astonishment of the town's citizens. But Philip's wars and religious passions had exhausted both his energies and money. Thereafter, says Richard Ford, 'the project dozed until 1641 when two other *foreigners*, Julio Martelli and Luigi Carduchis, in vain roused Philip IV from his siesta, who soon afterwards losing Portugal itself forgot the Tagus.' In Charles III's time a start was made, seven locks were built and beside the Tagus at Aranjuez stands the *Casa de Marinos* which was to be the system's headquarters. The project got no further. Until the age of railways it was occasionally revived but by 1845 the plan for serious navigation of the Tagus could fairly have applied to it the well-known Spanish proverb: 'In Spain things were begun late and finished never.'

Aranjuez seems even more associated with Charles IV (1788–1808) than with the three Bourbons who preceded him. Here, a mile and a half up the river, he built that most French of all Spanish buildings, the miniature palace known as the *Casita dei Labrador*. In its carefully decorated rustic cellar, to which the Tagus waters have added genuine decay, the royal family could play at being poor, as a change from their elegant posing in the gilded and painted little state rooms upstairs.

To Aranjuez the Madrid mob pursued Charles, his queen Maria Luisa and their minister and lover the plump Godoy, when Spain at last began to see the alliance with Napoleon for the abject surrender it was. On the night of 17 March 1808 they attacked Godoy's house, threw its furniture out of the windows, and would have killed the king's minister himself if he hadn't stayed hidden for thirty-six hours in a roll of carpet in the lumber room. The king, surrounded in the Royal Palace and suffering from gout into the

OPPOSITE *The* Puente de Alcántara *at Toledo which crosses the Tagus to the huge granite fortress of the Alcazar and the castle of San Servando. The ornamental Moorish-influenced gateway with its massive portcullis and the defensive tower guard the bridge and the approaches to the fortress and castle*

LEFT *The Tagus flowing through central Spain near Toledo, its course shaped by the granite never far below the surface*

OVERLEAF *Toledo, a natural stronghold almost encircled by a deep, cliff-sided gorge, was to the Romans, the Visigoths, the Moors and the Christian Emperors both a capital and the key to the conquest of Spain*

BELOW *The Alcazar of Toledo in ruins during the Civil War (1936–9) after a group of Nationalists, among them cadets and young children, had held out for nine weeks against starvation and the bombs and gunfire of the Government army*

bargain, could do nothing to help, and his plotting son Ferdinand refused to act. A month later Charles abdicated and king, queen, prince and minister were hurried from Aranjuez to Bayonne to have their exiles arranged by Napoleon.

There could be no greater contrast than that between the Tagus at Aranjuez, flowing gently among the bird-filled woods of this oasis in dry Castile, and the Tagus twenty-five miles below at Toledo. Here, the granite under the surface of the tableland of central Spain emerges from its thin sandy covering to grip and twist the river in a fantastic three-quarter circle of gorge. The dramatic setting of the town on its hill top at the centre of this loop is El Greco's best remembered landscape. He painted it under dark thunder clouds, which are commoner and therefore less self-consciously dramatic than one might imagine.

From the lip of Toledo's deep gorge, the men who work the ferry on the river far below have the smallness and precision of the figures of a Chinese painting. Possessing such a natural moat, Toledo was a self-made choice for a capital in the days when moats mattered. It was the capital of the kingdom of the Visigoths when they had driven out the Romans, and here, on the banks of the Tagus, legend sets what, if it were real, would be the most decisive event in Spanish history: the seduction of Florinda by the Visigoth king Roderick.

ABOVE LEFT *'This far and no farther' was the Duke of Wellington's challenge to Masséna's superior French army at Torres Vedras, a prepared defensive system on the Tagus north of Lisbon. Frozen and starving in a land laid waste by the defenders, the French were finally forced to retreat from the British entrenchments, in one of the decisive manoeuvres of the Peninsular War (1808–14)*

ABOVE RIGHT *Francisco Goya's drawing in red chalk of the Duke of Wellington (1769–1852), on which his three famous portraits of the Duke were based*

LEFT *A statuette presented to Wellington to mark the victory of Talavera, on the Tagus, in 1809. After this spectacular victory over a French army of 50,000 men Wellington – then Sir Arthur Wellesley – was created a viscount*

OPPOSITE *A scene from the battle of Talavera at which Wellington's army, rallying after a retreat had become a rout, held and defeated a French force in a two-and-a-half day battle described by Wellington himself as 'the hardest fought of modern times'*

To Toledo a certain count Julian, probably governor of Ceuta in North Africa, sent his daughter Florinda to be brought up at Roderick's court, and presently the king saw her bathing by the Tagus. The window and palace from which he watched have disappeared, but a picturesque ruin below *Peunte de San Martín* is known as Florinda's bath–it turns out to be the foundations of an old bridge. Here she was measuring the shapeliness of her arms against those of the other princesses. Far from enjoying the honour of the royal seduction which followed, Florinda complained to her father who applied for help to the North African Moors.

Whether or not this was the real cause, the first Moorish expedition landed in Spain in A.D. 711 and though heavily outnumbered defeated Roderick in two decisive battles. In the surprisingly short period between then and 718 the Moors conquered the whole of Spain except the northern fringe.

Toledo was a principal prize but, on its hilltop with its moat, it was the most obstinately rebellious of Spanish towns. For two hundred years reconquest alternated with periods of semi-independence. In one of several sieges the Sultan advanced on Toledo, occupied its bridge and undermined the piers. When his troops withdrew the Toledans rushed out and it collapsed. This was an effective defeat for the city, even if the Arab poet exaggerated when he wrote, 'Bereft of her citizens, Toledo is sad and deserted as a tomb.'

The present bridge over the Tagus at this point, the *Puente de Alcántara*, is not the Moorish reconstruction which followed this military episode but another built four centuries later by Alphonso X. Fine though this later bridge is with its unequal spans and imposing *mudéjar*, or Moorish influenced gate towers, it depends more for its effect on its setting. High above to the east stands the castle of San Servando, while to the west dominating Toledo, stands the Alcazar. The Tagus, dark brown in summer or a foaming yellow in winter, passes below.

At the opposite side of the town is *Puente de San Martín*, a narrower, taller and more impressive bridge of five spans. A Toledo legend tells how its architect confessed to his wife that he had made an error in its design. When the wooden centreing was removed he believed the whole thing would collapse. That night the wife set fire to the centreing, the bridge fell, an accident was assumed and presently work could be begun again to the architect's amended plan. But the wife's conscience troubled her and at last she confessed to Tenorio, Toledo's archbishop. Instead of punishing her he commended her for wifely loyalty. The great central arch to which this legend refers is 140 feet wide and 95 feet above normal river level. At such a height it is well above the flood waters which build up in winter in this narrow gorge.

Toledo fell to the Christian reconqueror, Alphonso

VI, in 1085 and its military and political significance seemed finally to leave it in 1560 when it ceased to be the Spanish capital. The Tagus, which had given it its importance, also constricted its growth – and incidentally made it the museum city it is today. But siege and rebellion seem endemic to the place. In 1936 it was on the heights above the Tagus that one of the most remarkable episodes of the Spanish Civil War took place.

In the old Alcazar, then a military academy, a body of Nationalists, part cadets, part instructor officers, part *Guardia Civil*, held out for nine weeks against all Government efforts to storm or bombard them into surrender. Their defence commands a respect which overrides political loyalties. From every side they were under fire: on the north, west and south from nearby buildings, on the east from the rocky escarpment across the Tagus. Not only was a rain of small arms fire poured at the building for the whole of these nine weeks, but the Alcazar was under continuous short range artillery bombardment from several batteries of 55, 75 and 155 mm guns. The defenders lived in its subterranean passages, on one roll each a day of flour ground by a motor cycle engine and on a ration of horse and mule stew. Water was a particular problem, for that mechanical wonder of the seventeenth century, designed by the engineer Juanelo, which raised water from the Tagus and delivered it to the Alcazar in a flow 'as big as the

body of a cow' had long disappeared. They collected rain water and used wells abandoned for years as unfit for drinking. For many weeks they had no knowledge of any army that could possibly relieve them.

On 18 September the Government staged a set-piece assault. Journalists stood on the hills across the Tagus to watch the taking of the Alcazar. Two huge mines were exploded, blowing thousands of tons of masonry including the south-west tower into the air. A rain of bricks and concrete fell on Toledo and into the gorge of the Tagus. On four fronts the assault troops advanced clambering over the ruins, but after a day of continuous fighting the Alcazar still held.

Relief came on 27 September from the troops of the Army of Africa which had advanced with astonishing speed from the south. For both sides the Alcazar at Toledo had become a symbol of success. On the very day of the relief a third mine was exploded, creating a huge crater at the base of the already collapsed northeast tower. Today it seems a symbol of the war itself, not only because of the courageous obstinacy of both sides, but for the story, now fairly well authenticated, of the shooting by Government troops of the defending commander's son when he refused to surrender the building. The siege had the added importance that it forced the Army of Africa to turn aside to relieve the Alcazar and so allowed the Government time to prepare the defence of Madrid. Some historians believe this prolonged the war by a year.

ABOVE *The many-arched Roman Bridge at Alcántara, built by the Emperor Trajan in the typical Roman fashion of huge blocks of granite without mortar, with a level roadway 190 feet above the river*

BELOW LEFT *The defensive tower over the central pier commands all approaches to the bridge from the river and the land, and is itself protected by the fortification high up on the mountainside*

BELOW RIGHT *Near Alcántara, where in winter the Tagus has been known to rise 140 feet above its normal level, a dam is being built to provide much-needed power*

OPPOSITE View of Toledo, *one of El Greco's powerful paintings of the granite city where he lived and as he often saw it, with its Moorish towers framed by gathering storm clouds*

OPPOSITE *The medieval castle at Malpica, a small village near Talavera on the left bank of the Tagus near its junction with the Rio Pusa*

RIGHT *Wide and deep when it enters Portugal from the wild, uninhabited country along the Spanish border, the river surges through the narrow Portas de Ródão between two mountain ranges*

Appropriately, the craft of military Toledo from Roman times was the making of swords. The water of the Tagus, in which they were tempered, was thought to give their steel its quality. The industry was systematised by Charles III and a mile below the town stands his arms factory, the *Fabrica de Armas Blancas*.

At Toledo the Tagus is still 1500 feet above sea level and has over 300 miles to flow to the Atlantic. Here it begins its steady descent across the sloping plateau of central Spain. Almost at once the grey rocks of the gorge widen, red hills appear then fall back, and within a few miles give way altogether to an expanse of flat country. Silver-green olives grow in wide sweeps and vines stand each on their little hillocks of sandy earth. The Tagus in summer, with its scrubby banks and occasional green islands is again as gentle as an English river.

Presently it reaches the small town of Talavera de la Reina. At Talavera and at El Puente del Arzobispo a little below, the more peaceful craft of pottery is practised. The sands and clays of the Tagus valley provide the materials. The craft is ancient and still in the hands of small potteries employing ten or a dozen artists. El Puente and Talavera each have their traditional styles, motives and colours–blue and yellow predominate at Talavera and strange prancing hares set off across the landscape. At El Puente primitive green parrots parade under curly green trees.

On the banks of the Tagus at Talavera the Duke of Wellington fought one of the decisive battles of the Peninsular War. It was also one of the fiercest. He wrote to a friend, 'The battle of Talavera was the hardest fought of modern times. The fire at Assaye was heavier while it lasted; but the battle of Talavera lasted for two days and a night. Each party engaged lost a fourth of their numbers!!!'

It was the summer of 1809 and Wellington in command of the second British expeditionary force to the Peninsular, had advanced this far up the Tagus valley towards Madrid. The first army, under Sir John Moore, had already been driven out of the country at Coruña. Ahead lay the French Marshal Victor, protecting the Spanish capital with a powerful force, while to the north on Wellington's exposed flank, was Marshal Soult, defeated at Oporto two months before but now recovered and far closer than Wellington knew. Wellington's plan was to attack at once but Cuesta, the aged general who commanded his Spanish allies would only agree to a reconaissance of the enemy positions beyond the Alberche tributary. An odd military party they must have appeared. Cuesta refused to go anywhere except in a coach drawn by six horses. Wellington rode like a cavalry man; Cuesta, for patriotic reasons, spoke only Spanish, which Wellington understood but did not speak.

After three days of manoeuvring the French attacked. The Spanish at once fell into confusion and 6000 of their troops fled, never to return. But the main French attack fell on the British. Throughout the summer afternoon the roar of cannon fire, the rattle of musketry and the shouts of fighting filled the river valley while the blue coated French came on valiantly again and again through drifting smoke and a hail of shot, only to be driven back.

When another violent French attack failed at dawn

the French command took council. If they had decided to leave the battle unfinished and wait for a flank attack by Soult it is hard to see how Wellington could have escaped. A new Peninsular disaster might finally have discouraged the British government from such ill-fated expeditions with incalculable consequences to the whole war. In this fateful interlude British and French soldiers wandered down to the stream bed which separated their positions to drink together and find shelter from the burning sun in the shade of some mulberry trees.

But at noon the French drums rolled. Half an hour later, under a deafening artillery barrage, they resumed their attack. Till six that evening the battle continued. By then the French were everywhere in retreat. The British expeditionary force had survived, to fight and win in the next four years a series of battles which took them through Spain into France and led directly to Napoleon's downfall.

Mountain and rock close on the river again and at Alcántara it is in a gorge as deep as that at Toledo. Here the Emperor Trajan bridged it and left what is today one of the finest surviving Roman structures in Spain. The Moors, Wellington and the Carlists each broke the bridge but now it stands again as it stood in A.D. 105, built of granite blocks without mortar, 617 feet in length, spanning the gorge 190 feet above the river.

Through a wild, uninhabited region, where for 30 miles it forms the national frontier, the river Tagus flows into Portugal. Almost at once it passes through the dramatic *Portas de Ródão*, a fifty-yard gap between two mountain ranges. Golden Tagus it is called, but it can be many colours, green and clear in its upper reaches, green and milky at Aranjuez, sea blue in its lakes. Often in summer it has the dark green-blue of oil as it glides in its rocky channel. But in winter it earns its name, when its rushing waters are filled with sand and its roar can be heard a mile away. At Alcántara the bottled up torrent has risen 143 feet above normal level. Whole bales of cork have been thrown from the bridge below *Portas de Ródão* and no fragment ever seen again.

Still among rock and mountain, the river passes two of its finest castles: Belver, dominating the valley from its cliff top, and later Almourol, perched on a fairy-tale rock at the river centre. This must have been a formidable position even before it was fortified. The Romans built a castle on it, but the present structure, with high keep and ten turrets, is a rebuilding by the Templars in 1171. Romance and Moorish legends are all it has for

TOP LEFT *A contemporary portrait of Christopher Columbus, the Genoan explorer who almost failed to embark on his voyages of discovery through lack of support from the sceptical rulers of Spain*

TOP RIGHT The Santa Lucia, *the flagship of Columbus' little fleet in which he set out on 3 August 1492. Less than a year later he sailed up the Tagus with the news that he had discovered a new world*

BOTTOM LEFT *Henry the Navigator (1394–1460), the Portuguese prince who discovered Madeira and the Azores and whose genius for navigation transformed a nation's passion for exploration into an age of discovery*

BOTTOM RIGHT *Vasco de Gama (1460–1524), the Portuguese navigator who was the first to discover the sea route to India in 1497 by rounding the Cape of Good Hope. He came home two years later still wearing the beard he had pledged to leave uncut*

The Tower of Belem, the granite stronghold built in 1520 to defend the Tagus near Lisbon was the starting point for many of the voyages of exploration. The carvings on the parapets represent the shields of the Knights of Christ

heroic history – no force ever attempted to take it in real life, perhaps because the task appeared impossible.

Beyond Almourol the Tagus, now definitely a Portuguese river, passes into a pretty section, one of the few to which such a mild word can be applied. The hills on either side are dotted with olives above the white houses of small villages. Presently even the hills fall back and the country spreads out flat and wide. The crops which grow on the rich, fertile soil are thick and luxuriant, no longer a miracle against nature as they so often seem in Castile. A continuous thicket of willow fringes the river which in summer has the thick heat and slow swirling power of some great river of the tropics. *Portas do Sol* at Santarem gives the finest view of these calmer reaches. High on its hilltop, this town was the key to the valley and for 200 years Christians and Moors struggled for it.

The plain between Santarem and Villa Franca de Xira is the centre of the Portuguese bull and horse breeding businesses. Herds of black bulls graze on the low fields and across the bridges go pairs of horsemen, hatted and pole carrying, costumed characters from the Middle Ages. Horses and bulls meet in the bullring at Villa Franca which stands by the river side, for in the Portuguese bullfight the emphasis is on the mounted matador, a brilliant horseman on a highly trained mount, who plays the bull with fantastic skill, a spectacle which in part compensates for the fact that the bull is not killed and the ritual thus left unfinished. At Villa Franca, too, one begins to see the sails of the Tagus barges. From a distance the river is hidden so that they seem to sail smoothly through the flat land itself.

At Alhandra, a mile lower down, on a hill of round topped pines, stands a monument to J. M. Das Neves Costa and Lt. Colonel J. Fletcher. Wellington's name does not appear, but it was his master stroke of the Peninsular War which they executed: the building of the Lines of Torres Vedras. The Tagus made them possible.

Its course here is nearer south than west, so that it flows parallel to the Atlantic and forms a large promontory protected by ocean on one side and river on the other. The lines crossed this promontory, from Alhandra through Torres Vedras to the ocean, and to them Wellington retreated in the autumn of 1810.

He was pursued by French armies, newly released

A tapestry depicting the Spanish Armada, Philip II's vast naval expedition against England which set out from the mouth of the Tagus in 1588 with almost 25,000 men. The Armada arrived off the English coast in perfect formation, but was scattered by fire ships, the long range cannon of the English, south-westerly gales and superior seamanship

from Austria, outnumbering his by two to one. As he went he took with him the Portuguese population of the countryside, ordering them to destroy all possessions which they could not carry. For a month in the early winter of that year the armies faced each other, Wellington's behind his lines, the French in the country outside. They never risked an attack and in mid-November retreated up the Tagus to Santarem. Wellington's stratagem had worked: there had been insufficient food in the denuded countryside for them to live on.

Last but one of the metamorphoses of the Tagus is the huge inland estuary or 'Straw Sea' into which it flows beyond Alhandra. So like a sea is this expanse of water that, looking across it, the distant sun haze often appears to be a landless horizon. Here the sailing barges operate in numbers, carrying cork or salt, local products

since the twelfth century. And here, on the right bank, just before it narrows again, stands Lisbon.

Such a site of many small hills beside a sheltered inland sea could hardly have failed to produce an important town. It was a Roman provincial capital, and a rich city for 430 years under the Moors. On the feast of St Peter the Apostle in 1147 the combined fleets of the Second Crusade – 164 shiploads of knights, squires, men-at-arms and bowmen from England, France, Germany and the Low Countries sailed into the Tagus to drop anchor opposite the city. The story of their attack, told by an eyewitness, is one of the most vivid of medieval siege chronicles.

The crusaders landed to the west and soon drove the Moors out of the suburbs and back behind their walls. The siege proper then began and lasted almost four

months. After many failures the Flemish crusaders and those from Cologne mined thirty cubits of the walls, but by this time the mutual distrust was so great that they refused to allow the Normans and English to join their assault through this gap. Though the Moors in the breach are said to have looked like hedgehogs from the numbers of bolts and arrows sticking out of them, they drove back the attackers.

So Normans and English built their own siege tower and ran it towards the walls. A miscalculation about the Tagus almost proved disastrous, for when they temporarily left it with a garrison of only 100 the tide rose cutting it off from reinforcements. Desperate fighting followed, the Moors attacking with burning pitch, flax and oil. But seven youths from Ipswich skilfully manoeuvred a protective pent house round the base of the tower so that the burning material could be beaten out under its shelter while others at the top poured a continuous stream of water down its cow-hide sides. After two days the crusaders forced their tower to within four feet of the walls, a bridge was set across and the Moors called for a truce. The capture of Lisbon opened the way for Christian reconquest of the south of Portugal, though this took another 100 years to complete.

From earliest times the Tagus at Lisbon has been the scene of great sailings. Few were so dramatic or to be so significant as that of the Portuguese expedition of 1415 which carried the crusade against the Infidel to Ceuta and established the first European colony of modern times in Africa. But it was the voyages of the explorers of the last two decades of the fifteenth century which finally opened Africa, the East and America to the countries of Europe and set them on their imperial courses. The Tagus was the starting point or point of return of all but a few of these adventures.

In 1482 Diego Cão sailed from here down the African coast to the Congo river and in 1484 on a second voyage reached Cape Cross in South West Africa. Four years later Bartolomes Dias, also from the Tagus, discovered the Cape of Good Hope. Most famous of all, the Genoese Columbus, under the patronage of Ferdinand and Isobel of Spain, returned in March 1493 to drop anchor in the Tagus after his discovery of America. He was received with so little enthusiasm that the king had to intervene to stop a plot to murder him.

Second only to Columbus's achievement was Vasco

An aerial view of Lisbon on the Tagus estuary. Once the store-house of treasure from the Spanish Main and the richest town in Europe, it became a modern city almost overnight when it was replanned by the Marquis of Pomba (1699–1782) after its destruction by the earthquake of 1755

The city of Lisbon, built like Rome on seven hills, as it was in 1640 at the height of its ancient wealth and power

da Gama's discovery of the sea passage to India. In the summer of 1497 his three ships and their store ship – the largest probably not more than 120 tons – lay at Belem near the mouth of the river waiting for a wind. When it came the crews attended a final mass in the church of Nossa Senhora, founded by Prince Henry the Navigator, before moving in procession to the shore. Priests carrying candles accompanied them and a great crowd from Lisbon called out the responses to the Litany. Eighteen years later the Tower of Belem was built at the point where they finally embarked. The king, lying off shore in his barge, watched till their sails sank below the horizon. Watchers on shore told each other that no more severe punishment than this voyage could have been found for Gama and his seamen if they had confessed to the most horrible crimes. So many tears were shed that the scene, according to contemporary chronicles, was like a funeral.

Two years later, wearing a huge white beard which he hadn't cut since the day he sailed, Gama returned safely to the Tagus. He had passed twice round the Cape of Good Hope, reached Malindi in Kenya, and crossed from there to the Malabar coast of India. Two of his ships had been abandoned and the remaining two were so rotten and warped by the heat of the tropics

that they could only be kept afloat by continuous pumping. Many of his seamen, infected with fever and suffering from scurvy, died from this heavy work.

Lisbon as it stands beside the Tagus today, bears less resemblance to the city the discoverers knew than most cities do to their past, because in 1755 it suffered the severest disaster in Portuguese history: the great Lisbon earthquake. So deep was the impression this made that twenty accounts of it had been published in London within a year; two and a half months after it had happened the Portuguese ambassador in Vienna was asking his government to confirm rumours that Coimbra (100 miles north of Lisbon) had been reduced to ashes, that Madeira was entirely destroyed and that the Azores had disappeared.

It was the Feast of All Saints, a morning of warm sunlight, and the people of Lisbon were filling the churches for mass. At nine-thirty, with no warning, there began a strange frightful noise underground, resembling the hollow distant rumbling of thunder. Two violent earthquake shocks followed and during these the captain of a ship at anchor in the Tagus saw the houses and churches of Lisbon waving backwards and forwards like corn in a field tossed by a breeze.

Many collapsed, burying their occupants. In less than

ten minutes a large part of the town was in ruins, a thick dust cloud hung over everything and through this rose the smoke of starting fires. An hour later the Tagus itself, rising and falling in three enormous surges twenty or thirty feet in height, inundated the lower streets of the town, drowning many of the survivors.

For three days the fires raged. Estimates of the killed vary from 5,000 to 80,000. The prisons had been broken open; escaped criminals joined looters and ranged the town, stealing, murdering and raping.

The emergency produced the man. If it wasn't the Marquis of Pombal himself who gave the terrified king the advice, 'bury the dead and feed the living', it was he who acted on it. He took charge of the city as he did of Portugal for the next 22 years, issuing 200 decrees in a week, many of them written in pencil on his knees in his coach, ordering everything from the closing of the Tagus to escaping ships, to the immediate hanging of looters. Pombal is responsible for the appearance of central Lisbon today, for the buildings which surround the *Praça do Commercio* on the water front and the grid-iron of formal streets which lie behind were his sensible reconstruction of the city.

Golden Tagus it is called and in the years of Portugal's commercial prosperity gold and silver poured through the city to pay for the spices of the East. It was a rake's progress, followed by debt and decline. Today Lisbon is again prospering, if on a more modest scale. Where the Tagus narrows to flow through that bottle-neck of sunny resorts, Estoril, Carcavelos, Cascais, the piers of an enormous bridge are evidence of this new prosperity. It has never before been bridged below Lisbon.

In its higher reaches the Spanish have sifted its sands for real gold but it has seen more of battles and sieges than of the ways of commerce. Most typically it has stayed hidden even from Spaniards, striking a solitary course across the remote tableland, a river for its own sake, the finest of Spanish rivers.

Time may change this. Irrigation schemes are now making fertile wide stretches of country on either side of its course. Lake-side chalets are rising at Entrepeñas. The Portuguese have dammed it successfully at Belver and the Spanish are building an equally impressive dam in the gorge above Trajan's bridge at Alcántara. Perhaps in the twentieth century the upper Tagus, too, will cease to be the flamboyant but unharnessed gesture it has been for so many centuries.

Sailing boats in the Tagus estuary where the river opens out into the sea, the gateway through which Portugal sought and found wealth and fame

THE THAMES

NIGEL NICOLSON

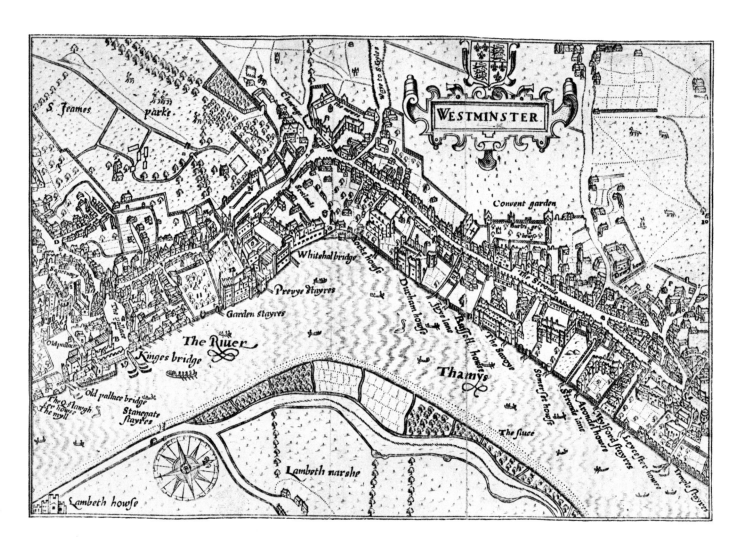

The Thames at Westminster in the time of Shakespeare. A map taken from Speculum Britanniae *published in 1593*

BUCKINGHAMSHI

OXFORDSHIRE

GLOUCESTERSHIRE

Blenheim Palace

St Martin's Church
Bladon burial place of
Sir Winston Churchill

River Cherwell

River Leach

River Coln

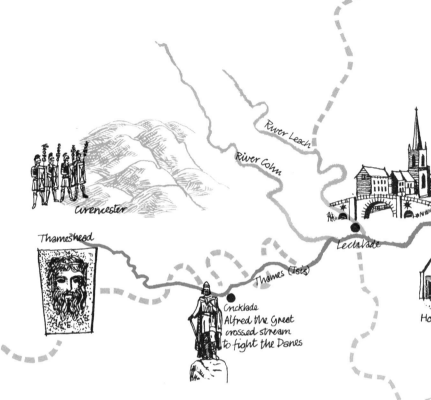

New Bridge
Radcot

Oxford

Kelmscott

Cirencester

Lechlade

Christ Church College Tom Tower

Thameshead

Thames (Isis)

Abingdon

River Thame

Cricklade
Alfred the Great
crossed stream
to fight the Danes

Home of William Morris

Dorchester

Medmenham Abbey

Wallingford

Marlow

Henley

Cookham

WILTSHIRE

Streatley

Goring

Sonning

Maidenhe

The Swan Inn
Streatley

Reading

BERKSHIRE

Windsor Castle

Kilometres 0   5   10   15

Miles 0 1 2 3 4 5   10

HAMPSHIRE

HERTFORDSHIRE

King John sealing
Magna Carta
at Runnymede

The Houses of Parliament

St Paul's Cathedral

THE THAMES

MIDDLESEX

ESSEX

Julius Caesar
crossed Thames 54 B.C.

LONDON

Eton
Windsor

~ Runnymede

Brentford

Richmond

Hampton Court
Henry the VIII

Kingston

Battersea
Power Station

The Globe
Theatre

Greenwich

Tilbury

Gravesend

Southend

NORE

Sheerness

Kingston Apple Market.

SURREY

KENT

LEFT *Sailing barges and fishing boats at Shillingford, a few miles from Dorchester, in the eighteenth century*

OPPOSITE *Radcot Bridge, a crossing between Oxfordshire and Berkshire and one of the oldest bridges on the Thames. Repairs to it are recorded as early as 1208. In 1387, during a battle between Richard II's army and the supporters of Henry Bolingbroke, Robert de Vere, Henry's favourite, leapt his horse over the parapet of the bridge and escaped by swimming downstream*

BELOW *Thames Head, the traditional source of the river in Trewsbury Mead near Cirencester. In the background is the mast of a ship on the Thames–Severn canal, completed in 1789. A circular stone wall enclosed the source when John and Josiah Boydell made this engraving in 1793 for their* History of the River Thames. *Today the source is dry except in the wettest weather*

RIVER only 215 miles long from source to mouth, with an average fall of twenty inches in a mile, cannot in purely geographical terms be counted among the great rivers of the world. The Thames has no stretches of gorge or torrent. Its tributaries are little more than brooks. Apart from the one barrier of the Chilterns, it flows through a passive countryside. Even its source in a flattish Gloucestershire meadow is a circle of stones as dry as knucklebones except in the wettest weather, and a statue of Father Thames gazes down upon it with a melancholy indolence that is typical of the upper reaches of the stream itself. In summer the first water is encountered several miles below the source in puddles agitated by despairing minnows, puddles that grow longer and more frequent until one of them begins to shiver and then to flow. Thenceforward it meanders lazily and weed-strewn between fields, and its central and most joyful passage is nothing more dramatic than a slipway between thickly wooded bluffs and the occasional hump of a down. It is a river without challenge except by its moderate floods, so calm that its bed has remained unchanged for millenia, so lovely that writers and painters have never exhausted its charms.

But if the Thames has created a landscape that sums up the character of the country and its people, it is also one of the most historical rivers in the world, since England's history has been rich and many of the greatest events have occurred on or near its banks. The reasons are not difficult to find. Its valley is the

215

A lock-keeper closes the gates at Hambleden Lock, about a mile below Henley-on-Thames, famous for its regattas

RIGHT *The weir machinery at Goring in Berkshire is typical of the precision and elegance of the machinery controlling the trim white locks and tumbling weirs of the upper Thames*

most fertile and accessible in the southern part of the country; it reaches across the island almost from sea to sea at the point where natural communications were most needed; and the capital city was founded upon it. 'Of all the rivers in England,' wrote John Buchan, 'the Thames has played the most notable part in her making, and its valley has been the cradle and nursery of most of her institutions.' A man's whole career, it was once said, could be profitably spent on the banks of the Thames, from his school at Eton, to his University at Oxford, to the City of London, to the Houses of Parliament. If this aphorism stamps the river as aristocratic, it is not inappropriate. It was adorned and exploited by the rich but remained open to the poor, a civilising, unifying influence throughout the centuries. Because it is short and flows through no wasteland except near its estuary, the places strung along its banks are close together and each has contributed to the prosperity and culture of its neighbours. The Thames is not only liquid history; it is history compressed like a concertina.

With the one overwhelming exception of London, the economic and commercial importance of the river has declined, and its military significance waned soon after the coming of the Normans. In later centuries it attended events rather than attracted them. The greatest single fact in the constitutional history of Britain

A view across the Meadows to Christ Church, the largest of the Oxford colleges, founded by Cardinal Wolsey in 1525. From the tower on the left the Great Bell of Oxford rings out 101 times every evening. This drawing was made by Turner in 1799

was the signing of Magna Carta in 1215, and the conference between King John and his barons took place in a Thameside meadow called Runnymede, between Windsor and Staines. There was no special reason why this place should have been chosen, apart from its nearness to the King's castle. The Thames was a silent witness of the event; it did not create it. But who could deny that the occasion gains something from the recollection of its site, and that its appropriateness as a memorial to President Kennedy is increased by its contiguity to a river that has meant so much to the English? A river is historical as much by association as by function. Cities, towns and villages may originally have been sited on the river because of the river, but later developed in importance for reasons other than the river. Their story remains part of the river's story nonetheless.

The modern Thames is divided into two sections by the lowest of its locks at Teddington. Below stretch the 69 miles of the tidal waters; above, the 146 miles of the middle and upper valley. The river changes completely in character at the point where the sea ceases to exert its influence. Below Teddington the great mass of London is accessible to ocean-going ships and their attendant tugs; above it the river has become a pleasure stream. Until some fifty years ago the distinction was not so evident. Barges would make their way with laborious economy as far as Oxford or even Lechlade, extending the traffic of London's port into the heart of England and drawing the produce of the country-

side down to the metropolis. Today railways and improved roads have reduced the commercial traffic to an occasional coal or timber barge travelling as far as Chertsey on the outer rim of London, and the remainder of the river is given up to launches, skiffs, racing-eights and other pleasure craft with their concomitant riverside villas, boat-houses, rowing and fishing clubs. The forty-four locks have become recreational shuttles, and the stretches of river between them are lakes of unpolluted water sliding imperceptibly towards an unimagined sea. It is the greatest, lushest and least-spoiled playground in Britain.

London is the weight near the bottom of the pendulum. It has always been the most important town on the river, and today it is the only town of any size to whose life the river significantly contributes. Staines, Windsor, Reading and Oxford regard the Thames as little more than a scenic and recreational asset. They have no river trade. But for London the river has formed a port of such profound significance throughout its history, that any account of the Thames must dwell on the reasons why the capital of Roman Britain was sited at precisely that point and why the choice has proved to be one of such unchallengeable excellence.

There was no London before the Romans came. The river emptied into the sea between marshes which to this very day are of little use except for the dumping of the city's refuse and the storage of its fuel; and the middle river was a boundary between tribes constantly

Ducks and canoes share the river at Cookham, a village near Maidenhead, where Stanley Spencer, the famous modern painter, lived and worked

at war. There was no bridge in the neighbourhood of London, but scattered fords are mentioned in near-contemporary accounts of the Roman invasions or presumed on archaeological evidence. One was at Westminster, on the line of the later Watling Street; another near Brentford, by which Julius Caesar forced a crossing in 54 BC; and a third in the estuary by which Claudius crossed nearly a hundred years later. London itself was founded by the Romans soon after A.D. 43. It became the main military depot for the conquest of Britain, and the communications centre from which eight of their major roads radiated to all parts of the island. In describing the events of A.D. 60, the year before it was sacked by Boudicca, Tacitus could already refer to *Londinium* as 'crowded with merchants and greatly celebrated for its commerce'. It is the first recorded use of the name, and the description has remained apt ever since.

The site of London is in a double sense due to its river. It was the highest point to which sea-going ships could penetrate upstream, because in Roman days the land level was some fifteen feet higher than it is today and the tide did not reach much further inland; and it was the lowest point at which the river could be bridged. The ideal port and the ideal bridging site coincided. Ships could be carried up to London on the flood tide and carried down on the ebb, and the water was deep enough in what is still called the Pool of London for them to berth in the very heart of the city. Downstream there was no suitable crossing point, not so much because the increasing breadth of the stream would have daunted Roman engineers, but because at no lower point did firm ground approach it on both sides simultaneously. Purfleet, on the north bank, for example, was faced by Dartford marshes opposite; Gravesend was confronted by the hard knob of Tilbury which became an island at every high tide. But at Southwark a spit of sandy gravel pointed directly towards a hard ridge on the north bank, and it was here that the Romans built their bridge, a few yards east of the present London Bridge. The town clung to its northern end, its limits roughly defined by the sites of the Tower of London and St Paul's.

This explains why London was founded there, but it does not explain why it soon became the most important town in England and eventually one of the

OPPOSITE *Hambleden Mill, parts of which date back to the early seventeenth century. The mill was in regular use until 1960, but has now passed into private ownership*

greatest cities in the world. Again the river determined its future. A bridge over so formidable an obstacle (matched in Roman times only by the bridge at Staines) would naturally make London a place of importance to the country on each side of it, and its position as the port where sea-borne traffic gave place to river-borne made it a natural point for storage and trans-shipment, both for import and export. To the south were the harbours on the Straits of Dover, the shortest crossing place from the Continent to England; to the north lay the heart of Celtic England, its capital successively at St Albans and Colchester, which could otherwise only have been approached by difficult fords or a long detour. To the west was the great valley watered by a river which formed an easy and capacious highway leading uninterrupted to the Pool. To the east was the funnel of the estuary opening across a simple sea passage towards the corresponding mouths of the Scheldt and Rhine, which in turn led to the heart of Europe. Thus London was bound to become a nodal point in British communications both by land and water. Once this elemental fact had been seized, everything else followed automatically from it. The Roman road system made London the political and financial centre of Britain; the port, facing in two directions, inland and out to sea, attracted traders and shippers, and eventually the bankers, exchanges and insurance companies. As the population grew, so did the traffic. London had to eat and to earn its living by its trade. The scale of the tidal Thames was equal to every demand made upon it for many centuries, and because its capacity was so huge it encouraged hugeness in population and enterprise. The spirit of the people, and centuries of relatively stable government and freedom from invasion, did the rest.

Between its capture by the Danes in 872 and the air-bombardment of 1940 there was no military assault upon London. William the Conqueror entered it unopposed in 1066, having crossed the Thames at Wallingford, and the defence-works hurriedly thrown up by the citizens during the Civil War were never tested. London grew unmenaced except by fire and plague. The city burst the bounds of the Roman walls soon after the accession of the Tudors, and between 1485 and the death of Queen Elizabeth, the population leapt from some 40,000 to about 220,000. By 1660 it had doubled again. It was still bigger in area than a modern

Eton boys, called wet-bobs if they row, and dry-bobs if they play cricket, passing through the lock at Cookham on an expedition up the Thames

ABOVE LEFT *Windsor Castle seen from across the river. Built by William the Conqueror and extended by his successors over the centuries, it is one of the most magnificent royal residences in the world. When the Queen is in residence the royal standard flies from the battlemented Round Tower in the centre*

LEFT *A painting by Canaletto of the Chapel of Eton College, the most famous of English Public Schools, founded by Henry VI in 1440. It stands on the banks of the river about a mile above Windsor*

OPPOSITE Swan Upping *by Stanley Spencer, who lived and worked at Cookham until his death in 1959. By tradition the swans on the Thames belong to the Queen and to two City Companies, the Vintners and the Dyers. Every summer the swans are caught and their bills nicked as a sign of their ownership. This custom is known as 'Swan Upping'*

cathedral city of average size, though its population was considerably more cramped. Riverside villages like Chelsea and Putney were to seventeenth-century London what Windsor is to us, a day's excursion; and at the end of the century the asthmatic William III needed to escape no further than Kensington to breathe country air.

Scores of witnesses, cartographers and artists have recorded their wonder at the wealth and splendour of the city throughout the middle centuries of its growth, and always the Thames figures prominently in the foreground of their accounts. It was not only the port that excited their admiration, but the skyline of medieval churches which changed abruptly after the Great Fire of 1666 to an even more dramatic fretwork of Renaissance spires, the old and the new St Paul's standing sentinel over each period in turn. The only bridge, until Westminister Bridge was opened in 1750, was London Bridge, with its double row of houses leaping the river like a street. Its nineteen narrow arches ('for wise men to go over and fools to go under') created

a tide race as dangerous as a weir, and although it incorporated a drawbridge, it effectively divided London's river into two. Below was the Pool, in which Defoe counted as many as two thousand ships on a single day; above it, an open-ended lagoon criss-crossed by watermen exchanging jovial insults, and the scene of splendid water·carnivals at the installation of a Lord Mayor or the coronation of a Sovereign. It was for one such occasion, in July 1715, when George I went by water to Chelsea, that Handel composed his *Water Music*. When, as not infrequently happened before the removal of Old London Bridge, the river froze from bank to bank, the festivities continued on the ice.

The London to which Canaletto gave the romantic glow of his native Grand Canal did not survive the eighteenth century. The Pool became too crowded for easy commerce, and upstream the building of new roads and bridges decreased the importance of the river as an urban highway. Old London Bridge was replaced in 1830 by the present bridge, the oldest survivor among London's many bridges, and the wharfs were supple-

mented and soon overshadowed by the system of great docks excavated from the low-lying banks on either side and approached from the river through lock gates. Throughout the nineteenth century London's old buildings dropped off like husks. There is almost nothing on the immediate river banks to recall the London that Dr Johnson knew. He could just have seen Somerset House (1776–86) in its uncompleted state, but the embankments, bridges and the present skyline of office blocks would have left him at a loss. Tudor London was as unknown to him as it is to us, for the Great Fire had destroyed four-fifths of the city in four panic-stricken days. Barely twenty medieval buildings, mainly ecclesiastical, survived. But three of them are among the greatest and most historical buildings in the country: Westminister Abbey, Westminister Hall and the Tower of London, all three within a hundred yards of the river's edge and symbols respectively of religious, political and military greatness.

The broad right-angled bend of the Thames between Westminster and the City is the indestructible link be-tween the centuries, its shifting waters paradoxically permanent, an axis broad enough to stamp upon London an unchanging topography. Enter London at dusk up the darkening tideway from Greenwich, and you will recapture something of the tension with which these many generations have approached the capital. The stream becomes tauter as the warehouses crowd in upon its channel and the arrested shipping in the Pool extends the city into the water. The silhouette of three great monuments rise beyond: William the Conqueror's Tower of London, Wren's St Paul's and Sir J. Wolfe Barry's Tower Bridge, opened in 1894, 'the noblest bridge I know', wrote E. V. Lucas, 'although its stone-work is but veneer and iron its heart', the only gateway that London retains. As its heavy roadway lifts up-wards in two pieces, the full muscularity of the city and its river is suddenly revealed.

Downstream from the Pool the river has not much to show the visitor in search of evidence of its past, for it is an unbridged approach route and the few settle-ments on its banks like Gravesend and Purfleet have had

The Great Seal of King John used to ratify the Magna Carta on 15 June 1215

Strawberry Hill, Horace Walpole's 'little Gothic castle' on the Thames near Twickenham, where he wrote his famous letters and his gothic novel The Castle of Otranto. *The house no longer exists, but it has given its name to the exuberant Gothic style of architecture, which was one example of the interest which eighteenth-century Englishmen (notably Walpole himself) took in things medieval*

ABOVE RIGHT *Hampton Court in the reign of George I. The palace was built by Cardinal Wolsey, who gave it to Henry VIII, and for centuries it was a favourite Thames-side residence of English sovereigns. The famous Fountains Court and south and east façades were added by Christopher Wren in the late seventeenth century*

RIGHT The Music Party, *one of a series of river groups by Zoffany. Kew, where Zoffany lived, was a fashionable meeting place for London society in the late eighteenth century*

OVERLEAF *Westminster Bridge on Lord Mayor's Day 1746 by Canaletto. Lord Mayor's Day was one of the most popular water festivals on the Thames, made colourful by the richly decorated barges and liveried watermen of the Aldermen, merchants and wealthy citizens. At this time the building of Westminster Bridge was in its final stages*

little significance compared to the stream itself. Tilbury was an isolated Tudor fortress covering the river entrance with its guns, and at Deptford and Woolwich Henry VIII established the most important naval arsenals in the country. London's docks were extended in the nineteenth century as far as Barking, with a vast outrider for liners of deepest draught at Tilbury, but the barren character of the banks below London is emphasised by the survival of only two small medieval churches, at Rainham and West Thurrock. Today the flat marshland supports much of the apparatus by which London lives – the gas works, power stations and sewage outfalls – as well as the occasional factory like the huge Ford works at Dagenham. All are on a scale appropriate to the widening stream. Prettiness is not expected near

the mouth of any great river: the silt, the greying, cooling, flooding stream and functional needs of mariners forbid it. That the Thames should finally lose touch with the land at Southend comes as a surprise. It is a holiday resort, half seaside, half riverside, its mile-long pier making hardly an impression upon an estuary that is by then barely distinguishable from a bay of the North Sea. Steel cupolas on stilts, erected in the Second World War as part of the anti-aircraft defences of London, march out to sea to extend the river line a few miles beyond its natural bourne.

The 50-mile stretch of the river that includes London, from Windsor to Woolwich, could be stigmatised as suburban and industrial; but historically it is the Royal Thames. Even more than their subjects, English Sovereigns have displayed a preference for riverside sites for their palaces. The earliest, like Windsor and the Tower of London, owed their positions to military strategy, but the later palaces, Greenwich, Whitehall, Sheen and Hampton Court, were placed on the river because it afforded an easy approach by state barge and the dignity of the stream added to the splendour of the buildings. Each from its own period embodies the greatest contributions that Englishmen have made to architecture. The Tower of London, in turn the nation's treasury, mint, state prison and place of execution, remains the most splendid survival from the Norman age. Hampton Court is without question the finest marriage of two supreme moments in England's artistic history, those of Henry VIII and Wren. At

The 1965 Cambridge University Boat Race crew. The Oxford and Cambridge Boat Race between Putney and Mortlake has been an annual event since 1845, interrupted only by two World Wars

Greenwich in the Queen's House, and at Whitehall in the Banqueting House, we have the two buildings by which Inigo Jones introduced his countrymen to the refinements of classical architecture. At Greenwich again, four of the greatest architects that England ever produced, Wren, Hawksmoor, Vanbrugh and Colen Campbell, collaborated on an unrivalled group of Renaissance buildings which open their arms to the river. At Windsor, the most venerable of them all, Sir Jeffry Wyatville undertook for George IV a reconstruction which gave the Thames its most dramatic silhouette. But the importance of these buildings lies not in architecture alone. If one adds to their number the royal palace of Westminster, which was occupied by the Kings of England until 1512, they have been scenes of immense events. One can illustrate them by a single life, that of Queen Elizabeth I. Born, like all the Tudor monarchs except Henry VII, at Greenwich, she was imprisoned in the Tower, was crowned at Westminster, heard at Hampton Court the news of the defeat of the Spanish Armada, held her court at Windsor and died at Sheen.

The courtiers and clergy, and then the dilettanti and artists, followed the royal fashion. Up the river from London can be seen the survivors among the great houses which at every period garnished its banks: Lambeth and Fulham, Kew and Chiswick, Syon, Ham and Strawberry Hill. The palaces and houses are sited a little way back from the water's edge, for privacy's sake or from fear of flood, but their lawns and parks sweep down to the river and elegant boat houses stand like water lodges on the common highway. The river becomes secluded and almost rural soon after leaving Mortlake, and London's suburbs are screened by dipping willows and long wooded islands as slim as triremes. Perhaps in all England there is no single view as beautiful as that from the summit of Richmond Hill. The

OPPOSITE LEFT *Sunset and evening mist on the river above Chelsea*

OPPOSITE RIGHT *An impression by Gustave Doré, the famous nineteenth-century engraver, of Penny Steamers embarking passengers at Westminster Bridge on Boat Race Day*

BELOW *The Thames by night from the South Bank, with Big Ben glowing from the Gothic silhouette of the Houses of Parliament, and to the east Westminster Bridge and the City*

whole of the eighteenth century seems to be within one's glance. Just below, at Twickenham, Pope had his villa with its Thames grotto, half a joke, half a work of art; and there Zoffany painted his charming water scenes which take the conversation piece out of doors. 'Ah, David,' Dr. Johnson once remarked to Garrick after spending a day at his villa at Hampton, 'it is the leaving of such places as this that makes a death-bed terrible.'

To understand the importance, and in its most literal sense the 'influence', of the upper river in England's history, something must first be said of its geography. It is a river without eccentricities. Apart from the northern swoop between Reading and Oxford, its upstream course is generally westward and its source lies on a latitude only a few miles north of its estuary. In medieval times it was but a day's march from the highest navigable point at Cricklade to the valley of the Severn. There are no great rivers in continental Europe whose unnavigable headwaters are so short as those of the Thames, fifteen miles at the most until the construction of the Thames–Severn canal lowered the water level between Lechlade and Cricklade to a depth that will rarely support anything much heavier than a canoe. Even before the first locks were made in the late eighteenth century the fall was so little that it could be controlled by navigable weirs, and the current was so slight that a boat would have little more difficulty in making its way upstream than down. The English climate always filled the river, even in summer, with sufficient depth of water for navigation and riverside wharfs. Finally, its course was constant. The bends most exposed to water erosion, like those at Abingdon and Dorchester, have

ABOVE *A late seventeenth-century scene showing a carriage being ferried across the Thames from the steps of Lambeth Palace, the residence of the Archbishop of Canterbury, on the right, to what is now known as Horseferry Road. Until 1750 London Bridge was the only bridge across the river*

LEFT The Ferry Boat, *one of the famous caricatures by Thomas Rowlandson, satirizing London society in the eighteenth century when it was fashionable to cross the Thames to the dark walks and bright lights of Vauxhall Gardens and the firework displays of Ranelagh, the two famous pleasure gardens on the south bank*

OPPOSITE *An illuminated page from a collection of poems written by Charles d'Orléans, the last and greatest of the courtly poets of France, during his twenty-five years' imprisonment in the Tower of London. He was captured in 1415 at the Battle of Agincourt, where he commanded the French army. Charles is depicted three times: seated writing, at a window, and handing a letter to a servant*

Es nouuelles dalbion

remained unaltered for thousands of years; the most striking proof of it are the pre-Roman earthworks at Dorchester, which still exactly slice off the peninsula formed by the confluence of the River Thame and the bend of the main stream. Thus the Thames has always formed a waterway on which travellers could rely to take them in the direction which was economically and strategically the most useful.

The river's banks, however, were not so helpful. While there was no place where steep cliffs barred access to the stream, the lowness of the surrounding land exposed it to constant flood. The few places where hard shoulders faced each other on opposite sides determined, as at London, the sites of crossing places, by bridge, ford or ferry. The Streatley–Goring gap through the Chilterns was one such crossing place from the earliest times, but the Romans knew only five main crossings throughout the river's length, at Cricklade, Dorchester, Wallingford, Staines and London, and only the last two were bridged. The map of Roman Britain shows how sparsely the middle and upper river were settled. Dorchester and Staines alone supported towns, and those were small. Oxford and Reading did not exist. Only a single Roman villa has been identified on the banks, at Hambledon near Henley. That the Thames should rise at the foot of a temporary Roman encampment, 'Trewsbury Castle', and be crossed by the Fosse Way within half a mile of its source, is a mere coincidence. The upper reaches were of no significance to the Romans, who were only anxious to press on across its marshes.

The military history of the river is remarkable for its meagreness. The only prehistoric camp is Sinodum, the huge British earthworks at Wittenham Clumps below Abingdon and nearly opposite the Dorchester fosses already mentioned. In Roman times the valley was far from the scenes of military operations once the country had been unified in the first century. The Saxons and Danes made use of the valley as an invasion route, but left no military memorials. It was

OPPOSITE *A view across the river of the 366 foot high dome of St Paul's Cathedral, the 'parish church of the British Commonwealth' and the cathedral of the See of London. It was designed by Wren to replace the church burned down in the Great Fire of London in 1666. The building was completed in 1710 when Wren was 78 and for most of that time he lived in Southwark, near where this photograph was taken, so that he could watch the progress of his cathedral*

RIGHT *Seagulls on the walls of Chelsea embankment near Battersea Bridge*

not until the coming of the Normans that any fixed castles were built, and these were few, at Oxford, Wallingford, Reading, Windsor and London, too far apart to form in any sense a fortified line. Apart from those at Oxford and Wallingford, which played some part in the wars between Stephen and Matilda and later in the Civil Wars, none of them fulfilled the military role for which they had been intended. In later periods the river was too frequently bridged, and too long and narrow, to form a serious obstacle. Even in 1940, when after a gap of eight hundred years England was in danger of invasion from the south, the Thames was not regarded as a main defence line. The key land battle would have had to be fought south of it to protect London, and Churchill's main fear was that the bombing of the bridges might prevent his land forces to the north of the river from intervening further south.

One should therefore picture the upper river through most of its history as primarily a highway, developing gradually, as the floods were tamed, into an area of agricultural and religious settlement. Agriculturally the valley became important for its timber, wool and wheat, and later for other articles of export and import to and from London. Defoe's account of Reading, written at the end of the seventeenth century, illustrates the importance of the river's economy in his day:

A very large and wealthy town, handsomely built, the inhabitants rich and driving a very great trade. The town is situated on the River Kennet, but so near the Thames that the largest barges which they use may come up to the Town Bridge where they have wharfs to load and unload them. Their chief trade is by this water-navigation to and from London, though they have necessarily a great trade into the Country, for the consumption of the goods which they bring by their barges from London; and particularly coal, salt, grocery-wares, tobacco, oils and all heavy goods. They send from hence to London by these barges very great quantities of malt and meal and timber.

LEFT *London Bridge in 1616. For 1700 years until the opening of Westminster Bridge in 1750, it was the only bridge over the Thames. It survived the Great Fire of 1666, but was replaced in 1832. The old bridge was lined with rows of houses and had the appearance of a street with a narrow carriageway between. At each end were fortified gates on which the heads of traitors were exposed. In the foreground is the tower of St Mary Overy, the cathedral church of Southwark*

OPPOSITE *The fair on the Thames on 4 February 1814. Until the destruction of old London Bridge in 1832 the river froze from bank to bank during a hard winter and became the scene of carnival. Hawkers set up their stalls, oxen were roasted whole, and all kinds of entertainers gathered on the ice. In the background is the dome of St Paul's*

THE FAIR ON THE THAMES, FEBY 4. 1814.   LA FOIRE SUR LA TAMISE, FEVRIER 4. 1814

OPPOSITE On the Thames, *one of nine river paintings made by André Derain when he visited London in 1905 and 1906. This shows shipping in the Pool of London, with Tower Bridge in the background*

BELOW *Tower Bridge at the entrance to the Pool of London is a masterpiece of engineering. It was built in 1894 and its twin drawbridges, each weighing 1,000 tons, can be raised in 90 seconds to allow shipping to pass through*

But neither Reading nor Abingdon nor Oxford, nor several other of the greatest names in Thames history, would have become the places they are but for the religious communities to which they owed their foundation. It is in this sense that we can call the middle Thames monastic and medieval.

These religious houses were of great antiquity. The three greatest, the Benedictine monasteries of Abingdon, Chertsey and Westminster, date from the seventh century. All three were sacked by the Danes but rose again within a few decades and lasted till the Reformation. The Cluniac monastery of two hundred monks at Reading was founded by Henry I in 1121, and Osney at Oxford shortly afterwards. Dorchester's Abbey was also twelfth century, and Lechlade's priory thirteenth century. To these should be added the lesser foundations, places like Eynsham, Godstow, Cumnor, Bisham, Wallingford, Sonning and a dozen others. All of them stood on the river banks, whether there was a crossing at that point or not, and all communicated with each other by the river, so that a traveller was seldom out of sight of a religious settlement. Some were of very great size. Chertsey, for example, was as large as Windsor Castle. Between the religious houses were the parish churches, their towers and spires spaced like sentinels along the stream. Many of these churches have survived practically unchanged from medieval times – Lechlade, Inglesham, Iffley (the finest small Norman church in the country), Henley and Bray.

The importance of the religious houses cannot be exaggerated. They bridged the Dark Ages. Having by the rules of the Orders every inducement to accumulate wealth and none to spend it, they became rich at a time when a reviving civilisation needed above all capital for development. They were centres of the arts and learning. They had close ties with the Continent. They possessed manors strung out along the banks of the Thames which for their time were models of agricultural management. Until the reign of Henry VIII

An eighteenth-century satire by a celebrated French engraver Philippe Boitard, showing Thames wharfs choked with imports from France. Among those he lists are French cooks, female dancers, milliners, tailors, disguised Jesuits, quacks, valets de chambres, and cargoes of French wine, cheeses, perfume and gloves

they seemed to be immune to destruction. And each of them attracted a civil community at the monastery's gates which in turn became the kernel of a thriving town.

Oxford is one example. It was an important town even before the Conquest, and it was there that Harold held his final Council before the Hastings campaign. But its University had its origins in the three Norman monasteries of Osney, Rewlay and St Frideswide. If only because it was a place early associated with holiness, learning and beauty, it attracted the English students whom Henry II's quarrel with Becket and the Pope excluded from Paris in 1168. A century later Oxford was second only to Paris itself among European universities. Its later history hardly belongs to the Thames. The University, separated from the river by Christ Church meadows, was confined within medieval walls. Only in the nineteenth century was the river rediscovered by the undergraduates and dons. One recalls the boating parties when a mathematical tutor, known to the world as Lewis Carroll, began to tell Alice Liddell, the young daughter of his Dean, the stories that grew into *Alice in Wonderland*. Or those more formidable expeditions when Benjamin Jowitt, Master of Balliol, would select from among his students a companion for his daily walk along the Cherwell. 'Master,' said one such quailing youth at the beginning of their walk, 'do you not consider Euripides to be a greater dramatist than Aeschylus?' There was a long silence. 'That, young man,' replied Jowitt four miles and one hour later, as they turned back into Balliol lodge, 'was a very foolish remark.'

In the seventeenth and eighteenth centuries great houses like Nuneham Courtenay, Culham Court and Cliveden began to turn some of the loveliest natural stretches of the river to aristocratic advantage. 'There are two things scarce matched in the Universe,' exclaimed Sir Walter Raleigh, 'the sun in heaven, and the

ABOVE RIGHT *The Free Ferry which carries vehicles and passengers from Woolwich to North Woolwich on the opposite bank. During the air raids of 1940 it carried thousands of people to safety from their blitzed and blazing homes*

ABOVE *Ships in Gravesend Reach in the early nineteenth century, when steam was still an auxiliary of sail*

LEFT *Low tide at Barking showing the huge mud flats visible when the water recedes*

Thames on earth.' Two centuries later a poet's encomium could be expanded without losing its rapture:

> Succeeding each as each retires
> Wood-mantled hills and tufted spires,
> Groves, villas, islets, cultured plains,
> Towers, cities, palaces and fanes.

Such, in essence, the Thames remains. The quietness of the middle Thames is not wholly lost on the tideway. The spirit of Henley Regatta is carried by the Oxford and Cambridge Boat Race into the centre of the metropolis. The non-tidal Thames has never been, like most Continental rivers, an industrial river. It need feel ashamed of only two miles in its whole course, those that flow between the gasworks and railway yards of Oxford. To this day there are no factories on its banks except at Staines and Reading, and these barely affect the character of the river. No railway follows the stream for more than a few miles. Not a single railway bridge crosses its course above Oxford. If the non-tidal stretch has lost its economic importance except as the source of London's drinking water, it has gained in solitude. The Thames is well-kept. Long reaches of placid water controlled by small white locks and tossing weirs, mile upon mile of meadows, wooded hills and untroubled banks– these are the essentials of the river's personality. But its importance must be measured by less romantic standards. Its value to the British people has been incalculable. When Charles I, in a rage with the Lord Mayor of London, once threatened to ruin the City by removing his court from Westminster, he received the memorable answer, 'But your Majesty cannot remove the Thames.'

The pier at Southend, the Londoner's seaside resort, where the Thames reaches the sea

THE TIBER

GEORGINA MASSON

*The river Tiber, named after Tiberinus, King of the ancient
city of Alba Longa who was drowned in its waters, was
worshipped as a god by the early Romans. This statue of Father
Tiber was discovered by Michelangelo and placed on the steps
of the Capitol in Rome, near the place where Julius Caesar
was murdered in 44* BC

THE MARCHES

TUSCANY

UMBRIA

Pieve S. Stefano

Sansepolcro

Arezzo

Città di Castello

Umbertide

Lake Castiglione

Perugia

Deruta

Todi

Procession at Basilica
of Saint Francis

Saint Francis

River Nova

River Crisani

The Cathedral (1305-30)
Orvieto

THE TIBER

LATIUM

TYRRHENIAN SEA

River Aniene

Terni

Augusto Bridge Narni

Orte

Magliano Salomo

Monterotonde

Mentana

The Esedra Fountain

The Forum

ROME

Tivoli

Villa d'Este Temple of Vesta

The Colosseum

Fiumicino

Ostia Lido di Roma Ruins of Roman Ostia

Kilometres 0   10   20   25

0 1 2 3 4 5   10   15

Miles

RIGHT *The rare patches of shingle formed where the clear waters of a tributary join the muddy Tiber are sought out by both laundresses and boatmen. The river's tawny colour, which painters call Umber and writers the* flavus Tiberis, *comes from the silt washed down from the Umbrian hills*

Rising eleven miles away in the Apennines, the Tiber is little more than a mountain stream when it reaches Pieve San Stefano, the first town along the river to be ravaged by the starving and brutal mercenaries of the Count de Bourbon as they fought and plundered their way to the Sack of Rome in 1527

EVERY year, for how many centuries we do not know, on 14 or 15 May a small group of people assembled on a primitive wooden bridge, high above the waters of the Tiber. The men wore purple-bordered togas and curious conical caps surmounted by wooden spikes. Of the women one alone had coloured robes, and her unkempt hair was covered by a scarlet veil and purple fringed kerchief; the other six were clad in white. One or two of these last might be mere children, less than ten years old, but with great solemnity they helped their elders throw manikins of reeds or straw, dressed in archaic Roman costume, into the tawny flood below.

This strange scene presented as great a mystery to the Roman crowds of classical times, watching from the banks, as it would to us today. Even men like Cicero and Livy could only resort to supposition to explain why, in the presence of the priestly *Pontifices* and the *Flaminica* – whose hair remained uncombed as a sign of mourning – the Vestal Virgins cast these manikins or *Argei* into the Tiber. Some people thought the *Argei* represented the Argive chieftains who came to Rome with Hercules; others believed that by Hercules' command the dummies had replaced human sacrifice. Most modern authorities agree that this token was intended to appease the river god, and propitiate him on behalf of those who used the bridge.

To the Romans the bridge itself, the Pons Sublicius, was sacred. Its maintenance was the special charge of the Pontifices, whose name seems to indicate that their order was founded for this purpose. The Romans in classical times believed that the bridge (the oldest in the city) was built by the fourth king, Ancus Martius, who reigned before 600 BC. As long as Rome lasted, whenever damaged or carried away by flood, it was rebuilt again and again in the same archaic fashion.

The Romans were an eminently practical people and many of their religious rites evolved from purely practical functions. The complicated ritual surrounding the Vestals' guardianship of the sacred fire was based on the domestic duties of primitive times – the fire itself was symbolic of the food supplies of the state. So it is not surprising to find that modern historians agree that Rome owes her development, from bronze age village to city state and eventual world supremacy, primarily to her position on the Tiber – the only Mediterranean river with a navigable estuary – and more particularly to being sited at the lowest point where the river could be bridged in early times, beside the Forum Boarium, originally the cattle market of the primitive tribes who founded Rome.

In fact the importance of the Tiber in history is due to the role it played in the development of Rome, and not, like other great European rivers, to its use as a means of communication through a vast area. Indeed the Tiber is only navigable for a small part of its 250 mile course – the comparatively short stretch between Orte and the sea. Even here the current is so strong that in early times the traffic can only have been one way; from the imperial era right up to the last century barges had to be towed upstream by oxen. Before the development of tow-paths, therefore, the return journey must have been made overland, giving rise to primitive trails which naturally followed the valleys of the Tiber and its tributaries through the mountainous mass of central Italy. Several of these trails met at a point on the Tiber, where the current of smaller tributaries or streams created firm shingle landing grounds on the river's otherwise muddy banks. At this point too, a series of hills provided good defensive sites for the villages which grew up at this primitive communication centre. Traditionally about 754 or 753 BC these villages were amalgamated to become the infant city of Rome, and here the river was later bridged.

The Sublician Bridge first owed its sacred character to the recognition of its importance to the infant city,

The golden brown of autumn trees merges with the tawny waters of the Tiber above Citta de Castello, where the turbulent, fast-flowing mountain stream broadens and deepens in the wide valley of the Roman Campagna

The wooded banks of the Tiber above Perugia, an ancient hill city whose walls, built in 370 BC of huge blocks of Travertine stone without mortar, are the best surviving example of Etruscan masonry. Perugia, now a university town, was the birthplace of the Perugian school of painters which, most notably, included Perugino, or Pier de Vannucci (c. 1450–1523)

The Tiber above Rome: Evening Effect by Claude Lorrain, the most celebrated French landscape painter of the seventeenth century. In his day the whole area was a malarial swamp, although in Roman times it was well drained and fertile, with a genial climate that reputedly attracted invaders while sapping the energies of its rightful defenders

The Shores of the Tiber by Nicolas Poussin, the French painter who came to Rome in 1624 and, except for three unhappy years in France, lived there until he died

but it soon acquired another significance in Roman minds as the scene of the famous defence of the 'immortal three'. Even today what child has not heard of Horatius though if he really lived it was nearly 2500 years ago. To the Romans of the classical era he was already a legendary figure, personifying all that they held most dear. Courage apart, he represented the spirit which had ousted the kings and created the republic to whose name Romans clung in later times, even after they had long been ruled by despotic emperors.

Writing five centuries after Horatius' legendary defence of the city, Livy himself was carried away by his vision of the scene, though he admits that his hero had 'given a proof of valour which was destined to obtain more fame than credence from posterity'. He describes Lars Porsena's Etruscan army charging down the Janiculum towards the vital bridge, the consternation reigning in Rome, and Horatius Cocles' command to destroy the bridge 'with steel or fire', while he himself would 'receive the onset of the enemy as far as it could be withstood by a single body'. Livy also recalls how Horatius was joined by Herminius and Spurius Lartius, 'both famous for their birth and deeds', and the desperate stand of the three against showers of javelins and repeated charges while the Romans hacked away frantically at the bridge behind them; then the last dramatic moment when, from the crashing timbers of the bridge, Horatius invoked the river god before leaping fully armed into the flood.

Whatever the historical veracity of this tale, it is certain that the expulsion of the last of the kings in 509 BC, and Lars Porsena's failure to reinstate the Etruscan hegemony, left Rome free to evolve her own inimitable character and institutions which eventually resulted in world dominion. But level-headed though they were, the Romans were the first to recognise the part which the glamour of heroism had played in their greatness. Even in the peaceful reign of Antoninus Pius, in the second century AD, Horatius was still a name to conjure with. His famous exploit was represented upon coins, showing him swimming beside the old humpbacked bridge which the Romans of that day believed was still built in this fashion so that it could be easily destroyed before an invading army. Though by then, of course, the Tiber was spanned by many magnificent bridges that carried the great consular roads into the heart of the city. Of these, two of the most notable in the whole history of Rome led, and still lead, along the Tiber valley in their early stages – the Salaria along the left bank, the Flaminia along the right.

The Via Salaria, as its name indicates, is an ancient salt road. Probably it was the earliest of the trails along the Tiber valley by which this precious commodity was carried in prehistoric times from the estuary to the Sabine hinterland. It was down this road that the Gauls advanced on Rome in 390 BC. The furious onslaught of their cavalry crushed the Roman army drawn up to meet them in the Tiber valley, between what is now Marcigliana and the river bank. That same night the city's terrified inhabitants looked out upon the plain dotted with Gallic camp fires and, knowing that the walls would not withstand an attack, prepared to flee. The sack of Rome which followed added to the city's stock of legends much as Lars Porsena's attack and Horatius' stand had done; divine intervention was seen in the legendary warning cackle of the sacred geese that saved the Capitol. In after years, however, the Romans' sense of shame at their defeat was somewhat mitigated by memories of the heroic gesture of the magistrates who, refusing to abandon the city, stoically awaited death seated on their ivory chairs of state.

Significantly, the bridges also played a dramatic part in these events. It was by the old Sublician that a humble plebian, L. Albinius, found the Vestal Virgins escaping on foot, carrying the sacred fire. Leaving his own family to fend for themselves, Albinius loaded the Vestals and their precious charge on to his wagon, bringing them to Caere (Cervetri) in safety. Thus the flame, upon whose unsullied continuance it was believed the prosperity of the state depended, was saved to burn for close on to another 800 years; it had been extinguished forever before Rome was sacked again in 410 AD. In that momentous year it was also by way of the Via Salaria that the Goths advanced on Rome. They passed over the self-same Salarian Bridge, near the junction of the Aniene and the Tiber, where Titus Manlius (afterwards surnamed Torquatus) had killed the Gallic giant and clasped his torque around his own throat. Some strange fatality always seems to have haunted this spot, for several times during the next 1500 years it witnessed events that decided the future of Rome.

The Via Flaminia, which crosses the Tiber by the Milvian Bridge, had almost as eventful a role in Roman history. Its 222 Roman miles–connecting the capital with Rimini on the Adriatic–were built between 223 and 220 BC by the Censor Caius Flaminius. After his election

ABOVE LEFT St Francis of Assisi *from a fresco attributed to the early Italian painter Cimabue (c. 1240–1302?). The Tiber runs through St Francis' life like a thread. In its valley are Assisi where he was born and the Basilica of Santa Maria degli Angeli where he died, Alviano where he rebuked the swallows, Citerna where he saved the inhabitants from a plague of ants, and Borgo Sansepolcro which he visited for the last time bearing the stigmata received at Verna*

ABOVE RIGHT *The Battle of Anghiari, fought between the Visconti of Milan and the Florentines under Francesco Sforza, was painted by Rubens from a copy of Leonardo da Vinci's hidden masterpiece in the Palazzo Vecchio in Florence*

OPPOSITE The Water Mill *by Claude Lorraine. Claude, a pastry-cook turned painter, was one of many famous artists and writers–among them Goethe, Byron, Browning and Henry James–who found inspiration in the romantic wasteland of the Campagna, with its abandoned temples, broken aqueducts and luxuriant vegetation*

249

OPPOSITE *Luigi Vanvitelli's* View of Rome *in the eighteenth century is one of many Roman scenes he painted with a care and precision that matches Canaletto's paintings of Venice. His picture shows the Castel Sant' Angelo with the Sant' Angelo bridge leading to it, and behind, the dome of St Peter's*

A sketch of a mosaic in the dome of an ancient mausoleum shows life in a Roman villa on the Tiber in the time of Constantine the Great (c. 280–337). The pillars of the loggia, the infant genii and the fruit and flowers are typical of the ancient Roman art which strongly influenced the school of fresco painters led by Cimabue and his pupil Giotto

as Consul, it was by this route that Flaminius secretly made his way to Rimini to take command of the army with which he hoped to defeat Hannibal, a campaign that ended in one of the greatest catastrophes to Roman arms – the Consul and his whole army were wiped out at the battle of Lake Trasumennus (Trasimen) in 217 BC.

Ten years later, with the threat of Carthaginian occupation still hanging over them an anxious crowd gathered on the Milvian Bridge, straining their eyes to catch the first sight of another horseman galloping along the Via Flaminia. News had begun to filter through that a great battle had been joined on the Metaurus (Metauro) River. The scenes that followed had no parallel in Roman history; senators and plebs actually fought each other over which should be first to hear the courier when he arrived. Finally a place was cleared in the Curia for him to read his dispatches; then his listeners realised that the threat to Rome's existence, which had begun with the Punic wars forty-seven weary years before, was ended. Hannibal's Carthaginian reinforcements had been destroyed and his brother Hasdrubal slain at the eighth milestone on the Via Flaminia outside Fanum (Fano). True, Hannibal himself remained to be dealt with, but it was the beginning of the end for Carthage; fifty years later the plough passed over her ruins and Rome's galleys sailed from the Tiber mouth to her new colonies in Africa.

As Rome's power spread beyond the shores of Italy,

OPPOSITE *The Isola Tiberina, an island of great natural beauty with a macabre history. Here, during the reign of Claudius (41–54 AD), sick slaves were left to die. Two bridges link the island to the banks: the Fabrizio, nearly two thousand years old, and the Cestio, of which only two of the original arches remain. In the foreground is the single broken arch of the Pons Rotto*

For centuries medallions like this, struck in the reign of Antoninus Pius (138–161 AD), kept alive the legend of Horatius, the Roman who traditionally fought off the entire Etruscan army while his fellow Romans demolished the wooden Sublician bridge behind him, and then, despite his wounds, plunged fully armed into the Tiber and swam to safety. The Pons Sublicius was the first and for many years the only bridge across the Tiber

RIGHT *The vision of an angel that appeared to Gregory the Great in 590 as a sign that his prayers would be answered and that Rome would be delivered from war, flood and pestilence is commemorated by this fresco in the church of St Francis at Arezzo. To mark the event, Hadrian's Tomb, where the angel appeared, and the bridge leading to it were renamed Sant' Angelo, and a huge marble statue of an angel was placed on the roof of the newly named Castel Sant' Angelo*

it might have been expected that the Tiber valley would cease to be the theatre of such dramatic events. But the Punic wars had left a very different Rome behind them. Bitter internal political strife and ultimately civil war threatened the state. Now, it was not only rush dummies that were consigned to the waters of the Tiber: political factions awarded this same fate to their dead rivals, a fate which had previously been reserved for living parricides and abnormal prodigies believed to have contaminated the city.

In 133 BC the body of Tiberius Gracchus was the first to receive this ignominy. His land reforms and challenge to the vested interests of the Senate ended in his murder and that of his supporters. Thirteen years later his brother Gaius paid the same price for continuing Tiberius' policy. Tiberius and Gaius perished, but their name lived for ever in the hearts of the Roman people who inscribed upon their mother's tomb the proud epitaph, 'Cornelia mother of the Gracchi'. But the lament of Gaius' wife, Licinia, foreshadowed the

mourning of countless others when she cried, 'Now I must probably beg a river or a sea to show me the body that they will be charged to keep.'

Until the end of the Julia-Claudian house, it was the normal practice for the naked corpses of those executed in the Mamertine prison to be exposed upon the Gemonian steps before being flung into the Tiber. During Tiberius' reign this horrible practice became almost a common occurrence, and it gave rise to a pathetic incident that was remembered long afterwards. A slave of Titius Sabinus, who was involved in the fall of Tiberius' adopted grandson Nero, was executed with his master and his body exposed on the Gemonian steps. His faithful dog, who could not be driven away, sat there howling and when the crowd threw it scraps of food carried them to the dead man's mouth. Accompanying his master's body across the city, the dog jumped after it into the Tiber, vainly trying to keep it afloat. This story of fidelity was entered in the city records and mentioned by Pliny in his Natural History.

S. Croce In Herusalem

S. PAVLO

S. GIOVANNI LATRANO

S. MARIA MAGIORE

S. PIETRO

LE SETTE CHIESE DI ROMA
Per esser uenuto lanno del santo Jubileo con:
cesso da Nostro Sig.re Gregorio XIII secondo
lanticho consueto e fatto questo disegno, con il
circuito de Roma, doue si uedeno dette chiese
cauate dal naturale, et se non sono poste nel
suo luogo, ogni persona iuditiosa conoscera
depender la causa per non hauer piu spatio
Di queste sette chiese quattro sono le piuile:
giate segnate con li Santi á chi sono de:
dicate, et con una ✠ et in esse si piglia il
Santo Jubileo, ilquale i Dio ci dia sua Santa
pace per poterlo acquistare nel presente
anno. 1575. ANT. LAFRERII ROMAE

The conspirators had planned a similar end for Julius Caesar; no doubt Augustus would have done the same by them if they had not all died before he seized the reins of power. Happily, the first emperor's association with the Tiber valley was of a different nature. Nine miles out on the Via Flaminia, the ruins of Livia's villa still stand on a bluff overlooking the river. It was a favourite retreat of the imperial couple and believed to be particularly fortunate to them. This was because, before their marriage in 38 BC, an eagle, flying over the spot, had dropped a white hen with a sprig of laurel in its beak into Livia's lap. The augurs advised that the hen should be preserved and the sprig planted with religious care. The prodigious fertility of this remarkable fowl resulted in the villa being called *ad gallinas albas* after it; the laurel spring, meanwhile grew into a tree from which each succeeding emperor planted a slip. It was from this grove that the laurels for all the Caesars' triumphal crowns were picked. In the last year of Nero's reign the tree withered prophetically and the whole flock of poultry died, before that night in AD 68 when he met his ignominious end in Phaon's house across the river.

The site of Livia's villa was indeed a fateful one in history. It stood close by the Roman posting station of Saxa Rubra, where in 477 BC the Fabii perished to a man in the war against the Etruscan city of Veii. It was here too that Vespasian's supporters paused before advancing into the city to depose Vitellius in AD 69. This was a turning-point in the affairs of Rome, ending the nightmare period which followed Nero's death and leading on to that of imperial splendour. Vitellius was the first emperor whose vicious career ended in the Tiber – a dishonour from now on reserved for the imperial rank. The last, Maxentius, met his fate at this self-same Saxa Rubra.

Driven unwillingly by the jeers of the crowd from the games celebrating his accession six years before, Maxentius consulted the Sybilline books before leaving the protecting walls of Rome, on 28 October, AD 312. Mistakenly he put an optimistic construction on the Delphic answer he received – that on this very day 'the enemy of Rome' would perish. Maxentius and the rear guard of his army had barely reached the Milvian Bridge when Constantine's victorious charge broke the Praetorians' defence of the defile of Saxa Rubra, turning the battle into a rout. By the time the victor had reached the banks of the Tiber, the river was choked with corpses. Maxentius' body was found on a pile of dead who had been drowned in the panic retreat across the Milvian Bridge.

His head was severed and carried on a spear before the splendid figure of Constantine, who now made his triumphal entry into Rome, clad in shining armour with golden cuirass and shield, his helmet brilliant with aigrettes and glittering jewels.

Pious legends of later ages told how Constantine's jewelled standard – the famous Labarum, with the Cross and the words 'Conquer by this' – was carried in the battle. These legends do not altogether agree with the findings of modern scholars, but no-one today argues about the fact that the battle of Saxa Rubra, and the retreat at the Milvian Bridge, changed in one day the history of the world. The whole of the west now belonged to Constantine, and when he died in AD 337, a Christian, he ruled the entire Roman Empire.

One last drama of ancient Rome remained to be played out, and it was again heralded by an invading army marching down the Tiber valley in 410. Alaric and his Goths had besieged the city twice before, and twice been bought off. In their pride and decadence the Romans probably believed that nothing could really happen; Rome was eternal and would last long after these barbarian hosts had melted away. The Goths'

Two riverside scenes by Giovanni Battista Piranesi (1720–78), an artist dedicated to preserving in his engravings 'the splendours of the most famous city of the Universe'

LEFT View of the Port of Riva Grande, *a vanished waterfront near the old Sublician bridge*

BELOW View of the Port of Ripetta, *another waterfront that no longer exists, which shows, from left to right, the Church of St Girolamo degli Sciavonni built by Pope Sixtus V, the Customs House, the Palace of the Borghese and the Clementine College. The magnificent baroque steps were built by Pope Clement XI in 1703*

Veduta del Porto di Ripa Grande

camp fires burned all round the city, and Alaric himself had set up his headquarters on a hill overlooking the Salarian Bridge and the river valley. We do not know with whom he conducted secret negotiations, but it is certain that it was by treachery that the Goths entered Rome by the Salarian Gate, on the night of 24 August, set fire to the city, and so began the sack that sounded the death-knell of the ancient world.

During the Dark Ages the Tiber's role changed as completely as the magnificent monuments and villas which now crumbled on its banks. From being Rome's highway to her Mediterranean lake, the river became the route for sea-borne invaders. Genseric and his Vandals were the first. In 455 they plundered Rome for fourteen days, carrying away with them the Capitoline temple's gilded tiles and the seven-branched candle-stick that Titus had brought back from Jerusalem. Eighty-six years later this candlestick figured in Belisarius' triumph after his conquest of Africa, which was the prelude to his liberation of Rome from the Goths in 536.

The next year the Goths returned in overwhelming force, and Belisarius nearly lost his life in a surprise attack near the Milvian Bridge. The siege which followed was epic. Chains were drawn across the Tiber, and for the first time in its history Hadrian's great tomb, which dominated the curve of the Tiber flowing through the heart of the city, became the bulwark of Rome's defence. Stripping the mausoleum of its splendid statues, Belisarius' forces flung them down upon the attacking Goths. It was during this siege that the aqueducts were cut, making the Tiber Rome's chief water supply for centuries to come, and thus radically changing the city's life. By seizing Ostia at the river's mouth, from where supplies had reached Rome, the Goths nearly reduced the city to starvation. But after a siege of one year and nine days, their numbers reduced by war and pestilence, the Goths retreated the way they came – over the Milvian Bridge and along the Via Flaminia.

War, one of the worse floods in the history of the Tiber, and plague, had reduced Rome to a spectre of her former self, when on 3 September, 590, Gregory the Great was proclaimed Pope. One of his first acts was to lead penitentiary processions through the city, to ask God's deliverance from the pestilence which still raged. Just as he was about to re-enter St Peter's, Gregory had a vision of an angel standing on the summit of Hadrian's tomb sheathing his sword. From that moment the plague ceased and, in memory of Rome's deliverance, the statue of an angel was placed on top of the monument, which from then on was known as Castel Sant' Angelo.

As a German author has truly said of this great castle by the Tiber, 'its history is a picture of Rome in camera oscura'. Commanding as it does the approaches to St Peter's and the Vatican, it is the key to Rome. Charlemagne passed it by on his way to his coronation in St Peter's, on Christmas Eve of the year 800 AD. Exactly 424 years had elapsed since the last emperor of the west had been deposed. In the words of Gregorovius, 'this was the most eventful moment that Rome was to see for centuries'.

Water Sports on the Tiber *by James Vernet, a French eighteenth-century court painter famous for his sea- and water-scapes. With the grim fortress of Sant' Angelo as the only reminder of the Tiber's turbulent history, men tilt with javelin and shield from platforms built on the prows of rowing boats while men and women of fashion with their marshals, trumpeters and armed guards watch from canopied balconies*

During the thirteenth century the Tiber valley, rather than Rome itself, was associated with the life of a man who could not have been more different from the war-like heroes who had left their mark upon it hitherto. Yet this apparently insignificant little man left behind him a legend which still has power to move the minds of men. An extraordinary aura of peace surrounds the many places where St Francis of Assisi stopped on his journeys up and down the Tiber valley. These range in distance from the Monastery of Pantanelli (near the junction of the Paglia), where from a rock he blessed the fishes, to the sanctuary of La Verna, near the Tiber's source, where he received the stigmata.

In the 250 miles between its mouth and Monte Fumaiolo, where it rises on the confines of Tuscany and Romagna, the Tiber passes through so varied a landscape that at times it is difficult to believe it is the same river. The wide valley of the Roman campagna soon narrows after the Via Salaria branches off into the Sabine hills near Passo Correse. Above Orte the Tiber forms the boundary between Lazio and Umbria, flowing through a valley picturesquely dotted with small hill towns like Alviano, where St Francis rebuked the swallows for interrupting his preaching. Above its junction with the Paglia the Tiber turns east to the foot of the hill where Todi stands. From there until just above Perugia it flows through a landscape immortalised by painters of the Umbrian school.

In the valley below Assisi, not far from where the Chiagio joins the Tiber, stands the Basilica of S. Maria degli Angeli, which enshrines the Porziuncola and the infirmary cell where St Francis died in 1226. Indeed the whole of the upper Tiber valley is filled with place-names familiar to most of the Christian world: from the *Fioretti* Città di Castello and the nearby Hermitage of Buon Riposo, where in 1213 the saint found a 'Good rest'; the fountain and shrine of S. Giustino, and Citerna, which he relieved of a plague of ants. St Francis passed through Borgo Sansepolcro many times, the last in 1224 just after he had received the stigmata. He came by way of Anghiari, which in 1440 became the scene of the famous battle – the subject of Leonardo's lost master-piece in the Palazzo Vecchio in Florence. Another of St Francis' staging posts was Caprese, where Totila is said to have died after his defeat by Narses. But this wind-swept little town standing high above one of the Tiber's first tributaries, is best remembered as the birthplace of Michelangelo.

The wild mountain country between Caprese and La Verna forms the watershed between the upper Arno and

Tiber valleys. Rising from it like a natural fortress, the precipitous rocks surrounding the Franciscan sanctuary dominate the whole scene. Some ten miles separate La Verna from Pieve S. Stefano, the first small town standing upon the Tiber, where the river is little more than a mountain torrent. Pieve was sacked in April 1527 by the Constable de Bourbon, during his advance on Rome. Coming from S. Pietro in Bagno in Romagna, he had crossed the Appenines by the Monte Coronaro pass, at the foot of Monte Fumaiolo. Thus the army which inflicted upon Rome the most grievous sack in her whole history passed within a few miles of the source of the Tiber.

This same route was one of the medieval pilgrim roads to Rome, probably the one where the Welsh Bishop, Gerald of Barri was beset by robbers and snow-storms. Matthew Paris included it among his famous itineraries. By this and many other routes pilgrims from all over Europe flocked to Rome for the first Holy Year in 1300; so great were their numbers that in the *Divina*

OPPOSITE *An early photograph of the Pons Rotto, built on the site of the Pons Aemilius, the bridge from which the body of the Emperor Elagabalus was thrown – a fate reserved for fallen emperors. He was put to death in AD 222 by the Praetorians (traditionally the Emperor's bodyguard) for his worship of the Sun God, his unparalleled debauchery and his insulting behaviour (he gave command of the Praetorians to an ex-actor and put his hairdresser in charge of the food supplies). One arch of the bridge, not visible in this photograph, was carried away by floods in 1598*

In 1870 when the Tiber overflowed its banks in one of the worst floods in records that go back to 241 BC many families escaped death only by taking to the boats with their babies in their arms, and the few possessions they could seize as they scrambled to safety

OPPOSITE *The Castel Sant' Angelo, built as a mausoleum by the Emperor Hadrian in 135 AD and completed by Antoninus Pius after his death. It has been successively a fortress, to which Pope Clement fled for safety during the Sack of Rome in 1527 (a disaster which his vacillation provoked), a prison (from which Benvenuto Cellini escaped), a barracks, and, today, a military museum. Three hundred feet square at the base, and with its immense circular tower 225 feet high, it has been continuously enlarged, notably by Bernini, and supplied with cannon made from the bronze roof of the Pantheon*

BELOW *The Bridge and the Castle by Jean Baptiste Camille Corot, now in the California Palace at San Francisco, is one of the several almost identical pictures of the Tiber Corot painted during one of his early visits to Rome. Characteristically he depicts the Sant' Angelo bridge as it was before the disproportionately large statues of angels were added, and with the small arches at the end which have since been removed*

Commedia Dante described the one-way traffic instituted on the Ponte Sant' Angelo, then the bridge closest to St Peter's. This Jubilee was the swan-song of Rome's medieval theocracy; five years later – after the election of Clement VI – the seat of the papacy was transferred from the banks of the Tiber to Avignon for seventy-two years.

This was a disastrous period for Rome and the Tiber valley. The city and the surrounding countryside fell into such disorder that in January 1377, when Gregory XI eventually returned from Avignon, he dared not come to Rome by land. Instead the papal galleys sailed up the Tiber from Ostia to St Paul's Without the Walls. On 17 January Gregory made his entry into the city, the first Pope ever to do so by the Via Ostiense – the same old riverside road down which St Paul had gone to his martyrdom. Neither he nor St Catherine of Siena, to whom Rome owed the Pope's return, would have approved the pageantry of the occasion – the gorgeously caparisoned horsemen, with their trumpets and banners, the nobles in their silk, and above all the white clad mountebanks, who preceded the papal procession dancing and clapping their hands.

This Roman carnival was of short duration. After Gregory's death in 1378, the circumstances of Urban VI's election provoked the Great Schism. For the next fifty-three years Rome was split apart by the supporters of warring popes and anti-popes. At last, with the election of Martin V in 1417, the tempest subsided. Before the Pope could return to Rome in 1420, however, he had

to placate Braccio di Montone, who controlled the Tiber valley, by making him his vicar for the strategic towns of Perugia, Assisi and Todi. For Gregorovius 'the shabby festival of Martin's entry closed the long and memorable period of the medieval city'. But the great German historian continued his classic *History of the City of Rome in the Middle Ages* to cover the Sack of Rome in 1527 – an event that changed the future of the city and the Tiber valley for ever.

On his accession in 1523, the vacillating Clement VIII found himself heir not only to the Macchiavellian policy of his much more able kinsman, Leo X, but also the great Julius II's aim of ridding all Italy of foreign suzerainty. The net result of the first four years of Clement's reign was to bring down upon himself and Rome the invading armies of the Emperor Charles V led by the Constable de Bourbon. On 4 May the imperial heralds were at the city gates, demanding entry and supplies. By the same night some 40,000 men – mostly German Protestant *Landsknechts* and Spaniards – were encamped in a great arc between the Milvian Bridge and the Janiculum, on the hills commanding the Vatican and the Borgo.

As in the year 410, the Romans believed their city was impregnable; and when the attack came at dawn on 5 May, at first it looked as if they might be right. The Constable de Bourbon was mortally wounded when trying to encourage his men to scale the walls near the Porta Cavaleggieri; but shortly afterwards the *Landsknechts* gained a foothold by the Porto S. Spirito.

OPPOSITE LEFT *The bridge to the Castel Sant' Angelo was built by the Emperor Hadrian as the approach to his mausoleum. For many years it carried pilgrims in tens of thousands across the Tiber to St Peter's*

OPPOSITE RIGHT *The Sant' Angelo bridge is built of immensely strong Travertine stone. The giant marble angels spaced along the parapet each bear a symbol of Christ's Passion. Like the gilded angel on the castle roof, they commemorate the visitation to which castle and bridge owe their name*

The Milvian Bridge framed in an arch of Mussolini's Ponte Flaminia. Note the massive piers with protective cut-waters and extra arches to let flood water through. On the Pons Milvia, Maximentius was killed by Constantine in 312. Here too, in 210 BC fearful of the outcome of a battle being fought only eight Roman miles away, patrician fought with plebeian to hear the courier's news — and learned that the Carthaginian power had at last been broken and Rome was safe

263

Charging with shouts of 'Spain! Spain! the Empire!', the invaders had overrun and sacked the Borgo within three hours. The Swiss Guards were massacred in and around St Peter's, almost within sight of the Pope, who now fled to Castel Sant' Angelo.

By the afternoon Trastevere had been stormed and taken; there was still hope of saving the rest of the city if the Tiber bridges could be held or destroyed. But alas! Rome produced no more men of Horatius' breed; instead a delegation was sent to parley at the Ponte Sisto. Barely had they reached it when the imperialists rushed across. Unable to believe that a city of some 90,000 inhabitants would give up without further struggle, the imperial forces mustered in the city squares, standing to arms. For six hours Rome lay silent as if under a spell, then at midnight these soldiers, who had fought and starved their way across Italy by forced marches, flung themselves upon the city and sacked it.

The horrors of those three days and nights changed Rome for ever; gone was the gay city of the Renaissance, the magnet which had drawn artists and writers from all over Italy to the papal court. From the ramparts of Castel Sant' Angelo, Clement looked down on a scene of terror and destruction; churches and palaces blazed, the streets were piled with corpses and re-echoed to the screams of the tortured and dying. For a whole dreadful month the fortress held out; then on 5 June the Pope surrendered, throwing himself upon Charles V's mercy. He was kept in close custody in the castle until a treaty was finally signed at the end of November. By its terms the Emperor agreed to release the Pope and to return to him the Papal States, on condition that in future they should preserve strict neutrality. The ports of Ostia and Civitavecchia were handed over as guarantees, and three cardinals as hostages; a council for Church reform was to be called and a heavy indemnity paid.

As a result of the neutrality imposed by Charles V, Rome ceased to be a political power. From now on the canons of Sant' Angelo were fired only to salute the creation of a cardinal of royal blood – except on one

Roman bridges are no longer built to the massive proportions of the early structures. In the Ponte Victor Emmanuel, built in 1911, the strength and simplicity of the Roman fortified bridge has given way to a more fashionable design, with ornamental groups of white marble in place of protective 'starlings' and floodwater arches

OPPOSITE *The Ponte Fabrizio, built in 62 BC, is the oldest bridge in Rome over the Tiber. It leads to the Isola Tiberina*

occasion for the amusement of Queen Christina of Sweden. Still the conversion to Roman Catholicism of this daughter of the great paladin of the Reformed faith was a measure of how far-reaching had been the effects of the Counter Reformation which followed the sack of Rome. For more than two centuries the city slumbered and it seemed as if old Father Tiber had forgotten his role in the destiny of nations. But the year 1798 brought a rude awakening, and what looked like the beginning of another 'babylonist' captivity of Avignon. Pius VI was deported and Rome declared a republic, though this was of short duration. A British naval squadron, under Captain Troubridge's command, landed at Civitavecchia; Tarquinia and Tolfa were also occupied, and the French forces had to evacuate Rome. A flotilla of boats then sailed up the Tiber and the Union Jack was hoisted on the Capitol. Incidentally this naval occasion resulted in saving many of the treasures of the Vatican Museum from being shipped to France; also in Captain Troubridge receiving the unique privilege of adding the keys of St Peter to his arms. In 1809 the temporal power of the papacy suffered another eclipse; Rome was declared 'the second city of the Empire' and Napoleon's infant son its king. But in 1814 Pius VII returned, crossing the Tiber by Ponte Sant' Angelo which was decorated with triumphal arches for the occasion.

In 1870 the diehards of the papal regime reacted much as their classical predecessors would have done, when it was noised abroad that during a terrible storm on Christmas day lightning had struck a sacred picture in the Pope's private chapel in the Vatican. Sure enough, calamity followed within twenty-four hours, with one of the worst Tiber floods ever recorded. Rome was paralysed for days: the main Post Office was shut and the city was without gas, while boats rowed down the Corso bringing food supplies. It was in the muddy aftermath of this disaster that on 31 December, Victor Emmanuel, King of united Italy, made his first visit to his new capital.

Naturally schemes for the protection of the city from future floods were soon instituted by the new government, though the energetic intervention of Garibaldi was necessary before the matter was taken seriously in hand in 1875. Much that was old and beautiful was destroyed to make way for the new embankments, but at least Rome was spared the fear of flood which had been recurrent throughout her history. Perhaps the greatest loss was the beautiful riverside port of the Ripetta, with its curving baroque steps leading to the water. However, when Augustus Hare wrote his classic 'Walks in Rome' about this time, a ferry service still existed, and until the

OPPOSITE High up in the Tiber valley, a boy fishes from the river bank

A Roman mosaic showing the lighthouse at Ostia, the main port of Rome, where the Tiber enters the Tyrrhenian Sea. From Ostia Mark Antony embarked for Egypt and the Nile. To Ostia the unpopular Pope Gregory XI came on his way from Avignon to Rome, preferring the safety of a journey up the Tiber in a papal galley to the welcome that might await him in the villages and towns

end of the century steam boats plied up and down the Tiber, from its mouth nearly to Orte. Quicker means of land transport finally killed the river traffic, and during this century the Tiber has been used for shipping only on exceptional occasions, such as for the transport of the obelisk for the Foro Mussolini (now Foro Italico).

Enclosed by its towering embankments, the river now seems to slumber peacefully, dreaming of its great past. However, during the German occupation of 1943–44 it again played its part in history; then an Allied wireless transmitter was for long concealed on what appeared to

be an innocent barge. Boats are now a rare sight on the Tiber. The last notable navigation of the river took place in 1949. Two American archaeologists, Louise and Lester Holland, descended it in an inflatable rubber boat, from Orte to the sea. They used this modern equivalent of a primitive raft to discover what were the natural landing places in early times. Floating on the current, they found that the only easy landing places occurred at the junction of the tributaries, because there backwaters are created where firm shingle strands jut out into the river; elsewhere the banks are covered with sticky mud.

No less than three of these landing places must have existed where Rome now stands, indicating that it was probably a favoured stopping-place from neolithic times. Moreover the Hollands' observations showed that the existing roads up the Tiber valley follow roughly the same lines as the primitive trails of prehistoric times. Thus modern research confirms the fact that thousands of years before Chaucer wrote 'yit by diuerse reules, rihte as by diuerse pathes leden diuerse folk, the rihte wey to Roome', the Tiber and its valley were the first of all roads to lead to Rome.

The Tiber is the second longest river in Italy and the only one with navigable estuary. Two hundred and fifty miles from where it rises in the Apennines, small boys in Ostia keep watch on fish traps suspended on booms from wooden platforms

THE VOLGA

LIONEL AND MIRIAM KOCHAN

The reality behind the Song of the Volga Boatmen is illustrated in this painting by the nineteenth-century Russian artist Repin showing men and women wearily dragging heavy barges through the sluggish waters of the river. Shown in one Russian village after another, it became a symbol of the suffering of the Russian peasantry

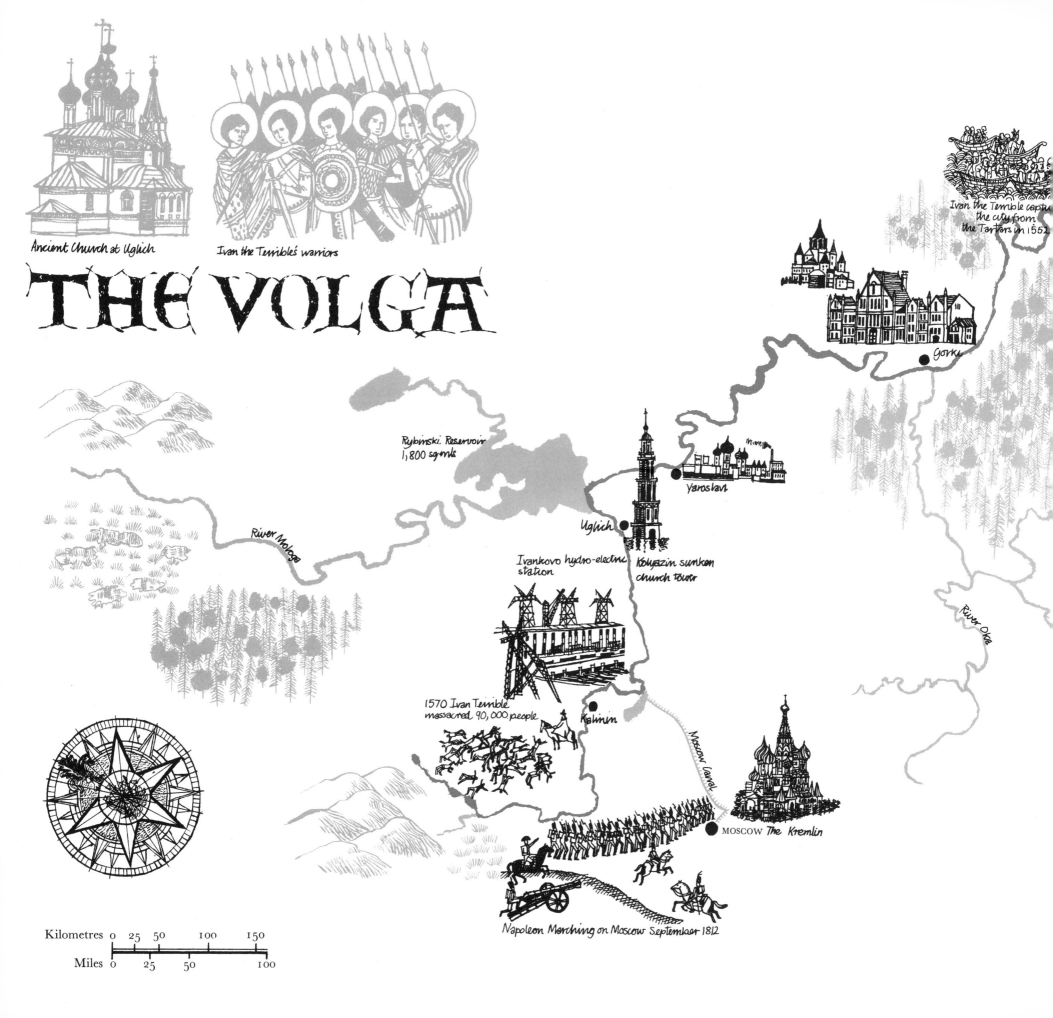

Ancient Church at Uglich

Ivan the Terrible's warriors

THE VOLGA

Ivan the Terrible captures the city from the Tartars in 1552

Gorki

Rybinski Reservoir 1,800 sq.mls

Yaroslavl

River Mologa

Uglich

Ivankovo hydro-electric station

Kolyazin sunken church tower

River Oka

1570 Ivan Terrible massacred 90,000 people

Kalinin

Moscow Canal

MOSCOW The Kremlin

Napoleon Marching on Moscow September 1812

Kilometres 0   25   50   100   150

Miles 0   25   50   100

Kazan

River Kama

Kuibyshev Reservoir
Greatest man made lake
in the world
(floods 2,3000 sq mls)

Ulyanovsk

Bend of Samara

Kuibyshev

River Samara

River Irgiz

River Tsna

Bridge at Saratov

Saratov

CASPIAN SEA

Battle of Stalingrad
1942

Volgagrad

Volga-Don Canal

Astrakhan Tartar City
captured by
Ivan the Terrible in 1556

To THE TARTARS and Arabs it was known as '*Itil*'; to Ptolemy and the Greeks its name was 'Rha'; the Finnish tribes called it 'Rau'. But to the Russians it is 'Mother Volga', an ineradicable symbol and personification of Russian history. In the thirteenth century the river's banks resounded to the thundering hooves of the Tartar Golden Horde; in the seventeenth century it was along the Volga that the Cossack rebel Stenka Razin set sail from Astrakhan with 200 barges in the forlorn hope of establishing a free republic; in the nineteenth century the Volga region was the scene of the worst famines in Russian history; in the twentieth century it was at the Volga town of Stalingrad (now Volgograd) that one of the most famous and bloodiest battles in history was fought.

If the Volga flows through the scenes of some of the most macabre and also most heroic episodes in Russian history, the Russians themselves are comparative new-comers to the river. Great empires rose and fell along its banks before the Russians secured control. The name 'Volga' itself betrays the river's ancient history–it is a legacy of the Finnish peoples of Bulgary who founded a state along the river in the early centuries A.D. Their capital, Bulgar, lay near the site of present-day Kazan. To the south at this time lay the Khazar state, with its capital, Itil, near the point where Volgograd now stands. But Khazaria fell victim to the Arabs and when Itil lost its importance as a trading centre the focus of power moved northwards. By the tenth century, when the Bulgars embraced Islam, their capital city was a flourishing commercial centre and the meeting place for traders venturing up the Volga from as far afield as Arabia, Persia and Byzantium. Even merchants from Scandinavia traded at Bulgar.

In the thirteenth century the Mongol invasions shook the Bulgar kingdom to its foundations; and at the end of the fourteenth century it finally succumbed to the onslaught of Tamerlane. The Mongols controlled the river for three centuries. Not until the 1550's when Ivan the Terrible led the new state of Muscovy to victory over the Mongol Khanates of Kazan and Astrakhan did the Russians at last dominate the whole length of the river.

It was a prize worth fighting for. The Volga is the longest river in Europe and the most important in Russia. It has its source among the lakes, marshes and low wooded hills of the Valdai plateau, only 1000 feet above sea-level, some 200 miles north-west of Moscow.

Here also two other great Russian rivers originate–the Western Dvina, flowing into the Baltic; and the Dnieper, flowing into the Black Sea. The Volga, the greatest of all, travels 2300 miles before it reaches its delta in the land-locked Caspian Sea. These rivers and their tributaries linked the territory they watered to the countries beyond the seas. Portages connected one river system with the next.

The Volga is a mere streamlet when it leaves its source, oozing from bog to bog for more than twenty miles. By the time it turns eastwards to Lake Volgo it has become quite a considerable stream. Three miles further on, the first rapids are encountered. Near here, the Volga is nearly doubled by the intake from another river and from this point, the navigable stream as such may be said to begin. The Volga descends the slopes of the plateau through a series of rapids which do not prevent navigation; and beyond these rapids it winds unimpeded through the great Russian lowlands, receiving numerous navigable tributaries, most significantly the 1000-mile long Oka from the West and 1200-mile Kama from the East, and communicating by canal with the Baltic basin.

In the lower part of the river, south of Samara (now Kuibyshev) and Saratov it is over a mile broad. At its delta it swells to over 110 miles wide.

Along this mighty waterway–the gateway to much of Russia–a constant flow of shipping–steamers, barges,

From earliest times the merchants of Persia and India brought their goods by camel to the shores of the Caspian Sea, where they were loaded on to ships and barges which carried them up the Volga to trading stations on its banks. A sixteenth-century woodcut

OPPOSITE *Timber cut on the banks of the Volga is lashed together to form huge rafts – sometimes as much as a quarter of a mile wide and half a mile long – which are floated downstream and broken up on arrival. The raftmen and their families live aboard in huts, their world bounded by the river and the raft*

RIGHT *A curious sport practised on the banks of the Volga in the nineteenth century. The participants climbed up steps cut into the side of a sandy hill and then hurled themselves down the slope*

An old paddle steamer with an unexpected name, Missouri, used to carry sightseers up and down the Volga. In Nizhni Novgorod (now Gorki) and Kazan these steamers were used for fashionable society outings

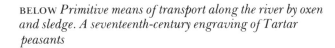

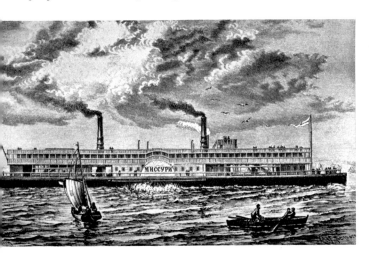

BELOW *Primitive means of transport along the river by oxen and sledge. A seventeenth-century engraving of Tartar peasants*

rafts, lighters and tugs – has always moved. The Volga is the most heavily traversed river in the Soviet Union – particularly where low-cost, bulky goods are concerned. Northwards flow wheat, coal and pig iron from the Ukraine, fish from the Caspian, salt from the lower Volga and, until recently, oil from the wells of Baku. All these commodities are destined for the Central Industrial Region, the Urals and the north-west. Southwards flow timber and finished products for the lower Volga and the Ukraine.

But the Volga presents several natural obstacles to successful navigation. Ice forms in solid sheets, often more than three feet thick, preventing all water traffic for four or five months every winter in the upper reaches and about three in the lower. There are large seasonal fluctuations in flow, with floods in spring and shoals in late summer and autumn. The river was always changing course and had to be dredged annually. Alexandre Dumas, the French novelist, journeyed down the Volga in the autumn of 1858 and found that the 'Volga boats do not travel at night at this season of the

year for the river bed is shifting sand and the water is very shallow, so that there is real risk of running aground.' Steamers in fact, were once stationed near the more dangerous sandbanks to help the stranded ships off. Nowadays, however, the flow of the river is controlled by a stairway of reservoirs. The song of the Volga boatmen no longer echoes and re-echoes from bank to bank. The old *burlaki* who in their tens of thousands once dragged their boats and barges along the banks of the river, chanting their melodious rhythm, have long since gone. Tug boats have taken their place.

Everywhere in fact the old is giving place to the new. In the early years of the century when Maurice Baring was in Yaroslavl he found it 'a sleepy town with trees and grass everywhere (the trees very dark in the twilight); the houses low, two-storey, all painted white (with pale green roofs), as white as ghosts in the dusk, ornamented with pilasters and Eighteenth Century and Empire arches and arcades. Every now and then one came across a church with the remains of the sunset making the gilt minarets glisten. The whole was a sym-

phony in dark green, white and lilac.' Today Yaroslavl is a centre of the synthetic rubber industry.

But perhaps the town on this part of the river that has undergone the greatest change is Nizhni Novgorod, now re-named Gorki, after the famous novelist. But far more important in the transition from the old to the new – it has lost its great annual fair, the Nizhnegorodskaya Yarmaka, founded by Ivan III, at the end of the fifteenth century. As late as 1910 goods worth 250 million roubles were sold at the fair and 400,000 visitors came from all parts of Asia and Europe. During the fair, Nizhni Novgorod stood at the crossroads of two worlds.

'The Volga itself,' wrote one visitor, 'seemed to vanish under a forest of masts flying flags of every size and colour. These were the cargo boats that had brought all the merchandise to the fair ... The scene on shore was like a great over-turned ant-hill, and on the landing stage at least a thousand drozhkys and carts were drawn up in line waiting to be hired.' Seen from above, the fair was clearly divided into four separate zones. One of these was occupied by between seven to eight thousand prostitutes who came from every part of European and Asiatic Russia for the six weeks of the fair.

Dominating the entrance to the fair was the Church of St Makarius (the patron saint of the great annual enterprise), with an Armenian church on its right and a Mohammedan mosque to the left, all three looking out over the central section, consisting of 2500 shops built of stone and roofed with sheet metal. Immediately in front of the saint were two diagonal rows of booths reserved for Chinese merchants and covered with fantastic ornaments–embroideries, hangings, banners covered with serpents, dragons, brilliant birds of scarlet, blue, orange. The roofs of these shops were built out with fretted strips of wood shaped to look like pagodas and painted with dazzling colours that never seemed to clash.

Millions of pounds worth of merchandise changed hands–precious stones were as plentiful as nuts, carpets and rugs, caviare, silks, leatherwork, damascened swords and firearms of every conceivable variety. The vendors were as fascinating as the goods they offered–Hindus displaying fine shawls, yellow-skinned men from Turkey unrolling silks and gauze, craftsmen with sensitive fingers proffering saddles, bridles, belts set with turquoises. All deals they made were completed solely by word of mouth–no written contracts, no bits of stamped paper. It was like a story from the *Thousand and One Nights*. At night the fair was lit up with torches, flares, every variety of illumination, and the prettiest sight of all was to see the little boats darting hither and thither on the canals, weaving a magic, ever-changing pattern like dancing fireflies.

Gorki today, however, is known as the 'Detroit of the Soviet Union'. It is here that Zim cars are manufactured in an automobile plant built by engineers sent to Russia by Henry Ford in 1932. Even so, the town still shows relics of its past–the small wooden dwelling where Gorki spent his childhood, and the political prison in which he found the originals of the characters for his play 'The Lower Depths'. At the other end of the scale the town also boasts the ornate building which the last of the Czars erected in 1913 when the third centenary

275

OPPOSITE *The ancient church at Uglich, named the Church of Blood in memory of the death of Dmitry, the youngest son of Ivan the Terrible. Dmitry is alleged to have been murdered at Uglich in 1591 by order of the Regent, Boris Godounov*

LEFT *The church tower of Kalyazin, 130 miles from Moscow, a village flooded by the building of the great dam at Uglich. The bell tower, the only visible remains of the settlement, is now used as an aid to navigation*

BELOW *In Yaroslavl, now a fast growing industrial city making trucks, tyres and paper, factory chimneys rise beside the onion dome of the centuries-old church. Some workers still make their homes in crumbling shacks near the waterfront*

of the establishment of the Romanov dynasty was celebrated.

These trading towns along the upper Volga–Yaroslavl, Kostroma, Gorki–in fact formed the area where the Romanov dynasty originated or at least where modern Russia first took shape. At Kostroma the Romanov house and the Susanin monument for decades symbolized this historic fact. In 1612, when the position of Muscovy had been rendered precarious by simultaneous invasion from Poland and Sweden, three men arose to save the country–Minin from Nizhni Novgorod, Pozharsky from Yaroslavl, and Patriarch Romanov. Romanov was twice taken prisoner by the invading Poles, thrown into dungeons, loaded with chains and tortured. But nothing could shake his faith in his religion and his country. He so typified the spirit of Russia that he became the focal point around which his countrymen rallied and it was from his family that Muscovy chose her next sovereign.

The monument to Susanin, on the other hand, expresses Russia's gratitude to a man of the people. In 1669, during a Polish invasion, the peasant Ivan Susanin was forced to guide a detachment of some 3000 enemy troops seeking a cross-country route to Moscow. Instead, he led them deep into an immense trackless forest. The soldiers battered him to death and so sacrificed their last hope of escape. No-one left the forest alive. The grateful Czar, Michael Romanov, decreed that henceforth no taxes were to be collected or men conscripted from Karabanovo, the village where Susanin was born. The monument was a column of pink granite from Finland, surmounted by the figure of Michael Romanov. Bas-reliefs on the pedestal depicted Susanin's story.

Kazan, to the east of Gorki, is traditionally the meeting place of Europe and Asia, 'the *ultima thule* of the civilized world,' as it was once called. A university city, it can boast Lenin and Tolstoy amongst its graduates. The students, according to Gorki, led a predictably bohemian life. For one rouble they could have a woman for a whole night in the brothels of Kazan. Amongst the tramps, thieves and stevedores of the Volga wharves Gorki found 'a whirling world where men's instincts

ABOVE *Russian families at leisure on the banks of the river near Kuibyshev*

OPPOSITE *A female labour gang repairs one of the dykes reinforcing the river bank near Kazan. The building of the huge hydro-electric dam at Kuibyshev has raised the level of the river and increased the possibility of flooding in places. The dam is part of the Great Volga Plan, which is transforming the river basin, harnessing its power, and irrigating its fields*

LEFT *The Kremlin of Kazan, built by the Tartar Khan of the Golden Horde in the mid-fifteenth century. Its capture from the Tartars by Ivan the Terrible in 1552 opened the way for Russian expansion eastward to the Caspian Sea*

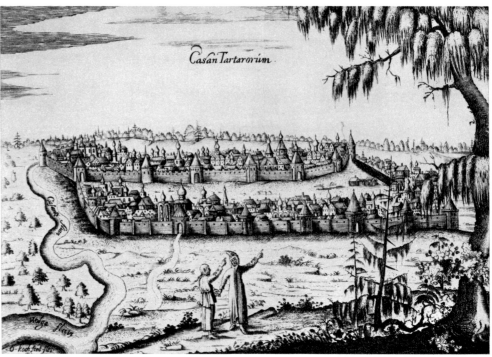

Casan Tartarorum.

NISEN. NAVGOROD

Occa fluu

Wolga fluu

ABOVE LEFT *At the Bend of Samara the Volga is joined by the river Samara. The town of Samara, now Kuibyshev, was built at the end of the sixteenth century to protect traffic on the Volga from the brigands who infested the hills overlooking the river*

ABOVE RIGHT *When Olearius recorded this scene early in the seventeenth century – one of many engravings from his* Voyages of the Ambassadors of the Duke of Holstein *– Kazan was a walled and fortified city. The two figures in the foreground are wearing the traditional Tartar costume – the woman a long white linen tunic with a pointed cowl, while the man has a shaven head with one long tress of hair, indicating he is unmarried*

LEFT *Nizhni Novgorod in the early seventeenth century, when it was the scene of an annual fair at which merchants from all parts of Asia and Europe met to buy and sell. Now called Gorki, after the famous Soviet writer, it is best known as the place where Zim cars are made – the Detroit of the Soviet Union*

OPPOSITE LEFT *Astrakhan lies in the centre of the fertile plain at the mouth of the Volga. It was founded in the fourteenth century and was the capital of the Tartar Khans until 1557, when it was incorporated into the state of Muscovy by Ivan the Terrible. An early seventeenth-century engraving showing men at work in the shipyards*

OPPOSITE RIGHT *For hundreds of years Astrakhan has been the principal commercial centre for catching sturgeon and for the caviare industry. The traditional method was to trap the fish behind barricades of wooden beams a foot apart and then catch them on unbaited hooks, after which they were towed away and killed*

RIGHT *A seventeenth-century traveller's map of the lower reaches of the Volga. The illustrations emphasize the importance of Astrakhan as a rich trading centre*

Steur vanast inde Rivier de WOSGA

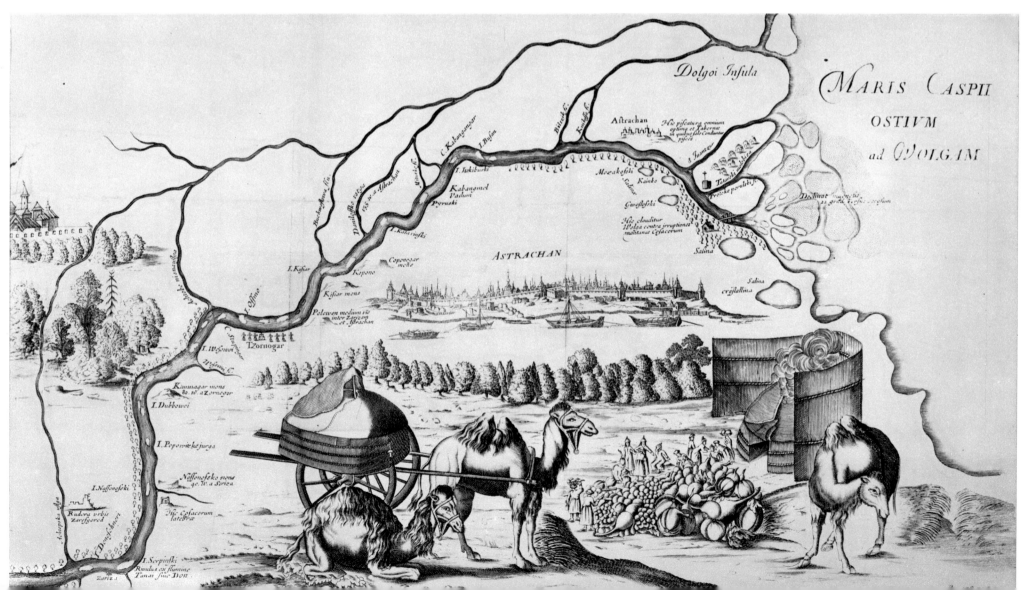

Dolgoi Insula

MARIS CASPII

OSTIVM

ad WOLGAM

Astrachan

ASTRACHAN

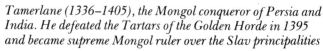

Tamerlane (1336–1405), the Mongol conqueror of Persia and India. He defeated the Tartars of the Golden Horde in 1395 and became supreme Mongol ruler over the Slav principalities

ABOVE RIGHT *The nomads of the Steppes, who once roamed far and wide, now live in reed-thatched wooden huts. They still wear traditional Cossack clothes and the men still shave their heads*

OPPOSITE *Ivan the Terrible (1530–84), the first ruler of Muscovy to be crowned Czar. He was a far-sighted but ruthless reformer whose strong, autocratic rule and policy of eastward expansion established his state as one of the European powers. Neurotically obsessed by the threat of treason, Ivan committed many acts of terrorism and was responsible for the murder of many thousands of people*

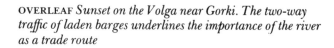

OVERLEAF *Sunset on the Volga near Gorki. The two-way traffic of laden barges underlines the importance of the river as a trade route*

were coarse and their greed naked and unashamed.'

Just below Kazan, the clear waters of the Kama River sweep down from the Urals and mix with the muddy Volga, changing the colour of the water from brown to white. In early Spring small snow-covered lumps of ice swirling along its surface look for all the world like a multitude of swans. Thereafter, the river's course is to the south and a high cliff cut by ravines lies to the west – the so-called Volga Heights. The highest part lies within the Samara Bend near Kuibyshev where the heights are known as the Zhiguli Mountains. The area was once the haunt of people seeking recreation in the hilly wooded area surrounded on three sides by water. Before the construction of the Kuibyshev dam, the short Usa river flowed northwards through this narrow band of hills into the Volga. It was a favourite trip of young people to leave Kuibyshev by rowing boat, float downstream on the Volga to the point opposite the headwater of the Usa, carry their small boat up over the hills for about a mile and then embark down the Usa bank to the Volga and down the Volga to Kuibyshev. This jaunt, known as the 'round the world cruise', took about a fortnight. Now the Usa valley is flooded by the great Kuibyshev sea, created by the dam, which stretches 500 miles along the Volga and 360 miles up the Kama.

This latter is perhaps the most striking manifestation

of a change which has been worked in the whole of the Middle Volga region, and which has made it the scene of a second industrial revolution. As late as the middle twenties this was a region subject to recurrent famines, and industries were few and far between. It was an agrarian backwater that has been hurled into the most advanced industrial development of the twentieth century. The oil from wells lying astride the great bend in the river at Kuibyshev is now being distributed by pipeline, railway and road all over European Russia. The wells will also soon be linked by a 2000-mile pipeline with the developing Siberian industrial complex. At Saratov natural gas has been exploited, and since 1946 this has been piped to Moscow.

But what is most amazing is what is known as the 'Great Volga' plan. This consists of a series of hydro-electric sites which will not only generate power but also conserve water for irrigation, eliminate differences in water level, and improve navigation up and down the Volga. Dams at Kuibyshev, Volgograd, at Balakovo (above Saratov) together with some smaller installations will eventually form a series of lakes along this whole stretch of the river. The Middle Volga now has in its centre the largest hydro-electric station in the world with a generating capacity equivalent to one-fifth of the power generated in the whole of Russia. It is this that explains

LEFT *One of the huge power stations that form part of Kuibyshev hydro-electric scheme*

ABOVE *The Volga–Don canal, opened to traffic in 1952, links two of Russia's greatest waterways*

BELOW *The monument to the river Volga by the Moscow sculptor Shaposhnikov, which stands on the shores of the Rybinski Sea, the great reservoir through which the Volga flows about sixty miles before reaching Yaroslavl*

the phenomenal growth in the size of Kuibyshev. The population in 1897 was 100,000. Now with a population of more than three-quarters of a million, it is one of the eight largest cities in the Soviet Union.

Canals have also been built to link the Volga with other navigational systems. The Moscow Canal, conceived in order to provide Moscow with a navigational waterway, was completed in 1937. It joins the Volga with the Moskva River in Moscow through a system of eight locks. The reservoirs in the upper reaches of the Volga, as well as regulating the river's flow, supply additional water to the Moskva River through this canal and so provide a deepwater route for navigation from Moscow to the Volga.

It was Peter the Great some 250 years ago who first envisaged a canal linking the Volga and the Don. The chief difficulty he encountered was the difference in height between the two rivers and he was forced to drop the project. It was not until December 1950 in fact that plans for this scheme were published and the work was carried out within a year and a half. The canal connects the two rivers at the point where they bend most closely towards each other and thus provides Volga traffic with an outlet to the Black Sea and the industrialized Ukraine. The canal begins where a huge statue of Joseph Stalin once stood on the left bank of the Volga a few miles below Volgograd and follows a looping course for 62 miles to reach the Don. It consists of 13 locks each with a lift of about 30 feet to raise the water 145 feet above the Don and drop it 290 feet to the Volga.

The left, eastern, bank of the Volga in this central section of the river is the antithesis of the right. It consists of very flat marshy lowland, the western edge of the steppe lands, where Kirghiz and Mongol once roamed between the Volga and China's Yellow River. The contrast between the two banks is greatest from Kazan to Volgograd. The river here also marks a climatic divide. The upland on the west is much more humid than the lowland on the east. On the west, the forests extend some way southwards, but to the east, they have almost entirely disappeared and the open, treeless steppe is not far away.

Along this central stretch of the Volga picturesque steamers ply their trade to and from no less than five seas–southwards to the Caspian, the Black Sea and the Sea of Azov; northwards to the White Sea and the Baltic.

Two features, one geographic, the other historical, distinguish this area. A few miles above Volgograd,

287

the river sends off a branch, the Akhtuba, which runs practically parallel to the main stream for 330 miles. As there are no low hills on the left bank, the Volga mingles freely with the Akhtuba and the country around is often flooded to a width of 15 and, in some cases 35 miles. The alluvial strip near the Volga and Akhtuba rivers is agriculturally by far the most favourable part of the whole Volgograd region. Poplar trees in this district attain a remarkable growth after only ten years and fruit trees bear for five years in succession. A threat to this agricultural prosperity is the frequent change in direction of the main water courses and connecting channels. A fertile garden can be rapidly converted into a waste of river mud. But much has recently been done to control this.

Historically speaking, this is one of the key strategic points in all Russia for it is here that the lower Volga reaches its extreme south-western limit. Below Volgograd the river turns sharply south-eastwards to flow through the low Caspian steppes. It is, as can plainly be seen by looking at the map, the gateway to Asia and the Russian hinterland. Hence the crucial part that this area has played in the history of Russia for the last four centuries.

Appropriately enough the first settlement to be erected there was a fort – Tsaritsyn. Put up in 1589 principally to hold the Tartars at bay it also protected the southward-trekking Russian traders from the violence of runaway serfs and Cossacks. In the seventeenth and eighteenth centuries Tsaritsyn was prominent in the great peasant revolts led respectively by Stenka Razin and Pugachov. In the less turbulent nineteenth century the original fort evolved into an important industrial centre with particular significance for the trans-shipment of goods from the Volga to the Don which at Tsaritsyn lie only some sixty miles apart. In the twentieth century Tsaritsyn became a key military strongpoint in the Civil War after the Bolshevik Revolution. Had it fallen to the White armies communications between Moscow and the south would have been broken and the Caucasus, the great Russian granary, lost to Lenin's forces. Some five years after this campaign the city was renamed Stalingrad, in token of Stalin's part in its defence, though his precise role was always contested by Trotsky.

It is therefore hardly surprising that the much embattled city should be the scene of the bloodiest and perhaps the decisive battle of the Second World War. From the Mamai Hills, originally a Tartar burial ground, a completely rebuilt city lies outstretched. A monument

in the form of a tank stands atop the hill. The raised concrete base bears the inscription: 'Here took place the most bitter and bloody of all the fighting in the great battle of Stalingrad.' In the terrible winter of 1942 the melting snows on the hills ran red down to the Volga. The destruction of the city began at 4 p.m. on 25 August 1942 with a forty-eight hour continuous bombardment from the air. This set the town ablaze. By the beginning of 1943, 85 per cent of Stalingrad had been destroyed. The German corpses that were found numbered some 147,000. There were 481,000 Russian dead.

The city is steeped in memories of the fighting. One landmark is the famous burnt-out house, which marks the furthermost advance of the invading German armies – only some 300 yards from the Volga. There Sergeant Pavlov and eighteen men held off the besieging German troops during 58 days of uninterrupted bombardment. On the walls, written in blood by Pavlov's men, are the words: 'We will hold on unto death.' In its original battered condition the house is to be preserved in an enclosure, as the scene of one of the key moments of the war.

One of the greatest problems for the defending Russians was how to reinforce their troops on the right, or western bank of the river. Stationed on the low-lying eastern bank, the main Russian armies had no hope of ferrying troops across – the German batteries would soon have made short work of them. They are therefore said to have tunnelled down to the huge Stalingrad sewers which run beneath the river, and filed through them, taking the enemy completely by surprise. The Germans capitulated a few days later.

Visitors to Stalingrad can also inspect the dug-out which was the headquarters of the German General von Paulus during the last desperate phase of the Stalingrad battle. In this dank miserable hole, with his beleaguered and eventually encircled soldiers dying like flies from typhus, dysentery and wounds, the general waited in vain for instructions from Hitler. On 8 January, 1943, an ultimatum was sent to von Paulus. He rejected it. When a Russian emissary went to his headquarters, von Paulus was found holding a revolver, inscribed 'From Hitler to Paulus'. He would not, could not, believe he had been defeated. Then 24 captured German generals were made to march before him and the terrible truth dawned. The first words he uttered were: 'Take me away from here to any place where I cannot see the ruins of the city.'

A rebuilt historical museum has a section devoted to the gifts later made to the city for its heroic resistance

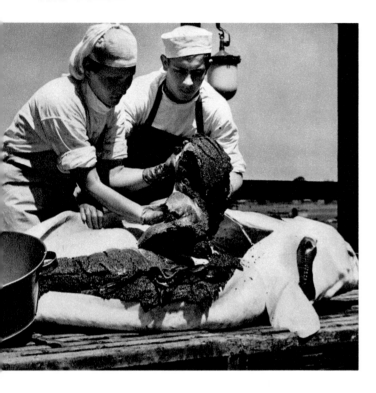

to the Germans. They include the Sword of Honour presented by George VI on behalf of the British people. The blade bears the inscription: 'To the steel-hearted citizens of Stalingrad, the gift of King George VI, in token of the homage of the British people.' President Roosevelt witnessed the sword's presentation during the Teheran Conference in 1943. He saw tears roll down Stalin's cheeks as he kissed the sword and took it from Winston Churchill. The exhibits also include a document signed by Roosevelt, proclaiming the debt of the Allies to the part Russia played in overthrowing the Nazis and praising particularly the heroes of Stalingrad.

The days are long since gone when the careless laughing citizens of old Tsaritsyn danced by the river on a summer's evening, pelting each other with sweet-smelling gardenias from the shrubs that sprawled along the banks of the Volga. Nowadays, in sunny weather, the Volga is alive with hundreds of tiny white-sailed yachts. These are owned or shared by innumerable workers, stern-faced men and women who have never fully recovered from the effects of war.

Between Volgograd and Astrakhan, the Volga becomes an exotic stream dividing into a series of intertwining distributary channels that make their way through sands and eventually empty into the Caspian. Between these two cities, the Kalmyck descendants of Mongols from Sinkiang used to live. They had migrated

westwards in the seventeenth century with tents, carts, and flocks, and seized the land. They were a lawless nomadic people, hated by the local inhabitants and also by the Czars. After the Revolution, Lenin tried to 'help' them but they refused to give up their Buddhist faith (they were for three centuries the only Buddhist peoples in Europe). They likewise refused collectivisation and refused to swear loyalty to the Soviets. They remained isolated and hostile, with most of their flocks taken to stock collectives until the Nazis seized Elista, their capital. Most of the Kalmycks collaborated with the Germans and, when they left, some 25,000 Kalmycks went with them. The Kalmycks were liquidated and their lands taken away.

In ancient days, Astrakhan was fabulously rich and prosperous, known variously as the 'Star of the Desert', and the 'Treasury of the Golden Horde'. After frequent destruction and rebuilding, the city was finally founded where it stands today and became the capital of a Tartar Khanate. Milton has written a poetic reminder of those days:

'As when the Tartar from his Russian foe,
By Astracan over the snowy plains.
Retires, or Bactrian Sophi from the horns
Of Turkish crescent, leaves all waste beyond
The realm of Aladule, in his retreat
To Tauris or Casbeen.'

It was taken by Ivan the Terrible in 1557. In 1660, it successfully withstood a siege by the Tartars only to be taken in 1670 by Stenka Razin, the leader of a peasant revolt. There is a wonderful song of the Volga which tells how Razin, when he found that he was forgetting his people and his campaign, out of love for the fair princess he had carried off from Persia sacrificed her to the waters of the Volga before leading his men in a final attack on Astrakhan:

'Volga, Volga, Mother Volga, take to thy bosom my lovely friend
With one sweep he lifts her, while a star shot o'er the sky . . .
And thus does Stenka Razin cast his princess overboard.'

Peter the Great in the eighteenth century made the town the base for his campaign against Persia, and constructed shipyards there. It is now used by several thousand ships a year and its outward and inward trade is important. But the prosperity of the town today depends almost entirely on the world famous Volga fisheries which employs over half the adult population.

In the nineteenth and early twentieth centuries sturgeon fishing stations along the Volga were a great spectacle. The fishermen's technique was traditional. An immense barrier of vertical beams, driven into the river bed a foot or so apart, prevented the fish from swimming back up the river, their instinctive urge during the late summer and autumn. Every three yards across the river a rope was fixed, and from it hung iron chains of varying lengths, ending in very sharp hooks, not baited. Boats moved up and down along the ropes, and the men, when they lifted the chains, could easily tell whether a fish had been hooked. It was a simple matter to heave it to the surface; but then the struggle began. To deal with a *beluga* weighing seven or eight hundred pounds taxes the strength of eight or ten men. But in less than an hour and a half, the fishermen could take 120 or 130 fish. These were then towed to a slaughtering pen where the caviare and spinal marrow were removed.

The town of Astrakhan is reminiscent of nothing so much as an Indian city. It has the same annoying flies, its flowers are equally sweet-smelling, its melons equally succulent and its dust equally pervasive. The distinguishing feature is Astrakhan's kremlin which stands on the highest point in the town and is surrounded by a loop-holed white wall with several towers. Within the wall there is also a cathedral with five green domes.

Astrakhan lies about fifty miles from the Caspian Sea. Between these two points is the Volga delta, covering some 5000 square miles, where 200 river mouths are intertwined with almost innumerable side channels. The delta itself is poorly drained and overgrown by a tangled mass of water-loving reeds. Myriads of wild animals and water-fowl occupy the region.

The sea here is quite covered by the golden-brown muddy water of the river, which mixes with the salt water. Moving upstream, the visitor passes many small light ships and many barges so large that they look like islands with a house set on top. Often a line of them can be seen, one behind the other drawn by a tug. Two-masted sailing boats, laden with dried roach, which lie in great heaps on the deck, also ply back and forth in the broad estuary.

In August the lagoon is covered with lotus flowers, from which a strange legend springs. One of the Tartar Khans of Astrakhan had a beautiful wife, Astra. She contracted a serious illness from which there was no hope of recovery. A fakir told the Khan that far, far away in the east there was a country in which grew a lovely flower, the fragrance of which would cure his wife. Thereupon, the Khan set off for India. After many adventures he managed to obtain the seeds of the lotus. He returned to Astrakhan, only to find that his wife was dead. Thereupon he cast the seeds upon the lagoon and it blossoms beautifully every year in the summer.

By now the Volga has left Europe far behind. It has reached the borders of Central Asia. It has not only travelled in the geographical sense. It has become a living link between the world of the Khazars and the world of hydro-electric generating plant, between the cruelties of Ivan the Terrible and the students of Kazan University, between the 'Lower Depths' of Gorki and the battle of Stalingrad. It has become a microcosm of Russia, past, present and even future.

OPPOSITE LEFT Sturgeon are caught by the thousand at the mouth of the Volga, mainly for the caviare they yield. The fish which can weigh as much as a third of a ton, are hooked as they enter the river to spawn, towed to the slaughtering pen and gutted of their caviare

OPPOSITE RIGHT Flamingoes feeding among the reeds and lotus flowers of the lower reaches of the Volga

A stranded sailing boat is repaired on the shores of the Caspian Sea. The level of the Caspian is steadily falling as the vast hydro-electric generating schemes and extensive irrigation of the Great Volga Plan divert water from this inland sea

ACKNOWLEDGMENTS

The collection of the illustrations was undertaken by Catherine Boswell Fried.

The publishers are grateful to the following for permission to reproduce photographs:

The names of photographers and photographic agencies are given in italics.

DANUBE

13 The Austrian State Tourist Office; 16–17, 30, 31, 32–3, 33 right, 34 left Österreichisches Nationalbibliothek, Vienna; 17 right, 18 top right, 19 *Toni Schneiders-Bavaria Verlag*; 18 top left *S. Lauterwasser-Bavaria Verlag*; 18 bottom Fine Arts Museum, Budapest; 20 left Naturhistorisches Museum, Vienna; 20 right, 25 right *C. L. Schmitt*; 22 by permission of His Grace the Duke of Marlborough; 23 right Heeresgeschichtlichen Museum, Vienna; 24, 28 left, 29, 32 left, 34–5 British Museum; 25 left *Christa Petri-Bavaria Verlag*; 26 *Paf International, London*; 27 *Foto Marburg*; 28 right, 34 centre *Interfoto MTI, Budapest*; 35 right *Keystone Press, London*; 36–7 *Michael Peto, London*; 38 *Ewing Galloway, London*; 39, 41 right, 45 *Black Star, London*; 41 right *Pressefoto Oscar Horowitz*; 40 left, 42, 43, 44, 46 *Inge Morath-Magnum*

ELBE

47, 61, 62 bottom left, 65 top British Museum; 50, 51, 52, 53, 54, 55 right bottom, 58, 59, 60 top, 64 bottom *Deutsche Fotothek, Dresden*; 55 left Österreichisches Nationalbibliothek, Vienna; 56–7 Gemalde Galerie, Dresden; 60 bottom The Antique Porcelain Company, London; 62 top left *Foto Marburg*; 62–3 Dr O. Thulin, Lutherhalle, Wittenberg; 64 top left, 65 bottom *Ullstein Bilderdienst, Berlin*; 64 top right *Roger Viollet, Paris*; 66, 69 left and bottom right *Kurt and Heike Hagen, Hamburg*; 67 Conzett & Huber, Zurich; 68 *Giraudon, Paris*; 69 top left and right, 70 bottom *Aart Klein, Amsterdam*; 69 bottom left and centre right *Odhams Periodicals, London*; 70 left *Toni Schneiders-Bavaria Verlag*; 70 top right *Réalités-J. Ph. Charbonnier*

LOIRE

71 British Museum; 74, 75, 77, 80, 85, 90, 92 left, 94 *Almasy, Paris*; 76 *Henry Grant, London*, 78 *Jack Scheerboom, London*; 79, 88 *Réalités-Roland Bonnefoy*; 87 *Réalités-Robert César*; 81 Caisse Nationale des Monuments Historiques, Paris; 82, 84 *Giraudon, Paris*; 86 left and right, 93 right *J. Allan Cash, London*; 83, 86 centre, 89 bottom left and right, 91 *Roger Viollet, Paris*; 89 top by gracious permission of Her Majesty the Queen; 92–3 *Edwin Smith*; 95 *René Jacques, Paris*; 96 top *Foto Bleuler-Bavaria Verlag*; 96 bottom *Fotogram, Paris*

PO

97, 100, 102 left, 103 left, 106 *Federico Arborio Mella, Milan*; 100 Conzett & Huber, Zurich; 102 right, 104 right *Alinari, Rome*; 104 left, 105 *Anderson, Rome*; 103 right *Mansell Collection, London*; 107 top *Hans Andres, Hamburg*; 107 bottom *Paf International, London*; 108 left by courtesy of Her Majesty the Queen; 108 right British Museum; 109, 111 *Giraudon, Paris*; 110 left, 113 *Roger Viollet, Paris*; 110 right Heeresgeschichtlichen Museum, Vienna; 112, 114, 115 right, 120 *Penelope Reed*; 115 left *Presse Seeger, Ebingen*; 116 left, 117, 118, 119 *Black Star, London*; 116 right *Douglas Dickins, London*

RHINE

121 *Rheinisches Bildarchiv, Cologne*; 124 left, 131 bottom, 142–3, 145 bottom *Ullstein Bilderdienst, Berlin*; 124 centre *Ruth Hallensleben-Bavaria Verlag*; 124–5, 128, 135 *Toni Schneiders-Bavaria Verlag*; 125 right *W. Suschitzky, London*; 127 Conzett & Huber, Zurich; 129 Compagnie Aerienne Francaise, Suresnes; 130 top left and right, bottom left, 131 top left and right, 140 top left and centre, bottom left, 141 top centre and bottom right British Museum; 130 bottom right, 141 left and top right *The Mansell Collection, London*; 132 left and right *Douglas Dickins, London*; 133 left, 137, 138, 139 left and right, 150 Life Magazine, ©Time Inc; 133 right, 145 top *Bildarchiv Foto Marburg*; 136 *Paf International, London*; 140 top right *Roger Viollet, Paris*; 140 bottom right *Radio Times-Hulton Picture Library, London*; 144 top *Keystone Press, London*; 144 bottom left *Fox Photos, London*; 144 bottom right *Black Star, London*; 146, 149 left and right *Walter Moog, Kettwig*; 147 *C. L. Schmitt*; 148, 151 left, centre and right, 152 *Aart Klein, Amsterdam*

SEINE

153 British Museum; 156–7 *Edwin Smith*; 157, 162, 178, 181 *Almasy, Paris*; 158 left, 159, 161, 165, 166 *Giraudon, Paris*; 160 top left The Art Institute, Chicago, *Roger Viollet*; 160 top right, centre left, bottom left and right, 179 right *Radio Times-Hulton Picture Library, London*; 160 centre right, 164 top *Roger Viollet, Paris*; 163 top left Caisse Nationale des Monuments Historiques, Paris; 163 top right Musée Carnavalet, Paris, *J. E. Bulloz*; 163 bottom, 164 bottom *J. E. Bulloz*; 165 Musée Calvet, Paris; 167 left Conzett & Huber, Zurich; 167 top and bottom, right *Collection Yvan Christ, Paris*; 168–9 *Roger Henrard, Paris*; 170 left *Henry Grant, London*; 170 right *Aart Klein, Amsterdam*; 171 *Photo and Feature, London*; 173 left and right, 174 *Willy Ronis, Paris*; 175 *W. Suschitzky, London*; 179 left *Ciccione, Paris*; 176, 180–81, 182 *Henri Cartier-Bresson-Magnum*

TAGUS

183, 186–7, 189 right, 196 top and bottom right, 198, 199, 209 left and right *Thomas Hinde*; 188 left, 194 top left *The Mansell Collection, London*; 188 top right and bottom, 194 top right, 200 top left and bottom right, 202–3, 204 bottom, 207 bottom *Radio Times-Hulton Picture Library, London*; 189 left *R. B. Fleming, London*; 190 *Bernard B. Silberstein-Camera Press, London*; 191 left, 201, 207 top, 210 *Almasy, Paris*; 191 right *Keystone Press, London*; 192–3 *Life Magazine, ©Time Inc*; 194 bottom Apsley House Collection, Photo Victoria and Albert Museum, London, Crown copyright; 195 *Brompton Studio, London*; 196 bottom left *Foto Mas*; 197 Metropolitan Museum of Art, New York; 200 bottom left Museu Nacional de Arte Antiga, Lisbon; 205 *Bavaria Verlag*; 206 *Michael Teague, London*

THAMES

211, 214 right, 224 left, 231, 239 bottom right British Museum; 214 left National Maritime Museum, Greenwich; 215, 219, 221 left *Pixphotos, London*; 216 left and right, 221 right, 228 top right, 234 *Eric de Maré, London*; 217 right Ashmolean Museum, Oxford; 218 *Stephen Harrison, London*; 220 Tate Gallery, London; 221 bottom left National Gallery, London; 222–3 *Central Press Photos, London*; 224 top right by gracious permission of Her Majesty the Queen; 225 *E. D. Lacey*; 226–7 by courtesy of His Grace the Duke of Buccleuch and Queensberry, *Royale Studios, London*; 228–9 *Henry Grant, London*; 228 top left *J. Allan Cash, London*; 230 top and bottom, 237 right London Museum; 235 Guildhall Library; 232, 233 *Penelope Reed*; 236 *Giraudon, Paris*; 237 left *Edwin Smith*; 238 *Aero Pictorial, London*; 239 top left British Travel Association; 239 top right and bottom left *Camera Press, London*; 240 *Keystone Press, London*

TIBER

241, 244, 245, 246 left, 247, 261, 262 left, 263, 264, 265, 266, 268 *Penelope Reed*; 246 top right British Museum; 246 bottom right, 249 right, 260 *Giraudon, Paris*; 248, 251 *Scala, Florence*; 249 left *Anderson, Rome*; 250 The Vatican Library; 252 *Federico Arborio Mella, Milan*; 253 left Bibliothèque Nationale, Paris; 253 right, 267 *Alinari, Rome*; 254 Istituto di Studi Romani, Rome; 255, 259 *Radio Times-Hulton Picture Library, London*; 256 top *Georgina Masson*; 256 bottom *Oscar Savio, Rome*; 257 National Gallery, Rome; 258 *Optique-Photo M. Porraz, Paris*; 262 *John Baker, London*

VOLGA

269, 288 top right, 290 left and right *Novosti Press Agency, London*; 273, 274 top left *Radio Times-Hulton Picture Library, London*; 274 right, 282 left and right, 288 left and bottom centre *Ullstein Bilderdienst, Berlin*; 275, 276 left and right, 277, 278, 279 top, 284–5 Life Magazine ©Time Inc; 279 bottom, 287 bottom *Fotokhronika Tass*; 280–81 except 281 bottom British Museum; 286–7 *Federico Arborio Mella, Milan*; 288–9 *Camera Press, London*; 291 *Black Star, London*

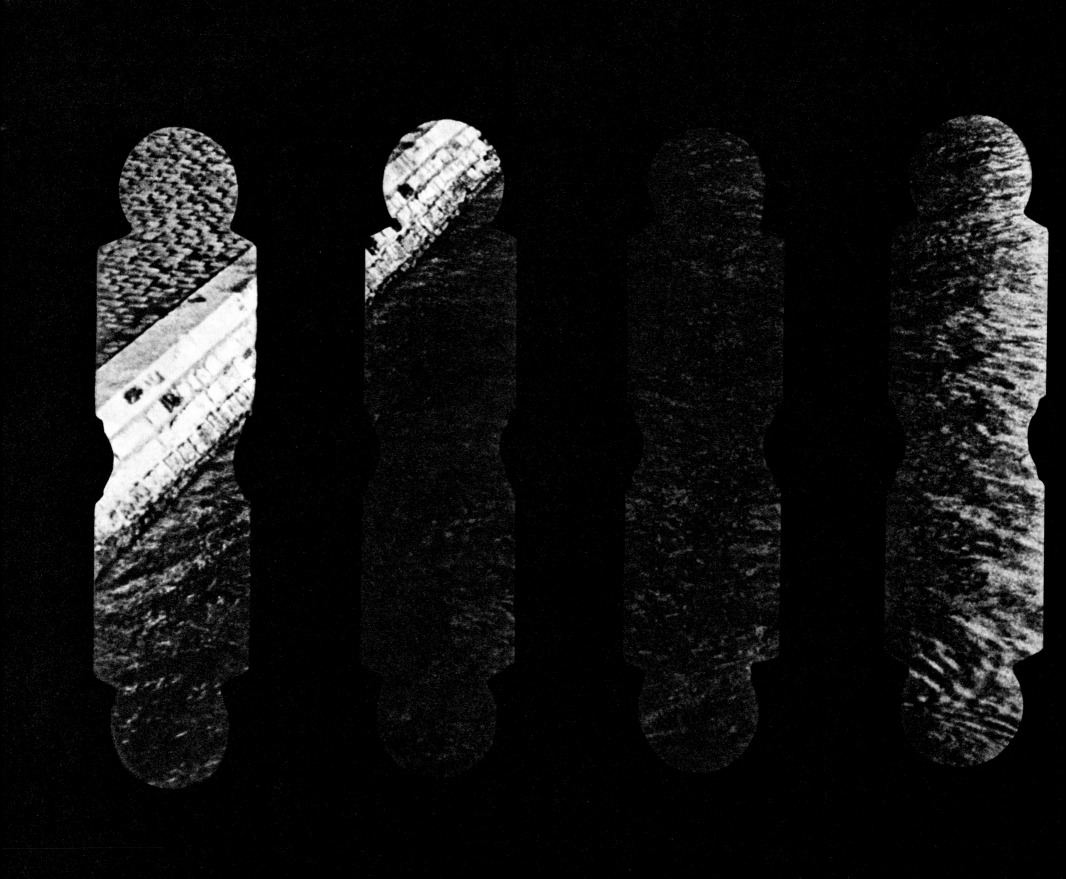